Ex Libris

Kindest Regards of
Manly P. Hall

Manly P. Hall
All Seeing Eye
Book Third
by
DARRELL JORDAN
Compiled and Edited

Athenaia.Co

Coeur D'Alene:
Printed and bound in
the United States, 2023

Manly P. Hall All Seeing Eye – Book Third. Compiled with graphics and edits by Darrell Jordan, Copyright © First Edition 2023. All rights reserved.

No part of this book may be reproduced in whole or in part without the written permission from the publisher, nor stored in any retrieval system or transmitted by any means, electronic, mechanical, photocopying, recording, or other, without the written consent of the publisher.

For bulk purchases, please contact the publisher.
Enquiry@Athenaia.Co

Library of Congress Cataloging-in Publication Data
Names: Hall, Manly P. | Jordan, Darrell
Title: Manly P. Hall All Seeing Eye – Book Third / Darrell Jordan, MPS
Description: First U.S. edition. | Coeur D'Alene, Idaho: Athenaia [2023]
Identifiers: LCCN (pending) | ISBN 979-8-88556-042-9 (First Edition hardcover)
Subjects: OCC040000: BODY, MIND & SPIRIT / Hermetism & Rosicrucianism, | PHI013000: PHILOSOPHY / Metaphysics, | SOC038000: SOCIAL SCIENCE / Freemasonry & Secret Societies
LC record available at https://lccn. loc.gov

On the internet: Parallel47North.com/collections/esoteric-books

Managing Editor: Darrell Jordan
Original Author and Essay: Manly P. Hall
Executive Producer: Yuka Jordan
Book Cover Design by Darrell Jordan
Image Credits: Manly P. Hall's personal collection
Printed and bound in the United States

Publisher: Athenaia, LLC
2370 N Merritt Crk Lp, Ste 1
Coeur D'Alene, ID 83814
The United States
Enquiry@Athenaia.Co

Manly P. Hall
All Seeing Eye

Book Third

by

DARRELL JORDAN, MPS

Compiled and Edited

Athenaia.Co

CONTENTS

INTRODUCTION: 3

JANUARY 1924
THE UNBORN: 6
EDITORIALS: 7
PERSONALITY VERSUS PRINCIPLE: 10
A ONE ACT THEOLOGICAL TRAGEDY: 14
BROTHERS OF THE SHINING ROBE - VII: 16
LIVING PROBLEMS DEPARTMENT: 21
THE TOWER OF TEARS: 24
OCCULT ANATOMY: 29
QUESTION AND ANSWER DEPARTMENT: 32
THE TEAPOT OF MANDARIN WONG: 35
THE VOICE: 38
SOLD: 41
ASTROLOGICAL KEYWORDS: 46
SPIRITUAL HEALING: 48
THE FLOWERS THAT BLOOM IN THE SPRING, TRA-LA.: 51

FEBRUARY 1924
THE CONSTANT THINGS: 54
THE PHILOSOPHY OF THE ABSOLUTE: 55
GENERAL GRUMP: 61
BROTHERS OF THE SHINING ROBE - VIII: 65
LIVING PROBLEMS DEPARTMENT: 69
THE MAN WHO FOUND GOD: 70
THE DANCE OF THE DEVAS: 77
QUESTION AND ANSWER DEPARTMENT: 80
THE HOMAGE: 81
OCCULT QUALITIES OF HERBS: 88
LITTLE CHURCH AMONG THE FLOWERS: 91
ASTROLOGICAL KEYWORDS: 98
GREAT SAYINGS OF JESUS: 100

MARCH 1924

VANITY OF REGRET:	102
THE ECONOMIC PROBLEM:	103
OUR DEMI-GODS:	109
BROTHERS OF THE SHINING ROBE - IX:	114
THE WINE OF LIFE:	119
LIVING PROBLEMS DEPARTMENT:	125
QUESTION AND ANSWER DEPARTMENT:	126
THE MAN WHO LAUGHED:	128
THE HOMAGE - II:	131
THE CHAIR OF DOOM:	135
ASTROLOGICAL KEYWORDS:	138
QUESTIONS AND ANSWERS :	141
GREAT SAYINGS OF ZOROASTER, THE PERSIAN:	144

APRIL 1924

SELECTED VERSES :	146
SHALLOW BROOKS ARE NOISY:	147
MENTAL ATTITUDE AS THE BASIS OF EFFICIENCY:	151
BROTHERS OF THE SHINING ROBE- X:	154
THE WITCH DOCTOR:	158
CONCENTRATION:	162
LIVING PROBLEM S DEPARTMENT:	165
QUESTION AND ANSWER DEPARTMENT:	167
THE TERROR TREE:	168
THE BREASTPLATE OF THE HIGH PRIEST:	172
KEY TO PHYSIC AND THE OCCULT SCIENCES:	178
ASTROLOGICAL KEYWORDS:	183
GREAT SAYINGS OF THE RABBIS:	187
AUTHOR AND MANAGING EDITOR:	189

INTRODUCTION

EDITOR'S NOTE

Manley Hall was born on 18 March 1901, in Peterborough, Canada, to William S. and Louise Palmer Hall. The Hall family moved to Sioux Falls, South Dakota, United States, in 1904. Manly Hall later settled in Los Angeles in 1919.

As a young man, he became interested in all forms of occult subjects. He subsequently joined a number of societies, among them the Theosophical Society, the Freemasons, the Societas Rosecruciana in Civitatibus Foederatis, and the American Federation of Astrologers.

In 1922, Hall wrote his first book: Initiates of the Flame and was collecting all form of esoteric/exoteric/mystical subject matter, in his own words: "late in the fall of 1922, the plan for a comprehensive work on the symbolism of western mystical societies began to take shape in my mind. It soon became apparent that research facilities for such a project were not available in Southern California... The only answer was to contact antiquarian book dealers and elicit their cooperation in the search for the items desired." In 1934, Hall founded the Philosophical Research Society, a research institute modeled on the ancient school of Pythagoras.

He was ordained a minister in 1923 to an occult/mystic congregation at the Church of the People in California. In that same year specifically in May 1923, Manly Hall began the membership/student based, not for sale magazine, all written, edited and published by Hall titled the "The All Seeing-Eye."

This Book series covers the first year of the All Seeing-Eye magazine for ease of reading. Bear in mind that Manly Hall at this time in 1923 was only 22 years old! Editing was minimal in terms of punctuation and spelling. In some cases, there are made-up words (or words that are no longer in use) in which case they were left spelled as is.

I'm sure that you will find, as did I, that Manly Hall was highly intelligent and possibly bordering on genius. Many of his stories that elucidate a particular subject were written in the first person. Whether or not this was the case, the stories demonstrate either a highly active imagination or perhaps he did, in fact, experience what he wrote in the first-person account stories or a combination thereof.

Suffice it to say, we are positive you will enjoy the many journeys Manly Hall takes you on.

JANUARY 1924

THE UNBORN

From behind the Veil of Maya
The faces of the unborn gaze,
Baby faces from the shadow
Of that blue unbounded haze.
Baby fingers play the heartstrings,
Baby hands reach out in love,
Baby voices hear them calling,
From the shadows far above.
In the yesteryear gone by
You were with them over there,
Longing through the silent ages
For a mother who would care.
One who would fulfill her duty
And give to you a chance to live,
That to you might come the blessings
Our old earth has power to give.
So the unborn through the ages
Wait behind their veil of tears,
And the ones who should be mothers
Wander childless through the years.
With mortal hands you still their hearts
And cast their broken forms aside,
Murdering souls and slaying bodies
With criminal thoughtlessness and pride.
On your hands is blood of murder,
On your soul a blacker stain
Mother of Mercy have compassion
On the slayer and the slain!

EDITORIALS

The time is coming for New Year's resolutions (which are usually made in the first week in of January and broken the second.) This year, let us aspire to hold through the entire span of months the resolutions which we make for the New Year. The occult schools are indeed mystic organizations and entrance to them is man's pledged oath and vow. Many people object to oaths and vows, but there are some which we must take as we go along the line. They are not, however, pledges made to others; they are moral obligations which the body must assume and live up to. We must pledge ourselves to ourselves; our life is our living oath of allegiance to the cause which we most cherish while the vows we take in the silence of our soul tie us to the Masters of Wisdom. No vows to other mortal things, but an endless vow of allegiance to our God.

Let this New Year bring with it these promises we make to ourselves, when no one demands of us that we shall do the best that is in us for the unfoldment of our nature and the glorification of the plan. All the books that have ever been written in this world and all the lectures given since earth began cannot bring you any closer to the realization of right than someone else's idea or at best a mental concept. But when man lives the practical life of regeneration, purification, self-mastery and harmlessness, the bodies attuned by their purification and the resulting improvement of organic quality are capable of finer ideals, nobler concepts and truer estimates than it is possible for us to make in our present condition.

Only a sage can make an honest estimate, uncolored by personality, only gods are capable of right analysis, only seers and patriarchs of right discrimination. These qualities are a basis of wisdom, which is not book learning but practical experience. In the ancient Mosaic law, the powers of being spoke unto the children of earth in the voice of wrath, saying, "Thou shalt not." This was the ancient law. But with the coming of the new law, this is changed to "Thou shalt." No longer does the prophet say you must not do evil, but now he says you must do good. These paragraphs are not affirmative and anyone who tries to make them into affirmations will destroy all their value. They are resolutions with which to open the new year that it may, in truth bring us closer to wisdom and understanding. Therefore, let us consider these resolutions as listed below:

1. Unto that Self which is within me and is the source of all, I send those greetings which the body can send unto the source of itself and pledge that this year I shall serve this spirit within myself with my heart, my mind and my hand, not to the glorification of matter but that all the world may know the

reality of spirit.

2. As the spirit in man is a friend of all things, one with the spirit of all things, knowing neither foe nor friend, kith or kin, race, or creed, I shall emphasize this during the coming year through that personality which is the finite manifestation of the infinite. I shall harm no living thing during this year but shall seek communion with that spirit in all living things, which is the universal solvent of inharmony.

3. My relationship with my brother man this year shall be based upon my own intrinsic realization of right and not upon their attitude to me. It shall make no difference to me how I am treated, for during this year I shall only do good, express charity, live fraternity, and follow the doctrine of non-resistance. I shall neither resist evil nor accept it but shall remain in poise while others are in turmoil.

4. No word of dissatisfaction, of criticism or of destructiveness shall be launched into the world this coming year from me. I shall meet and receive all things in the spirit of charity and will accept those responsibilities which the world gives me in peace, in poise and in placidity, no matter how hard my lot nor how sad my life.

5. I shall be clean in thought, word and action; in body, mind and soul; and nothing shall defile the temple of the living God within me; either that which goeth in or that which cometh out, but both shall be acceptable in the sight of the most high.

6. My voice shall not be raised in anger, nor my words be quick in tone or harsh in meaning, but shall be in perfect peace unto all things, realizing the fundamental unity of all life and that diversity is nature's illusion.

7. This year I shall labor. Every day, something useful must be standing when night falls to show that today has not been in vain. Someone shall smile who has not smiled before, someone shall be glad who is sad, someone shall be richer who was poor, each day that I am spared in this world of men.

8. Unto my younger brothers I also pledge in the spirit of helpfulness all that I have and am, that each year will come closer to realization of the oneness of all living things.

9. Unto those foes with whom my life has been beset, those thoughtless ones who have grieved me often, those friends who have been untrue, those of my own flesh and blood who have been false to me, to all these this year I send greetings that, while they may be false to me, I shall never be false to them. That one Power in the universe which is the basis of all bases and the cause of all causes, to that I renew the bond which is so easily broken by the thoughtless-

ness of life that I may each day be true and come closer to the ideals which I know but which the weakness of the flesh so seldom gives expression to. Brother, beast and God-all three of these in nature shall realize my realization of unity, for I shall live this year to serve those who alone have the power to reward in spirit and in truth.

Let us this year take unto ourselves these resolutions, build them into that eternal part of ourselves which was before the world was and shall be when oblivion dissolves all things. In the basic realization of human relationship and of man's relationship to God lies wisdom and the relationship between man and his body will be the base of his relationship with the Body Cosmic, and this relationship shall be emphasized in spirit and in truth during the coming months that past knowledge shall be changed to wisdom, intellectuality, and mind forces into soul powers. In this, the student fulfils that task which he is appointed to accomplish and passes successfully through that probationship which we know as life.

During the coming months let us endeavor to realize that the greatest instruction which it is possible for mortal being to receive is that which is woven into your soul during the everyday experiences of life. The restraint, the kindliness, the charity, and the innate understanding applied to the panorama of endless occurrences measures the growth which is really yours among the spiritual things of nature. Wisdom does not come with listening; it comes with living. Only when we cleanse the inside of the cup, can we receive the spiritual ordination which floats in it as the blood of the Christ. When we have cleansed this cup, then all may come and drink of the communion wine of spirit for instead of a man the Initiate has become a well of living waters springing up in the wilderness where the thirsty of the world may come to drink-not of things human but of things eternal.

Let us each reach the highest goal which man may attain by preparing our compound natures to receive the finer currents of natural force that are ever in the universe to nourish all who will attune themselves with the ever-subtle influences. Man is a great receiving station of natural force and thousands of messages pass through him every day, not mediumistic messages but the messages of natural force which express themselves in thought, action and desire. Those who would come into the light of actual knowledge must learn to realize that wisdom rests in the proving of things and in the finer and higher qualities of reason. The wise man knows and does and his actions being in harmony with his knowing emphasize the sincerity of his wisdom.

PERSONALITY VERSUS PRINCIPLE

INSTEAD of building our temple upon the rock of principle most of us trust the weight of our souls upon the fleeting clouds of personality, not seeming to realize that in this world of ever-changing things there is no perfection but just combatting, striving organisms that vanish from this mortal vale as soon as they have achieved and therefore are not to be found here. Be it saint or sage, all who dwell here are battling with faults and failings and seeking with the light of the spark within to read the mystic message of experience. There is no reality in matter, yet it is part of the great plan whereby man may achieve ultimate reality. We worship graven images and then, as time shows us their faults and failings; we turn away disillusioned blaming them but really responsible ourselves for having sought the ultimate in the transitory.

Wherever we find personality we will find traits that hurt us, qualities not true to the ideal, lives unable to express the true ultimate of their desire, unable to really show the feelings and ideals which fill their souls, for, as the Apostle said, when they would do good evil is ever with them, when they would be kind the sharp word comes, when they would soothe the hand is rough and callous, when they would give words to the dreams of their soul only harsh guttural sounds come forth. The beauty is within, but usually remains unknown.

Personalities are to principles what matter is to spirit and what lips are to the voice, they fashion its varying tones, but the source is ever the same. But we cannot learn, apparently, to overlook the personality, we accept lives because of a pleasing personality and reject truth if the bearer be uncouth, judging all things by the arch of a brow, the clasp of a hand or the tone of a voice. In other words, as did the children of Israel while Moses was upon the mountain, we worship the Golden Calf and ornament statues of wood and stone. The great struggle has always been between the personal and impersonal. We say: "I like Jones, but I do not like Smith." While the thing really like and disliked is neither Jones nor Smith but a personality through which the struggling rays of an individuality shine but partially, a glass darkened by the film of matter. We must learn to look for Truth, regardless of the bearer. We are not called upon to live the life of the teacher or to copy his mistakes, but when we turn from light because the bearer fails to please us we are merely cutting off our own nose to spite our face. The light shines through those instruments which are at hand. On the Potter's Wheel of being are molded many shapes of clay, some broken, some deformed, and yet into each is poured the Water of Life that to it others may come to drink if they will, all is the same water, though the vessels differ. If man waits for a perfect one to bring his light, he will wait forever, for perfection would be unrecognizable if seen. To us reality would be strange and weird, and a perfect man would be a curiosity, boresome, dull and uninteresting, and absolutely unusual because so typically usual. The greater a person is, the more he is scoffed at for his failings by those who know less than he does but he has no way of reaching his fellow creatures unless, like them, he is born in the vale of imperfection. However, we are not forced to judge upon the merits of form alone and those who do so are foolish, for they prove that the weakness is in their own souls, or they would not have found it in the soul of another.

When we hear our favorite teacher launch forth in a stream of profanity, we faint in our friends' arms, stricken with mortal horror, while a great big golden calf comes tumbling down to burrow its nose in the dirt. We are disillusioned, our hearts are "busted," our souls are shattered, and our dream fades into the shadows. And so it goes. The light shining down-to-earth shines into the unreal through many little windows. Some are open but a little way and a tiny shaft of light is all that it is seen, others are great stained-glass windows like those in mighty cathedrals, which, through the beauty of their forms and colors, send soft glows of mystic light that rest our souls and calm our spirits. Through other windows, the light glares out, injuring our eyes and bewildering us with its dazzling radiance. But wherever there is even a tiny little opening a beam shines through and that beam is the hope of glory to some soul, the promise of salvation to some otherwise empty life. And a man who turns from the light which shines faintly will never reach the light that shines brightly for, having found the gleam of possibility, it is his duty to seek to open the window himself that the light may shine more brightly.

This world is filled with hearts that are cold, with lives that are cold, with cruelty, with hate, with thoughtlessness, with perjury and with crime, yet in almost every heart there is one little spot where the light shines through. Shall we say the light is not good because the window is befogged? Are we here in this world to worship windows? Are we here to reject the messenger because of the door through which he passes? Shall we say the door is black and no white thing can come through it? Shall we say the messenger is weak, therefore the light is false? Or shall we follow in the footsteps of the wise ones, who, knowing that the flesh is weak, do not serve it but thank even the weakened personality for the little light that does come through and praise God that there is much as there is.

So, in our works, let us divide between the false and the true, between the weak and the strong. Let us be servants of the masterpiece and not the frame which borders it, for though the frame be broken and tarnished, the picture within is by the hand of an Artist. Let us glorify the picture and be thankful for the protection of the frame.

This world judges God by man because man is made in the image of God, but as men cannot live up to the Image, it is the privilege of man to forgive the weakness in his brother, for tomorrow he must be forgiven. The privilege of man is to overlook, only God has the privilege to judge. Let us create true charity within our souls, realizing that the light shines through many windows. Our duty is not to judge the window of our brother but to make certain that ours is open and the light passing through. Those who keep their souls clean will lose faith in nothing, but will gain faith in all things.

Upon the rock of personality, the noble vessels of the soul are shattered. We say the man is bad, so how can the light be good? We say that he is rough, coarse and ill-mannered—how can God speak through such a one? Surely, he is false in that he is not like his God? That in itself is a blasphemy, for what right has man to judge man by God? If man were to truly do like his God, his brother would then as surely denounce him as a blasphemer and hypocrite.

Therefore, thank God for mistakes and faults. They tie us together, but we need neither serve them nor copy them. To say: others do ill, why should I do better? is utter foolishness. Another's mistakes must be paid for by him and if we follow in his footsteps, we too shall have to pay for them. Our duty is to judge no one save ourselves and to always remember that even a thief can bring us light or that a murderer could aid in our redemption. When man falls through weakness, the world points its fingers at him and says, like the priests of old, "what good thing can come out of Nazareth?" In other words, it is what good things can an evil man do?

And yet with all his erring, a man may have light where we are in darkness, where he may have broken one law, he may have kept another we have broken. We do not need to copy his faults, but we should be big enough to aspire to his good qualities. Many a crook lives a more honest life than the "Christian" we usually meet. Many a heart cold to most things has the soft spot in it where ours is cold. Let us learn to live and know this truth, divide the good from the evil as we would the gold from the dross, keep the man or the woman out of the problem and serve the spirit of light which they have shown us. The idea that a man's word is wrong because he is not good himself is foolish and those who ostracize such a one and destroy his philosophies for his morals, or his intellectuality for his concepts, are only losing opportunities.

An individual who is unable to divide between personality and principle is unable to fully learn or know anything and there is no time in the universe for him. When a dear old lady comes up to us and says she has left the church because of the person's scandal, we are sincerely sorry, not for the church but for the old lady who has left the light because the window has specks on it and will wander in darkness rather than take bread from the hands of sinners.

The Master broke bread with the publicans and sinners, taught them, loved them, and worked with them and from them chose His disciples that they might carry on His laws. If those were His concepts, they should be good enough for His followers.

We should never be guilty of mixing our philosophy with our personalities, for when we do, we prove beyond all doubt that we are unworthy of the philosophy. The great test which few stand up under is the test of standing true to the ideal when the idol falls. Those who have reached that point are in the light, the rest are in the shade, not in the shade because there is no light but because they refused the light and sacrificed its gleams rather than accepting it in an undesirable personality.

The war of all the ages is between personality and principle. An individual who is still able to turn up his nose is still unable to enter heaven and you would be surprised at the strength of the nasal muscle in some people we know. The "holier than thou" doctrines of life were shattered by the doctrines of Christ, who, when speaking to a woman taken in adultery said, "Let him who is without sin cast the first stone," and afterwards, "Neither do I accuse you go and sin no more."

The modern world is basing itself not upon spirituality or honesty but upon concepts, creeds, and castes. If there is one person you look down upon, one religion you hate, one relative who has played you false and you refuse to forgive, if such a one there be, from them shall come the light and without them you shall be in darkness. God shatters the idols of man as fast as he raises them that man may learn to build for principal and not personality, for ideal and not for idol, and shall worship the light and not the bearer who, were he not in sin, could not bring it to you. So, thank God for the light He sends and do not criticize the one who brings it. In this secret lies the foundation of wisdom and the path of the law.

A ONE ACT THEOLOGICAL TRAGEDY

THIS story needs no name for under any title it would reach straight to the heartstrings and there twang out dolorous tones. In a small town three or four miles south of a large city, a young minister, fresh from a theological seminary and fired by ambition to redeem the world from its follies and foibles, was preparing for his first sermon. Our reverend friend wore a nice long, shiny, black coat and a brand-new celluloid collar while the beating of his heart well-nigh strangled him. In one hand was a neat bundle of notes -the sermon that he had prepared.

Just as he was passing down the aisle, the choir welled forth in the first verse of the opening hymn, a beautiful anthem of piety and consecration. He was about halfway to the pulpit when the eldest of the deacons tugged at his coat-tail very gently.

"Brother," he said soto voce, "I have been deacon of this church for many years, and I want to make a little suggestion. In your sermon today, do not attack any of the social evils-they are not popular in this church. We have some rather fast people-er-for example, Mrs. McSnubb down in the left-hand corner. But they pay very well, and we mustn't hurt their feelings-of course you understand, my dear sir." The small-town falsetto was leading the chorus of the first verse of the opening hymn when the second deacon, a little further down the aisle, held out his hand to stop the passing minister. Looking up very piously the good man spoke with a soft nasal accent.

"My dear young friend, take the experience that comes with gray hairs. The last minister who was here was-ah-er-a little blunt. In your sermon today I would suggest, merely suggest, my dear friend," the deacon beamed, "that you would refrain from discussing prohibition. The chairman of our board of trustees is a heavy drinker, but he pays well, exceptionally well-in fact he is having a stained-glass window put in now. It really would not do to hurt his feelings, of course, you understand."

The young minister was being rudely awakened from his dream of reformation but, as the basso profundo reached low G. in the second verse, he started down the narrow pathway again-only to be stopped by the third deacon whose shrill little voice was highly intensified by his false plate.

"My very good young man!" exclaimed the bewhiskered demagogue, making a trumpet out of his hand, "my long experience with this noble institution is" at this point his plate dropped but getting it back with a Herculean effort he continued, "my experience has been that it was far better to refrain from any discussion of gambling or horse-racing. You see that stout gentleman in the checkered vest sitting in the third-row aisle? He-er, what you call it, plays the ponies sometimes, but he is a pillar of the faith, my dear young friend, a pillar of the faith! I may say one of the main supports of the church."

The quartet launched forth into the closing chorus. The notes climbed up each other until they reached high C. then cracked and collapsed just as the minister reached the fourth deacon who sat in the front row right beside the pulpit. "My dear young sir," called the deacon, "come here a moment, please. If by any chance, you contemplated preaching against vice this morning, I would suggest that you change your subject. Years of experience have proven to me that our most successful clergyman are those who talk a great deal, but don't say anything. Quote Hebrew and original Syriac but if you want this church to be successful financially do not under any conditions attack any of the failings of the congregation. If you can't think of anything else to talk about, choose the twenty-third Psalm." And with a sly wink, he sat back, satisfied in the realization of duty well done.

The young minister's head was going round, and his breath was coming in short gasps. There was nothing left to speak about. As he stood bewildered in front of the Bible the old sexton bell-ringer hobbled all the way from the back of the church, down the aisle to the front, and motioned for the young minister to lean over the side of the pulpit.

"Young 'un," he said, "I just came to give ye a little advice, don't you say anything about..."

"Stop! Stop!" cried the minister in distraction. "Wait a minute! Do not give me any more advice about what not to do, just tell me some virtues that I can preach or some vices that I can attack!"

The sexton floundered mentally for a few seconds, then the gleam of a great idea spread over him and oozed from every corner of his countenance.

"Give the Mormons Hail Columbia!" he exclaimed. "They haven't got a friend in town!"

The Bible, as we study it, is a sealed book, and there are few who can read its meaning; but the keys offered by the oral traditions of the ancients unlock many of its hidden places and unravel its complicated story.

Only with the highest motives and purest ideals can the student hope to gain true knowledge of a science which contains the secrets of the soul, and when the seeker after spiritual illumination so lives that he proves by his thoughts and actions his worthiness to receive the celestial knowledge, only then will the keys of the sacred sciences, the silver key of the old and the golden key of the new, be entrusted to him.

The true student of music can never gain the inspiration of his art until the attuned keyboard of his being registers the music of the spheres. No artist has ever learned color, no lawyer or physician his craft, until its hidden side was understood, and no student of modern religion can unlock his sacred books without the two-fold key, heart and mind.

BROTHERS OF THE SHINING ROBE - VII
Chapter Seven
THE FIRST STEP

For several days after the incident related in the last chapter, nothing of great import happened. The newspapers were filled with bulletins concerning the health of the great king, whose fate hung on the threshold of eternity. I read these accounts with particular interest realizing that the hand of the great Brotherhood was pulling the strings, and that a great chess game, with humanity as the stakes, was being played out between the powers of light and the powers of shade.

I had not seen the Master since we parted that night, so I carried on my work, quietly and inoffensively as I had before, waiting for the plan of greater minds to formulate, holding myself in instant readiness to do whatever work was given me. The preparation necessary for my ever wider public work kept me to my studies more and more, outlining the various principles and concepts around which my work was woven.

I was sitting in the same old library, where he had come so often to talk to me when the voice of the Master sounded in my ear. He was not there himself, but was speaking from a great distance.

"The king has just died, and it has been decided that for the present I shall accept his body for his nation is the pivot upon which turns a great world problem that is appointed to me to take charge of, therefore you will not see me for some time. But there is a special work for you to do. There is now in London a man who has just invented the world's most terrible war contrivance. He has harnessed bacteria as war menaces and is now privately consulting a number of nations concerning this damnable invention which is capable of destroying whole races at once with the most terrible and loathsome diseases. I will give you directions concerning this man and it is up to you to in some way prevent this human beast from giving to the world this dreadful secret."

The Master then told me where to go and how I should gain entrance into the laboratory of the scientist whose fiendish discovery threatened creation. The voice then ceased speaking, and having made a note of the various points, I took my hat and cane and left the apartment. Jumping into a cab, I headed across the city and out into the country beyond.

* * *

For the purpose of his scientific research Professor Atherton had taken a long lease upon an old dilapidated estate, not far from London, where ivy-grown, unkempt gardens, overrun with weeds and creepers, concealed from sight of the world a long rambling manor-house. The gates to the grounds were always closed, but there was a small wicket on one side where one might enter. Stepping from my cab at this wicket I hurried along a torn down and leaf-path and climbed several flights of crumbling stone steps, at last reaching an entrance of the house.

My knock was answered by a gruesome looking man-servant, his face resembling a grinning skeleton, who introduced me into a musky room hung with ancient draping's and molding tapestry. Here, Doctor Atherson joined me a few moments later.

The doctor was a tall, rather slender, man with a fierce beard, a bald head, and very heavy glasses. Motioning me to sit down, he inquired pleasantly as to the cause of my visit. Obeying the instructions that were given me, I introduced myself simply as a gentleman who wished to speak to him for a few moments about an important problem; and then, as he opened the way, I expressed myself with the problem at hand.

"Professor Atherson," I began, "you are the inventor, I am told, of a great germ shell which liberates upon those within the area of its exploding mass the deadliest bacteria which as it passes from one to another, can destroy a whole nation in a few weeks."

Professor Atherson looked at me, a little surprised.

"How did you know that?" he asked.

Not answering this question, I proceeded with my point.

"I also understand, sir, that a number of nations are already bidding for this strange unearthly product which, in my estimation to be plain with you -is the most terrible thing human ever conceived of."

The professor smiled broadly.

"I appreciate your repugnance, my dear sir, but you realize that war is not a game of love anyway and that all is fair when man struggles for supremacy. The nation who becomes possessor of my secret can in sixty days rule the world."

"A world of corpses," I reminded him.

The professor beamed broadly. "They will give much less trouble than living men," he answered.

"By the way, won't you come into my laboratory and let me show you some of my experiments?" he asked.

I bowed in acceptance, and, rising, he led me through several ancient rooms into a large barn-like structure filled with scientific apparatus. Picking a small brass cylinder from the table, he handed it to me.

"This, sir, weighs less than two pounds and yet there are sufficient creatures bottled up in this brass tube to kill a hundred million men, for they spread and multiply at great speed. With a shudder, I laid the tube back on the table.

"One of these bombs dropped over a city would make a desert in thirty days," announced the professor gleefully, "and I am the inventor of it!"

The man raised his head and drew back his shoulders. "Yes, sir, I am the inventor of it, I am the greatest inventor that ever lived!"

It was slowly dawning on me that I was facing a very peculiar person, a giant intellect, a perfect egotist -perhaps a madman whom the whole world might fear. Returning to the great dingy sitting room, we sat down again, and the professor offered me a cigar.

"I have spent fifty years completing that device," he went on. "I have spent from fifteen to eighteen hours a day culturing those germs and bacteria until they are a thousand times more formidable than any known to science."

I waited until he was through talking and then I leaned forward quietly in my chair.

"Professor Atherson, I have come to you to bring a message, a message from someone whom you do not know, from a power greater than any of the nations who bid for your secret. I bring you the instructions of the Great White Brotherhood: Destroy your formula and give up your murderous investigation or your life will very probably pay the forfeit."

"What do you mean?" exclaimed the scientist, "are you threatening me, sir?"

"No," I answered, "not threatening, just warning, and carrying out the instructions of another. For fifty years, you have labored to produce something with which to slay and destroy your fellow creature. This is not permissible in the law of things and unless you accede to the demands of the Brotherhood, your secret will be wrested from your grasp. Is this the noblest thing you have to offer to a world crying out for light and understanding? Have not all the wars of the past shown the fruitlessness of war? Are not the battles of men but wholesale murder? Have you never thought that perhaps the divine powers might occasionally take a hand for the good of creation? I warn you, Professor Atherson, either destroy your formula before seven o'clock tonight or be prepared to face the consequences which are meted out to interferers with creation's plan."

The professor rose. "I do not understand your words!" he retorted sharply, "and what is more, I do not care to understand them. If you have come here to intimidate me, you have come on a fool's errand. I have spent a lifetime in producing this instrument and I intend to dispose of it to the highest bidder. It is absolutely perfect, and nothing can withstand it. I treated you like a gentleman and you have insulted me." He rang a bell. "Here sir, is your hat and cane, and there is the door. Goodnight."

I returned to the room I had left early in the evening with a down cast feeling in my soul. My first piece of diplomacy had not resulted exceptionally well. I sat in the room for some time wondering what I had better do when the voice of the Master again spoke in my ear.

"Get those formulas tonight."

Then I felt a strange throbbing in the pit of my stomach and the next instant I found myself floating in the air while sitting in the chair below me was my physical self, sound asleep. Obeying the commands of the Initiate I sped with the rapidity of the wind until I stood again in the laboratory of Doctor Atherson.

That worthy was sitting in his chair facing the safe as I glided through the wall and stood not far away, listening to his ravings.

"Give them up? I guess not!" he muttered, "they are locked in that safe and there will they remain until I am ready to use them. I am the world's greatest inventor and eternity will remember me as the master of men!"

Of course, I cannot tell just how Doctor Atherson felt but I believe I can understand the sensation that passed over him when before him a miracle appeared to have happened. Can you imagine the stoic scientist, deep in his own conceit, seeing a white hand form itself in the air in front of him, a hand to which nobody was attached. Can you imagine the expression of awe and amazement, of horror and terror on his face? But even then, he did not realize that I was reading the combination of the safe from his mind.

Slowly the ponderous steel door opened and with a scream Doctor Atherson jumped towards the portals, trying to protect his property. He saw the white hand open the little drawer and take from it the tiny bundle of formulas. He grasped at the hand, but his fingers closed over only empty air, yes there is no doubt Doctor Atherson was enjoying himself. Me strove to tear the formulas from the bodyless hand but suddenly both the hand and the formulas vanished. I had slipped them into my vest pocket.

With a groan, the doctor sank back in his chair, his eyes staring from their sockets and his hands clenched convulsively. I slowly walked away and passed out through the walls of the house. I never saw the professor again, but I understand that he disappeared from London to America, where he lived and died in an insane asylum. In all reality, he was a raving maniac when I met him, a great destructive genius used by the powers of evil to thwart the Brotherhood of Light.

Returning once again to my little study, I laid the papers upon my table and sent a mental message to my Master that I had them. I then busied myself about my labors for the next day and a few moments later when I looked back at the table the little bundle of formulas had dissolved into nothingness. But I knew that far away in the heart of Asia, is the Temple of Caves, they were laid away with many other strange documents where they could do no harm to the world.

The next morning, I bought a newspaper. The front of it was all splashed over in three-inch type announcing that a miracle had been performed and that a mighty king who had been given up for dead had returned to life and was rapidly recovering. Several famous European scientists were cited as the ones responsible for this miracle. It told of how they had dragged the monarch back from the gates of death. In the paper was a picture of the king-a hard, severe looking man, his chest covered with medals and medallions and his spare hair closely cropped.

"I like the Master better in his white cape and robe, but I do not suppose he is as useful that way in the world of men as he is in this garment of a king. How little does the world realize the strange mysterious things that are happening in its midst? Well, maybe it is for the best that they do not know, for the power of the Master is the power of silence."

I turned back to my labors, and that afternoon left for Glasgow where I was to meet a group of scientists and theologians to discuss the origin of the Christian faith.

(To be continued)

The study of man can only be approached successfully by those who have evolved the qualities of reverence and simplicity, with but one great ideal as their guiding star, that of the study of principles and not personalities. All abuses of man's opportunities to understand God's plans bring with them a karmic reaction.

LIVING PROBLEMS DEPARTMENT

THE PROBLEM OF EDUCATION

FOR a long time, we have been giving our young people a theoretical education which specializes upon cramming in two brains, each differently constituted and with a different interest, a cut and dried scheme of things, basing merit upon parrot-like repetition and not upon thought. Occultism is fighting this problem tooth and nail, seeking to change the cramming system of our modern education into the real meaning of the word education to draw forth. That is, to bring out of the scholar the ideals and qualities which his soul possesses as the fruitage of endless endeavor and not to cram into his mind millions of things he will never want to know.

A well-known New York businessman, when hiring young men, had a question he used to ask: "Young man, are you a man or are you a college graduate?" This little question contains more wisdom than wit.

Education does not consist of memorizing school yells, but there are some who seem to think otherwise. Many a parent is struggling desperately to educate a child who spends months in a hospital with a broken collarbone or smashed rib or comes home with his nose in a plaster as the result of football playing and similar things. Then, with the closing of a school year, the students leave their lessons and educative work to prepare Marcus Aurelius essays or Hamlet's soliloquy for the school play.

In other words, thinking people are beginning to wonder just exactly what form and heading modern education can be listed under. Children are individual problems and until a system is evolved wherein individual needs are considered, our educative systems are not going to profit us much.

OUR TRAFFIC PROBLEM

The one thing which the world needs more than anything else is to transform its veneering into a solid product. When we meet Smith on the street, he takes off his hat and bows low, but five minutes later when we meet him in an automobile, and he does not recognize us personally he pulls his hat down over his eyes and shoots in front of our car as though he were the only individual on earth. What we need more than anything else in the world at the present time are those little acts of courtesy which show breeding, education, and true knowledge. In this day and age of the world, there is little, if any, real courtesy shown. The slogan is, "each for himself and the devil takes the hindermost!" This is especially emphasized in our traffic problem where otherwise rational, respectable people become fools, lose all semblance of human instinct and like a lot of crying, scolding, kicking school children howl, fuss and swear, or else with their noses in the air sail through congested streets at about seventy-five miles an hour and then say that it is your fault if you happen to be alive when they appear and dead when they pass. Ninety percent of our ladies and gentlemen become low browed bowery toughs when they take their automobile out of the garage, disobeying all laws of courtesy and consideration, they make it impossible for either a fellow motorist or a pedestrian to exercise the privileges of a human being.

Church is not the test of Christianity but a few hours on the main street corners will prove that the average citizen is on a par with the orangutan monkey, the only difference being that the man glorifies in it, while the monkey cannot help it.

THE GREATLY SLANDERED PLAYING CARD

In this day and age of the world, the playing card is one of those terribly slandered things that is far more sinned against than sinning. Our churches look askance at us as if, when pulling out our handkerchief, some poker chips roll out or an ace of spades flutters to the floor. It is not realized that the deck of cards is the oldest known bible, having been inscribed upon the walls of the Temple of Seraphim in Egypt thousands of years ago. It is also a complete symbol of the Masonic lodge, of the Mystery Schools and the story of initiation. It is man who has made it into a gambling thing but of itself, like all other creations, it is good and remains good until we make evil out of it. Our modern dice are taken from the altars of the ancient gods and their faces, added up to seven, are the symbols of the Mosaic law. The roulette wheel was originally used in the temples to represent the motion of the planets, and practically all of our so-called gambling games and implements were originally sacred things. The evil side of them lies entirely in the minds of men and they could all get together, card, roulette wheel and justifiably sing that little song entitled, "You Made Me What I Am Today, I Hope You're Satisfied."

A BRIGHT OUTLOOK

Yes, it looks as though we are just about ready to have another war. Things are looking exceptionally favorable for it. The majority of people are still foolish enough to cooperate with it, there is still a little loose money which can he used to finance it, and bring more cash to a few and suffering to many. The problem of moral and principle no longer enters into war, for at the present time, it is the world's most scintillating graft. We did not learn much, apparently, from the last one, but probably in time we will learn more. As long as people do not think they will have to fight but if they will ever begin using the mental elixir and will stop to think long enough to realize what fools they are, they will not fight any more. The average individual today is behaving just as though he wanted a war and of course cosmos is divinely obliging and always has a couple of wars hidden away at bargain prices. If man does not learn to find the God in his brother and in himself, he shall hear the voice of his God in the thunder of cannon and the prayers of the dying.

FROM THE DAYS OF ROME

As you sit watching a football game and see the stretcher-bearers taking the combatants from the field or as you watch two pugilists mutilating each other, you begin to wonder where you are living, whether it is in 1923 America or Rome during the time of the Gladiatorial sports. Have you ever listened to a great cheer rise from the ring-side seats when men and women wildly applaud while a leading prize-fighter is spitting out loose teeth, plastering up a broken nose, or trying to pry open an eye which has ceased to manifest? Wherein lies the novelty of this procedure? Two games, it seems, which do nothing but bring back to the world the things it is better they forget, one is football and the other prize fighting. They are the most barbarous of our modern sports and have no place in twentieth century civilization. An individual who can enjoy a stream of stretches does not have to go to a football game, he can go down and spend an enjoyable afternoon at the city morgue.

AN UNDREAMED OF CAUSE

Few people realize that fifty percent of the ailments which man suffers from have their cause in his mouth, both the words that come out and the substances that go in. The teeth play one of the most important parts of the body and insanity and death, which have never been traced, have often had their origin in the teeth. An improperly filled tooth has a fifty percent chance of killing us. This little dreamed of cause of sickness is very important and an individual who has a healthy mouth has a pretty fair chance of getting along almost anywhere. If the mouth and the great colon are kept free from impurity, there is no reason why we should not fulfill the scientific ideal and live to four hundred, that is, providing traffic congestion does not get us when we walk across the street.

THE TOWER OF TEARS

FAR into the heart of the Arabian desert there was, ages ago, a kingdom ruled over by a cruel and heartless emperor who had usurped the throne of the rightful heir and filled the land with sadness and oppression. On every side of this kingdom, the great Arabian desert stretched out into the unknown wilderness which few have ever traversed. In this desert, five days by camel from the city of the king, was a lonely tower that had been built ages before by a people now long dead and unknown. This was a sacred tower and had once been an astrological observatory where an ancient priestcraft had studied the motion of the stars. In this tower was a child, imprisoned by the usurper king, that he might keep the throne of the nation.

Year after year the people of that land went to kneel at the foot of this tower, praying that the rightful heir to the throne of their nation might be released from his dungeon prison. A great wall of granite surrounded this tower and, as the years bore heavily upon the people and their king involved them more and more in war and dispute, this great wall became known as the Wall of Tears for here the people in their anguish came weeping, remembering the good king who was dead and hoping against hope that someday their prince would be liberated.

There were two great classes in this country, one class made up of the priests and nobles who surrounded the king, and the class of the working people. In this land, the working people had no rights for all rulership, and power rested in the hands of the nobles. These great nobles all owed their appointment to the usurper king and as they were the ones who led the armies and ruled in the cities and towns, they prevented the populace from securing the release of the prince whom they all loved. The child had been imprisoned there when less than a year old and slowly as time went by and the ancient calendars showed the span of thirty years, during which time the country became ever more involved in wars and its people ever more discontented.

At last, a great plague swept through the nation and the spirit of death walked in the streets, coming to all alike. The philosophers cried out that it was the vengeance of the gods for the wickedness and oppression of the king. This plague spread into all parts of the city and one night crept into the palace. When dawn came and the light shone in at the mighty windows, draped with finely tinted animal skins, it shown on the great twisted wooden couch of the king. There the evil monarch lay asleep forever with the fingers of plague upon his brow and his long gray beard upon his chest.

Great rejoicing went through the city even among the weeping of the populace who feel broken-hearted as the plague took from them their best beloved. A great caravan of camels was sent quickly out into the desert, for the usurper king had left no heir and the one so long imprisoned in the ancient tower was to be the king of the land. The bells and gongs of the city were sounded, and the ancient gates of brass were swung open as the gayly comparisoned caravan, headed by the mightiest in the city, lead its way over the desert to the Tower of Tears. Great dromedaries, prancing stallions, and dashing Arabians, their riders streaming whirlwinds of color, dashed in and out among the crowds. The priests in their litters, drawn by single hunched dromedaries, and a great cavalcade in armor of brass and with flashing spears, wound in and out among the sand dunes.

Four days they traveled. As the sun rose, a golden mass of splendor on the fifth day, they saw far ahead, rising like a needle of stone from the bare desert, the Tower of Tears in some chamber of which their rightful prince had been chained for thirty years.

* * *

Within the ancient building, its bare rocks battered by passing time, were many chambers and vaulted archways where once the priests of the ancient mysteries had chanted their songs. But the strangest of all the chambers was the one at the very top of the tower. It was like a great well, some twenty feet deep and the same distance around, without windows, and no opening save at the top. In this pit, a solitary form walked round and round on worn stones that grew more rugged each day with his pacing footsteps.

The figure was that of a tall, handsome, broad-shouldered man, with his long black hair uncut since the day of his birth, hung nearly to his waist and his heavy black beard, untrimmed and uncut, added force and power to the great character of his face. One would expect to see a wild-eyed prisoner, broken in heart and in body, but instead of this a great peace rested in his face and his eyes looked with tenderness and understanding at the lonely jailer who was his only companion.

On one side of his prison was a little heap of dirt in which was planted a wild trailing rose, which each day shared with him the water the jailer brought. The stem of this rose was thick and heavy for it had been there many years. It had trailed up the side of the prison wall and burst into bloom, filling the whole prison, with fragrance and beauty. This rose was the friend of the lonely prisoner. Year in and year out, he had watched and loved it. Brought as a little baby to the prison, all he could remember of that fateful day was one passing scene in the garden of his father's palace, a wild fusion of flowers in bloom. He could remember that as a baby he had played among them, cooing, and caressing the scented blossoms.

Since that time, he had never seen the world and the only thing besides the dungeon wall that had ever met his eyes was the blue sky above-the same every day, year after year, save when occasionally a great storm sent clouds of gray and black across the narrow opening. For twenty-nine years the prince had never seen the earth or any of mankind, so the tender-hearted jailer, who himself longed for the freedom of the prince, had tried to make the years of captivity sweeter by building only beauty into the mind of the growing youth. So, he had only told him of the gardens of the earth, of the flowers, and of the beauty. No word of sorrow, no tale of suffering, the prince had ever heard, and all the life he knew was the old jailer with the smiling face and the rosebush on the prison wall.

So, the prince had become a dreamer and the world, shut from his view by the gray stones of matter, had opened up to the eyes of imagination. He made of the whole world a garden of roses; he filled it with laughing people, with joy and with happiness, and fondly believed that all parts of it were as bright and true and beautiful as the rose hush that climbed on the prison wall. In his rose blossoms he saw the laughing faces of the world and in the soft fragrance the beauty and peace of nature. In the heart of his dungeon, he never heard the weeping and wailing at the foot of his prison, he knew nothing of the wars which had torn his country, or of the cruelty of the king and the spirit of death had not reached to that lonely tower. And so, while the world wept with its freedom, the prince was at peace in his prison; while the world in its freedom was in bondage, he, in bondage, was in freedom.

Then suddenly one day the silence of years was broken. There came voices, musical voices he had never heard before, there was a babble of sound breaking the stillness where before the shuffling footsteps of the old jailer fell in the air. The prince looked upward, for the voices spoke in confusion and the sound of them seemed strange after so many years of silence. As he gazed upward, a line of faces peering over the top of the shaft met his vision. Old faces, and young faces, some with gray hair and beard, and others with bright flashing eyes and ferocious men. The voices sounded down to him.

"Thank God! Our king is alive! God save the emperor -we have waited for so long! "What means this?" asked the prince in mild surprise. "It means," answered an old man from above, "that the usurper king is dead! The villain who placed you here has gone to his reward, and you are now free to come back into the world again. We have come to bring you back to your kingdom, for we remember well the goodness of your father whom we all loved. We remember too the night when the scimitar of the usurper slew him on his throne and how the sword ran through your mother's body. We have come to call you back to your throne that your people may have rest and peace again."

A ladder of silken ropes was lowered into the dungeon, and, in a dazed sort of way, the prince climbed up and out into the light. In a simple white robe of cotton cloth, the prisoner faced the gloriously arrayed group that had come to welcome him. These all bowed their heads and fell upon their knees as they gazed upon him, for never such a face had they seen before, it seemed not that of a man but of a god indeed.

"Oh, sire," murmured one, "thou art indeed a worthy king! Come, let us lead thee to thy kingdom."

Another came forward, bearing in his hand a pillow of tapestried lace upon which rested the jeweled crown with its silken draperies.

"Here, sire, is the crown that should have been yours many years before."

The prince looked around in amazement, first at the group surrounding him and then out over the desert with its rolling sand and utter deathliness. Slowly, a sad look came into his face.

"What is it, master?" one asked, "are you not glad?"

The prince pointed at the desert. "Where are the flowers?" he asked, "where are the roses and the lilies?"

An old man came forward and, bowing reverently, answered him.

"Sire, no flowers grow here, for this is the desert. For ages these sands have rolled here since eons ago, an ocean covered the land. Here there is nothing but sand and death and mayhaps the bones of many an unwary traveler.

"No flowers?" asked the prince in a wondering tone, "why I thought all the world was full of flowers like the roses on my dungeon wall. If this desert is all over the world, there is, do not take me away! Let me go back to my roses!"

"No, your majesty, that cannot be," answered the old man. "A kingdom awaits you. You have duties to perform, and millions of people look to you for their redemption from suffering and death. Come."

And leading the dazed prince by the arm, the party returned again, down the winding steps of the ancient tower to where the camels and horses stood. Here there stood a wondrous palanquin inlaid with gold and jewels, a noble cottage prepared for the return to the world of a lost prince.

Five days later, in the great palace of his father, with its domes and minarets, the prince was crowned king of his nation. Those five days had been days of torture for the prince, for all he had seen about him was but sickness and suffering. Dying people had held out their hands to him, falling unconscious in the path of the procession. All he had heard was the wail of the dying. The streets of the city were lined with the plague-stricken, poor ones who starved, and many left mutilated by the wars that had passed.

"Is this the world?" the king kept muttering. "No, no, it cannot be! This must be some horrid nightmare! Where is the world of flowers and love that I have dwelt in all these years? Where are the rose gardens that I faintly remembered in my youth? Are they all an illusion or is this world the death of an illusion?" He rubbed his hands across his eyes as though to sweep away the mist that concealed the real.

So, the years slowly passed. The new king was as great and good as had been his father before him, but from the first he was called the man who never smiled, for his noble face was always filled with a deep sadness. He wrote many great books, all of them whispering of the rose garden of his dreams, and he lived alone in a world of his own making which those around him never seemed to understand. Slowly, the years came upon him and his long hair, which he had never cut, turned gray and finally white like the snow on a distant mountain.

The laughing faces returned again to his people, for the weight of oppression was re· moved. They called him the Beloved King and in legend they named him the Prince of the Tower of Tears for they said that the tears of those who had wept in the desert had nourished the flower of his soul and that all the sadness of the world was in his heart. Yet they loved him, each and every one, for while he was king there were no wars, no plagues, no pestilence, and they said that he must be glad with the joy he had given others. But the king only smiled sadly, and his eyes kept turning to the desert, far away from the ancient prison.

One morning they sought in the city for the king. He had vanished from his palace in the night. None knew where he had gone. Day after day they sought until at last a wise man whispered, "I know! He has gone to the Tower of Tears."

So again, a great troupe of camels went out into the desert and at last reached the ancient tower. Again, they climbed the winding steps, again they gazed down into the dungeon pit. Surely enough there on the floor of the old stone well lay the body of the king, his white face, upon it a smile of peace, turned upward to the blue of the sky. He lay near the wall and one of his arms was twisted around an old dead stump that stood in a heap of dirt. Gaunt, leafless branches still twined upon the wall. It was the rosebush that had blossomed long ago. On the ground beside the king lay a little piece of paper, finely written upon in ancient characters, and this is what it said:

"I was a prisoner and longed for freedom. I was free and I longed to be a prisoner. While I was a prisoner, my soul was free and while I was free, my soul was a prisoner. So, I came back again and here the last of my dreams was shattered. During all the years that I was king of my people, I saw visions of my rose bush that I had planted here. When at last, through wandering and suffering, I came back and found that the picture was false, all was ended. While I could dream, there was something to live for, but when there is no dream, the world is cold. My vision of the flower garden made me happy for thirty years. My dream of the single rose bush filled an empty void for fifty more. But when a man no longer dreams it was better, he should die. As I lie here, I see the garden of my hopes and I rest again. Do not feel sad -a new king will come to you- I go again into the Garden of my Dreams."

OCCULT ANATOMY
THE HUMAN BRAIN

A very great number of analogies exist between the human brain and the Christian bible and also the other sacred scriptures of the world. The skull, of course, represents the temple on the mountain top and its dome is the dome of the head. It is up this mountain that the spirit fire climbs on its path of liberation, passing upward through the thirty-three steps of the Masonic initiation, which are of course the vertebras of the spine, it enters the domed room of the skull where the great mystery initiations are given. The Himalaya mountains can be correlated to the human body and the sacred temple that is somewhere upon their heights is again the brain. In the brain of the mountains there are caves where, according to the legends, the wise men are the great yogis and hermits. Here again the analogy is perfect for in the cave of the human brain are the spiritualized sense centers which are the holy men. These holy men are the Seven Sleepers of the Mohammedan Koran who remain in the darkness of their caves until the spirit fire vitalizes them and brings them into manifestation. The brain of course is the upper room referred to in the gospel where Christ met with His disciples and it is said the disciples represent the convolutions of the brain. These gather around the central opening, which is the holy of holies, the point from which the spirit finally ascends in Golgotha, the place in the skull.

The God in man dwells in his heaven while the Christ dwells in the heart and Jehovah in the generative system. These are the trinity in man and the unfoldment and transmutation of these three results in the sounding of A. U. M. the great Word.

In the cerebellum or rear brain, which has charge of the motive system of the human body, which is the highest brain of the animal, is found a little tree-like growth which has long been symbolized as a sprig of acacia referred to in the Masonic allegory. The skull is the little room with the hole in the floor so often referred to in the ancient mysteries, for the main opening of the skull is the foramen magnum through which the spinal cord with its nerves pass. Medical science now knows that the spinal cord is an elongation of the brain and is capable of intelligence like the brain. This cord is the flaming sword which stands at the gates of the Garden of Eden, which is in the human skull. The Greek god Atlas carried the heavens on his shoulders and the upper vertebrae of the spine is called the Atlas and the skull articulating with this bone which is provided with rockers gives us the back and forward motion of the head. This is in itself sufficient proof of the analogy that exists between the ancient and modern worlds.

The brain is filled with vaulted chambers and passageways which are in exact accordance with the spans and arches of the ancient temples, while the third ventricle is undoubtedly the great pyramid chamber. The spinal cord is the serpent of the ancients. In Central and South America, Quetzalcoatl is symbolized as a serpent with either seven or nine rattles. Nine is the correct number, for it represents the sacrum and coxgeal bones which contain within their nerve centers the secret of human evolution.

Every organ of the physical body is reproduced in the brain, where it can be discovered by anyone who wishes to exert the power of analogy. The two ductless glands of the brain are well worth consideration, for they play a very important part in the unfolding of human consciousness. They are the head and the tail of the dragon of wisdom. The pituitary body which rests in the Sali turcica of the sphenoid bone directly behind and just a little below the bridge of the nose is the female pole or negative center and has charge of the expressions of physical energy. It is known under the following symbols by the ancients: The alchemical retort, the mouth of the dragon, the virgin Mary, the Holy Grail, the sacrificial dish, the laver of purification, one of the Cherubim of the Ark, the Isis of Egypt, the Radha of India, and is the hope of glory of the physical man. Behind this and a little lower in the brain, is the pineal gland, which does not look unlike a pinecone from which it secured its name. It is the tail of the dragon and has a tiny finger-like protuberance at the end. This is Joseph, the staff of God, the holy spear, the evaporating apatoir of the alchemist, the spiritual organ which is later going to become what it once was, a great organ of sense orientation.

The third ventricle is the great place of initiation where the spiritual consciousness of man passes through a great series of purifications and where the essence is extracted from his food and transmuted into thought action and desire and returned again like the Prodigal Son to the house of his father.

Between the eyes is located the seat of the human spirit in the frontal sinus which phrenology knows as the organ of individuality, while the palatine bone at the roof of the mouth is the Palatine hill of the ancients upon which were built the temples of Jupiter and Juno which are the human eyes. The cross represents the human body. The upper limb of it is the head of man rising above the horizontal line of matter. The great churches and cathedrals of the world have been built in the form of a cross and containment, where the head should be, the altar where two or more candles burn continually. This is the sanctum sanctorum of the Masonic temple and is the temple of occult initiation to which only the pure in spirit can aspire.

The winged bone which medical science knows as the sphenoid is the Egyptian scarab while the spinal cord is the sacred tree of the ancients which had its roots in heaven and its branches on the earth. Man is an inverted plant and gains his nourishment from the sun as the plant does from the earth. So as the life of the plant ascends its shoot to nourish the body, the life of man descends to produce a similar result. Here it remains in the lower world until the regeneration of the three body centers pours three streams of spirit fire into the spinal canal where it passes upward, taking the degrees of initiation as it goes, until finally it enters the sacred temple where the twelve Masters sit in meditation and rule the world.

The gods of old came down from heaven and walked on earth. In a similar way, the god powers in man descend from the heaven of his brain to carry on the work of constructing and reconstructing natural substance. Man's body will slowly be resolved until nothing remains but the great globular brain, radiating seven perfect sense perceptions, which are the saviors he is bringing into the world to redeem it.

QUESTION AND ANSWER DEPARTMENT

What is the difference between the divine will and the human will?

Ans. The Divine Will wills to do, and the human will wills to avoid doing anything that is not pleasant. The realization of this great human ultimate.

Why do the sages spend so much time in silence?

Ans. Silence is the teacher of the sage. When he breaks the calm of soul and body, he destroys the teachers who only come to him when he has mastered the confusion of external things.

What is the purpose of life?

Ans. The Development and evolving of our partially awakened faculties is the purpose of life. When the spirit centers itself on this eternal work, man is harmonious, and this harmony is the basis of his only happiness.

What then is happiness?

Ans. Happiness is the natural effect of adjustment between conflicting poles of consciousness. Unhappiness, which is mental, physical, or spiritual discomfort, is the result of maladjustment of centers of consciousness either to each other or two bodies.

What is the duty of man?

Ans. Man's duty is to awaken the latent powers within himself and transmute them into active tools to be used in building his own temple and carrying on the labors of the universe.

Did Jesus ever live?

Ans. In spite of the fact that there is much dissension concerning this point, all the great schools of religion agree that the Masters lived. In fact, many of the great mystics and occultists have seen and talked to the Great Masters such as Jesus.

Was the earth ever destroyed by rain?

Ans. There have been many floods, but they covered only a small part of the earth at one time.

How may we know that we are saved for certain?

Ans. When we reach that sublime point when the knowledge and understanding of all the universes is at our feet; when we have gained consciousness upon all the endless planes of nature; when the spheres of the unknown are grasped within our span and cosmos has given up its mysteries; when every art and science is known and its workings completed, then will it be given unto us to know in our slowly expanding consciousness and that we will be saved if we

QUESTION AND ANSWER DEPARTMENT

keep on doing that well forever?

Should we allow our lives to be run or influenced by numerology?

Ans. We should be the masters of our own destiny and let our lives he run by nothing but the highest spiritual consciousness within ourselves. We should study and learn all the good in everything but never become servants to our own slaves.

Is heredity or environment the most important in forming a character?

Ans. It is not heredity but the law of attraction that attracts egos of similar characteristics into families. Environment molds individuals until they realize that they themselves are the creators of environment.

Will the white race ever be dominated by a superior people?

Ans. The white race, with its heartless domination over lesser peoples, has made the karmic debt which can only be paid off by our own race bowing beneath the heel of some coming conqueror.

When will we be able to heal as Jesus healed?

Ans. When we live as Jesus lived.

What is the meaning of service?

Ans. Service, from the occult standpoint, means to do something that will help somebody besides yourself without the hope of a reward.

Will conditions in Europe cause another World war?

Ans. The unsettled unrest which pervades the world at the present time, which is more filled with hate than the European conflict, will undoubtedly result in wars, crimes and pestilences.

What will be the result of the present conditions of capital vs labor in U.S.?

Ans. If the wrangling and dissenting continue, it will destroy the entire country without having secured the desired results.

Why are we so much in doubt as to what is right and what is wrong?

Ans. The reason why there is so much misunderstanding is that right and wrong are individual concepts and what is right for one is wrong for another. The only thing that is right for anyone is the very highest, noblest, truest, and purest that they can conceive of. Everything else falls short, regardless of other people's estimates.

What did Jesus mean when He said, "every laborer is worthy of his hire?"

Ans. It means that in all nature the law of compensation holds good, in all nature, we are paid according to our works and must reward others equally when they serve us. The idea that we can secure something for nothing is one of the most erroneous concepts and destructive slogans that man has created.

Why should an innocent person suffer for the sins of another?

Ans. They do not. They suffer for the mistakes that they themselves have made and the person whom they believe is injuring them is really only an instrument used to pay debts long over-due. Of course, this does not excuse the injury, but injustice is impossible with a just God.

Why is it so many elderly people lose their memories and mix dates, facts, etc.?

Ans. It means that the vehicle is running down, cogs missing, and the overcoat is about ready to be taken off and a new one put on. The higher intelligence is having more and more difficulty trying to manifest through a crystallizing body.

What is the meaning of the six-pointed star?

Ans. It is the interlacing of two triangles and represents the union of the threefold spirit with the threefold body.

What is the mark of Cain?

Ans. The mark of Cain is unbalance where one trait, organ or talent has been allowed to master and slay out all others.

Do we meet or recognize our friends after death?

Ans. It is very probable. It is a well-known fact that people passing out see around them those who may have gone many years before but who have come by the great law of attraction to assist their loved ones in the greatest adventure of life.

What was the Sphinx built for?

Ans. There is an ancient legend that says originally the Sphinx was the gateway to the Great Pyramid. There is also a temple dedicated to the sun between the great paws of the Sphinx.

What was the purpose of the building of the pyramids?

Ans. The Great Pyramid was built by the ancient Atlanteans as a temple of initiation into the sacred mysteries. The other pyramids in Egypt were built by the later Pharaohs as tombs. No one was ever buried in the Great Pyramid of Cheops.

Why is blood called a precious substance?

Ans. Because it is the vehicle of the spirit. The indwelling consciousness of man works through the blood.

How do you reconcile the fall of man with the doctrine of eternal progression?

Ans. There is nothing in the entire history of human progression which did as much to develop man as his so-called fall which was only a great dip into matter to learn the lessons that were necessary to his later perfection.

Explain the missing link?

Ans. The missing link is the point reached by humanity before it was divided and one part, through their development, became human and the other part degenerated into monkeys.

THE TEAPOT OF MANDARIN WONG

IT was a small room, but its furnishings were in keeping with the estate of its owner. The walls were richly taped tried and the subtle odor of the East pervaded the room. In the middle of this interesting apartment, every drapery of which seemed to enfold Oriental mystery, stood a carved table of teak inlaid with mother-of-pearl designed in the forms of beasts and birds. In the center of this table stood a teapot of rare Chinese porcelain. It was an odd teapot, diamond in shape, and its long nozzle was formed of the beak of a bird pointed at an outward angle. The handle was of twisted rattan and from the airhole in the lid a thin stream of steam was rising and the soft aroma of steaming tea buds, the first picking of the great crop, filled the air.

The apartment was without a light save a wonderful silken lantern, hung with tinkling hells and cut glass, which sent a soft shaded light over the table, leaving the corners of the room in impenetrable gloom. At the table sat three Chinamen, before each a tiny porcelain cup filled with the almost colorless tea of China's best. The first was a middle-aged man, the son of Mandarin Wong. He was inclined to be heavy in stature, and his long black coat stretched over a ponderous front. His slanty eyes were gazing at his cup of tea, and long yellow fingers toyed with the carvings on the tabletop. His face was immovable, and no sound escaped his lips.

The second was an older man of slender build with a massive brow. His hands were folded in his lap and the red tassel of his cap hung before his eyes, which you did not at first notice so abstracted was his manner, but they show like those of snakes. Once he lifted his hand and stroked the drooping black mustache, the corners of which hung down over his mouth.

The third member of this party was a very ancient Chinaman whose wizened features and leather like skin told that the years were heavy upon him. His hair was grayed, nearly white. In one hand he held his cup of tea while in the other was a long, thin Chinese pipe.

For a half an hour these three had sat together, no word had passed their lips, while cup after cup of tea alone proved that they were living things and not statues of ancient wood. They had met for a very important work. Two of them had come that justice might fall upon the head of the third who had in the silence of the night strangled with his cue Mandarin Wong, whose body lay upon a couch a few feet away. One of them had slain this mighty Chinaman whose power in the Orient was without limit and whose estates were bordered only by the Wall itself and whose grandsires lay buried beneath the mighty tomb of the Ming emperors.

Mandarin Wong was the last of a mighty line and now he had climbed to the celestial lands upon the cues of his ancestors while these three sat in a silent vigil that the justice of China might he fulfilled. No word passed their lips, no sound broke the stillness, but slowly they sipped their tea, each knowing in his soul that one of them was a murderer.

The old Chinaman leaned over and poured another cup. Even this motion seemed to startle the other two for they moved slightly and seemed to waken as from a sleep. Silence again descended, unbroken, as these three strange figures remained silhouetted by the gloom of the surrounding room bathed in a pale-yellow light from the swaying lantern.

Suddenly, the silence of the room was broken by a soft footfall. There was a slight squeaking sound, then a miracle happened. From his couch of death, buried beneath a wealth of Chinese silk, rose Mandarin Wong. The aged Chinaman, his frame broken by the weight of years, leaning upon a heavy staff, walked slowly across the room, and seated himself upon the great carved dragon chair facing the three Chinamen. They gazed stolidly at the figure and continued to drink their tea for they knew that the ancient law of China was to he fulfilled, as the dead would walk in the midnight hours to condemn their murderers.

Mandarin Wong sat facing them for several seconds, his long fingernails upon the edge of the table. Around his neck was a mark of purple where the rope of human hair had strangled out his life and in his eyes was a strange, glazed look which seemed to see nothing, but which gazed beyond the skyline of the infinite. Slowly the Oriental with the drooping mustache reached down to a shelf beneath the table and drew from it a tiny cup of chased porcelain. Picking up the great tea pot he filled it and sat the cup with its steaming contents before the shadow of Mandarin Wong. You could have heard a pin drop in the room, it was that silent. The aged Chinaman Lowed his head and his fingers, laden with jade rings and ornaments of old gold, picked up the tiny cup and drank with the three living men.

Silence was as yet unbroken and with the great stoic power of the East these three waited for their condemnation, for one of those with whom the old Chinaman drank had slain him a few hours before. The three gazed on the specter, not even the muscle of an eye moving, as the old man leaned over and, with his nimble hands, poured another cup of tea. The minutes passed as the four drank from the little cups. The low sound of their breathing was the only thing that broke the silence.

Suddenly Mandarin Wong extended his hand, and it closed over the handle of the teapot, which stood on a tiny tabouret of carved ebony. His long yellow fingers rested upon the pot, then slowly, so slowly as to be almost imperceptible, his hand moved, and with it moved the teapot. Softly it turned, its nozzle directed first to one and then the other, and finally it rested, pointing towards the portly Oriental who sat to the right of the dead man.

Then the hand vanished, the shade of Mandarin Wong disappeared in the shadows of the room, then silence, unbroken even by breathing it seemed, grew denser with the passing seconds. The three Chinamen still drank their tea, before them the empty chair where the spirit of Mandarin Wong had sat. All three were staring at the teapot, for they well knew what it meant. The nozzle was pointed at the heart of the son of Mandarin Wong.

The elder Chinaman with the gray hair reached down into the sleeve of his robe and drew from it a wondrous piece of carved ivory about seven inches long, traced upon it the most delicate flowers with tiny, twisted dragons wound among the blossoms. With his long forefinger and thumb, he separated the ivory stick and from the hollow of its case drew a fine steel dagger which he laid upon the table top its blade pointing with the nozzle of the teapot. Then, lifting up the wonderful porcelain container, he filled his cup again and sank back in his chair. A few minutes later, having finished this last cup, he rose and with him rose the other two. Crossing his hands in his sleeves, he bowed low to his companions. The Chinaman with the drooping mustache also folded his arms while the son of Mandarin Wong inclined his head also in dignified salutation. The two Chinamen then passed slowly from the room, leaving the teapot and the dagger on the table.

The son of Mandarin Wong sat down in the chair facing the porcelain nozzle with the flaming bird traced upon it. Then, taking the dagger in his hand, he played with it for several seconds. A shadow of gloom seemed to pass over the room, the lantern swayed, the floor heaved and twisted, the great teapot grew larger and larger before his eyes, lights danced in many colors and before him stood the face and form of Mandarin Wong, his yellow hands upon the teapot lid.

Then, slowly, things grew dark and darker around him. A great shadow descended and without a sound the son of Mandarin Wong fell forward his head resting upon the tabletop, in his heart the dagger of justice, driven by his own hand.

The gleam of the lantern still shone down, and it fell upon the black-robed form of the Chinaman, his head deathly still upon the table. It fell upon the carvings where his fingers had played but a few minutes before; it shed a faint light upon the body which lay upon the teakwood couch nearby, but it shone and gleamed mostly upon the teapot whose accusing nozzle still pointed at the heart of the son of Mandarin Wong.

THE VOICE

THIS is a little story that might have been. It concerns one Giovanni Cini, of whom one must hear more to better understand this story. Giovanni was called the ape man for he was a strange creature with a great misshapen head and body twisted and bent, long arms that swung nearly to the ground, a hunched back and legs that had never grown but, short and thick like those of a gorilla, carried him in along a strange shuffling walk. When children saw him, they ran in fear and trembling, while grown people shuddered as he came by.

Giovanni had never been wanted. His family, one of the greatest in Italy, had him carried away when just a baby and brought up among beggar folks and thieves. The mutilations of his body were the results of attempts to destroy his little life before he was born, and now, like some strange demoniacal ogre, he wandered around. Even the dogs and beasts loathed him and when he put out his great gaunt, misshapen hand to pet them, they ran away howling, their tails between their legs. He grew up in dirt and squalidness, could neither read nor write, and his life seemed a curse to all with whom he came in contact.

His foster-parents were paid great sums of money to keep his identity unknown, for if the world had known who he was, he would have been heir to one of the highest titles in the land. His mind was like that of a child, for the deformity of his body was reflected in his brain. But Giovanni was strangely different from the deformed appearance of his body for while his form spoke of violence and hate his mind and soul were full of love and charity to all living things. He lived his life alone, for none would go near save with beats and cuffs. He was a sad, broken thing who could never know friendship or have one soul in whom he could confide his childish tale of woe.

Giovanni was a grown man now, but all through his life, even to the time when death shall close his eyes forever, he will be a child. He loved to go out from the city into the meadows and valleys beyond and pick flowers, for flowers were the only things that did not run away from him. But he sighed, for even these seemed to wither at his touch. Gaunt and uncouth, Giovanni Cini wandered the earth, walking in the gutter and living with dogs and swine. He never knew why his body was distorted, of the cruel blows that sought to kill it; all he knew was that he was different from other things, was lonely and misunderstood.

One day, cowering away from the stones and sticks which the village youths threw at him, his cheeks wet with tears and his heart aching beyond expression, he came to the door of a little church in whose shrine dim tapers burned. As he huddled, brokenhearted, on the steps, an old man came out, dressed in a long gray robe, and for the first time in his life Giovanni Cini heard a kind word.

A hand was laid upon his shoulder, tenderly this time, and the poor boy looked up in amazement, for never in all his life had he known a soft touch. An old gray-haired man with a kindly face and a sweet smile gazed at him.

"Why do you weep here?" he asked the wondering youth.

"They all throw sticks and stones and tell the dogs to chase me because, oh, I am so hideous!" And the youth held out his long misshapen arms with their claw-like fingers. "No one cares for me, they all hate me, they tell me they wish I had never been born, and oh! how I wish I could die!"

The old man leaned over and helped the youth to his feet. "Come with me, my son, for when the world shall cast you down, then your God shall pick you up. Here none shall come to laugh at you, for there is a place far in the mountains which is called the Monastery of Sorrow. All who dwell in those stony cells have sorrow in their souls, broken hearts, broken bodies, and the cruelty of the world has forced them there, and there alone they sit to write and meditate. When you are tired of wandering these streets, you may go there to rest, for at this place all will be kind to you and help you to forget the coldness of the world. When you are ready to go into these mountains, come and tell me."

"Father, I am ready now!" answered the youth rising on his short-dwarfed legs. He turned his horrid face with its discolored teeth and flattened nose up to the priest, and, clasping the hem of the father's robe, he sobbed, "I am ready now, father, take me away, no one cares for me here, there are none to even ask. Take me away to the country where the flowers are for. They are the only things that do not run from me in fear."

"I am not afraid of you," answered the priest, putting his arm around the dwarfed figure, "nor is God afraid of you. Come with me and I will send you to the Monastery of Sorrow, where you can spend the rest of your life in nature, in prayer and meditation, and in peace."

Throwing his great cape about the figure, which toddled by his side, the priest entered the ancient church and the great door closed behind him. Giovanni Cini thus disappeared from the sight of the world and was never seen again.

* * *

In a distant land, there is a great cathedral where people come to hear a voice. Some say that it is the voice of God, but none knows what it really is. Each Sunday there breaks forth upon the air a song. It comes from behind a grating of curtained partitions and wells out with the strangest notes that ever mortal ear listened to. It is the voice of Fra Celestius, the great monk. Five notes higher than high C. that voice rises, higher even than the fine notes of a bird, then it swells out in a thundering baritone and bass voice without limit, high or low, it was called the god voice in man.

From all over the world, people came to hear that wondrous singer that no man had ever seen. The penitent came to pray, and sinners renounced their lives of crime as those notes hung upon the air. The very glory of God himself was sung in that voice which woke memories that were dead, revived hopes that were broken, gave peace to the sad of heart. The sick came on their crutches, the halt, and the blind, and as that voice sounded their eyes were opened, their ears were made to hear, and the halt of their tongues was loosened, they cast down their crutches, and rose from beds of sickness under the divine inspiration of the Voice.

From across the sea there came one, an artist. Day after day he came to the great cathedral to gain the inspiration for a masterpiece of art, and then, returning to his studio, painted the painting of a voice. It was a glorious canvas. In the center was a heavenly figure, as perfect as a Greek god, with eyes upraised and hands spread as though to grasp the infinite creation. The mouth was open, singing, and the air was filled with winged figures that seemed to pour in an endless stream from his mouth. Into this the artist put all of his soul and when it was finished, he called the picture Fra Celestius, the Voice.

A great one came to see him one day, and an old man in a gray cowl. The artist showed him the picture, saying, "Is it not wonderful, the dream, the inspiration that I gained from that voice? What a beautiful man that singer must be!"

The monk nodded his head. "Beautiful indeed," he answered softly. "Come with me next Sunday and I will show you the singer."

On the next Sabbath, the artist and his gray cow led friend entered the church by a side door and stood where they could look down upon the niche where the singer stood. As they waited there, a form stepped into the niche, concealed from below by the heavy draperies.

The artist stepped back in amazement.

"My God! That can't be he! Not the Fra Celestius!"

In the niche stood a short-deformed figure in the gray robe of a monk, with long arms like those of an ape, a strange fierce face and distorted body, unfinished or broken in the making. A few seconds later, the mouth opened. A beautiful soprano note hung in the air and a hush fell over the church.

"Indeed, brother, that is he," said the monk. "In the world, he was Giovanni Cini the man-ape; now he is Fra Celestius whose voice sings as the birds of the sky, whose heart is as sweet and soul as pure as the notes he sings. You drew a wonderful painting, signor; you drew not this body of Giovanni Cini, you drew his soul. Listen. How can such notes as those come from such a broken heap of clap? Ah, brother," the old man crossed himself, "God works indeed in a mysterious way His wonders to perform. Someday yonder brother will be a saint, while you and I are still sinners."

SOLD

"But, mother, he's old enough to be my father and besides, I don't even know him! Why should I tie myself to an old man like that? I could never learn to love him!"

"My dear child, you must get that foolish idea of sentiment out of your head. Children do not marry for love nowadays but for the general good of the whole family. Doctor Rix is a wonderful match for you and according to the Blue Book he is one of the richest men in the city, why he's worth millions and is so old he can't live very long, anyway. My dear, this is the chance of your life! Think what it will mean to all of us. It will mean that I, your mother, will again be surrounded by those comforts and conditions she has been accustomed to but which your late father by his foolish sentimentalism made impossible by giving his money away to beggars."

"But mother, I don't want to marry an old man who is so sick and dissipated he can hardly walk!"

"It is true that he is rather old to be eligible, but if you will think carefully, you will realize that he is entirely to too eligible to be considered old. If you do not think of yourself, think of your mother and the needs of her old age. Do you want her to live in some little country town all her life on the paltry pittance of your father's run-down estate, not even sufficient to supply us with a servant?"

"Mother, why do you keep after me day after day, month after month, when you know it is breaking my heart?"

"Because, child, this is not a matter of your heart, it is purely a matter of business. Dr. Rix is madly in love with you. Anything you ask for, he will give you and the future and happiness of the entire family depends upon your marriage to this man."

"Mother, I cannot. I will not marry that old tottering man in his dotage! It would be a lie before God and man, a crime! I will not sell myself for his money!"

"Tut, tut, my dear. You have not lived as long as I have or you would realize that I am giving you good advice, and what is more, I expect you to follow it."

"I will not."

"Edith Marlowe, it is my command that you marry Doctor Rix. I am your mother, and my word must be your law."

Mrs. Marlowe rose to her feet, her jaw set like a vice of steel and her eyes glinty with anger. She was a handsome woman with a tall, stately figure and gray hair, but the expression on her face was that of an empress demanding obedience. She ruled her home with a rod of iron, feared by her children whose spirit she had broken and whose lives she was bent on twisting into her own channel. The daughter looked at her mother for a few seconds and then her head, with its mass of tousled and disheveled brown hair, fell before the piercing eyes of her mother. Tears were in the girl's eyes and slowly she sank to her knees, clasping her mother's hands.

"Mother, mother! I will do anything in the world to please you, for I love you with all my heart." And she turned her big brown eyes, wet with weeping, to her mother's face. "But don't, you can't ask me to sacrifice my whole life in such a way! Mother, don't look at me like that I can't do it. I will kill myself first!"

"Nonsense, child. Get up and behave yourself. Remember what your father said: children obey your parents and if you love me, you will keep my commandments. I command you to marry this man for the good of the whole family, for your own sake and for mine as well."

"For months you have tortured me with that demand, but mother, I shall never marry Doctor Rix and that is final."

Mrs. Marlowe drew herself up and glared at her daughter, her face white with rage and her lips like two thin lines of purple.

"You shall marry Doctor Rix. I have already arranged it and when he calls this evening, you will become engaged to him. Do you understand? Now go to your room and remain there until he comes or until I call you. This is once where your mother is going to have things done the way she demands them. Now go!"

Edith Marlowe passed slowly from the room, her shoulders bent and her breath coming in short sobs. Reaching the door, she turned around with a look of desperation in her eyes.

"Mother, you shall regret this someday."

Turning, she ran up the stairs. Mrs. Marlowe stood for several seconds undecided, striking the palm of one hand with the fist of the other. She was a woman of the world, a woman of ambition, and she had reared her daughter for one purpose alone to fulfill her craving for riches, and at any price she would obtain her end. Her white head rose, and she became again the dowager empress, a woman bringing over from some past life the power of a breaker of men, in soul and in spirit one of Caesar's legions.

The moments passed, the great clock on the stairs ticked out and the dull gong told of a passing hour. Mrs. Marlowe sat down.

"She must, she shall, obey me. I have spent thousands of dollars on her education. I have brought her into the best society and all this for nought? No! My happiness depends upon her making a successful match. If she marries Doctor Rix, I can have my private car and a home. I shall not miss this opportunity!"

The gloom of evening. No sound broke the stillness save the old clock. Finally, Mrs. Marlowe rose, her face now set in repose, and pressing the switch flooded the room with light. She looked about carefully to see that everything was in order, for this was one of the most important moments of her life. That evening, Doctor Rix was to call. The moments passed while through the mother's mind schemes of the future were passing, schemes centered around her own ambition, absolutely thoughtless of her daughter's heart of woe. Then the ring of the doorbell sounded and, rising, Mrs. Marlowe passed with Georgian dignity into the hallway and opened the door to admit Doctor Robert Rix.

He was a little short, dry looking man of about seventy-two years of age. His complexion was the color of paste, and his entire system was permeated with scrofula and nicotine poisoning. He had been married four times, two of his wives had left him and the others had died. He spoke in a high, sharp voice and looked through old-fashioned gold-rimmed glasses at Mrs. Marlowe.

"Good evening, madame. I have come in reply to your note. Am I to understand that my plea for the hand of your daughter has found favor in your sight? This delights me."

Mrs. Marlowe closed the door behind the doctor, her eyes turning with envy to the beautiful automobile that waited before the door with chauffeur and footman in livery.

"Come in, Doctor Rix, and sit down. Here, let me take your hat and cane."

Seated across the living room table from each other, Doctor Rix and Mrs. Marlowe discussed the plan which their older heads had framed between them.

"I am fascinated by your charming daughter," squeaked Doctor Rix, "can it be that my charms have found favor in her sight?"

"I know she thinks very highly of you, Doctor," lied Mrs. Marlowe sweetly, "but you know the child is very young and hasty yet. However, I think we can come to a very amicable understanding of the subject. But there are two or three little things that must be considered. If I allow my daughter to marry you, I must have five hundred thousand dollars."

"You shall," answered Doctor Rix eagerly, "gladly shall you have it. I would give all I possess for her."

"Then that is settled," answered Mrs. Marlowe. "Will you please make that out on paper, Doctor, so that we will have no misunderstanding later?"

"Better than that, madame, here is my check." And with a shaky hand, the Doctor filled one out.

"I will announce the engagement at once. She shall marry you the first of next month. Doctor, this is one of the greatest moments of my life. At last, after years of poverty, I shall again occupy my proper position in society. This is the happiest moment I have known in years."

Mrs. Marlowe looked up and there standing with her back against the door stood Edith Marlowe, a strange expression in her face which her mother had never seen there before.

"Good evening, Miss Marlowe." Rising with difficulty, the old doctor stood. "It is a charming evening."

Miss Marlowe did not look at him at all, but her face was turned to her mother.

"Mother," she said slowly in a voice which seemed strangely different. "I have come to say two or three things to you, and you must listen to them. You have just signed on that table a paper which is to sell my life and soul to another. You say it is in the Scripture: Children, obey your parent. But it also says in the Scripture: Parents, provoke not your children to wrath. You have ruined my life, broken my hopes, shattered my soul, all for the sake of your own social position. YOU brought me into the world for no other reason than to sell me. But you do not own the soul of me, you but own the clay that you have broken. Life already stretched before me in the path that I had chosen to go, a path which is reasonable and true; I had already chosen one who was to walk that path with me, but he was poor, and you would not have him and turned him away to sell me to another. You are but one of many mothers whose eyes gaze longingly at their children's form, waiting until they are old enough to turn them into gold. From out of the Infinite, they came to you to love and cherish. You have sold God's gifts to you, you have blasphemed His plan, you have prostituted His offering like so many others have. Almost all the daughters who come into the world are for sale to the highest bidder, but you shall never own me, nor will you ever own the soul of another living thing. This old man, broken in body, too old for you even to consider, you would sell him to me and me to him. Well, sell that which was yours to sell, it is not much."

At that instant the sound of footsteps, heavy boot-treads, sounded on the porch of the little house and a ring came at the door. Mrs. Marlowe rose, a strange expression on her face, her eyes fastened to the accusing ones of her child, and slowly reaching the door, threw it open. Into the room came four figures, two men in rubber boots soaked with water. In their arms they carried a third while a youth, wild-eyed and disheveled, followed up the rear.

"Mrs. Marlowe, I believe?" said one of the men as he lifted the covering off his burden. "We have just dragged the body of your daughter out of the river at the dam, she must have fallen in, I guess. She has been dead about three or four hours."

"Impossible!" exclaimed Mrs. Marlowe, staring around. "There is my daughter." She pointed to the figure against the door.

Edith Marlowe pointed her hand to the white, water-soaked figure in the arms of the dam-keeper. "That, mother, is yours to buy and sell."

On the altars of ambition lie the bodies of the slain, youth and love together martyred in the cause of human gain; life and limb are bartered freely as the golden shekels flow while misery lurks in the shadow of each deadly hammer blow.

What is offered? Sounds the call-sorrow's song through every age lives for gold, youth for silver, and misery for the hammer's wage. Thus, are hopes forever slaughtered at the auction block of gain? Rosy cheeks are turned to ashen, noble lives by greed are slain.

Mothers, fathers of the races, sell not children's hearts for gold! They have come as trusts from heaven, not for profits bought or sold, and the curse of all the ages rests on those who buy and sell the lives and hearts of living creatures to chain them in ambition's hell.

Going, going, how much is offered? Still the traitor ply's his trade, the old buy youth, the rich buy beauty, "The Devil buys the soul 'tis said." The laughing eyes grow dim with sorrow, singing voices wail instead, youthful souls are aged with sorrow and seek peace among the dead.

Sons and daughters, buy them here! Your worthiness is proved by price. The highest bidder owns the soul, while death wins all with loaded dice. Gone! another soul is butchered for some ambitious parent's scheme. Gone! another life is ruined, broken is its golden dream.

But above the sadness brooding, a single star of light still gleams, for the spirit flees to freedom from the wreckage of its dreams. The God who loves His children buys each heart that's sold, they say, and those who pawn and sell His children barter only lumps of clay.

ASTROLOGICAL KEYWORDS

Scorpio is one of the most interesting signs of the Zodiac because of its deep occult nature. It is twofold and very decidedly so in its expression for it produces the greatest scientists, philosophers and occultists and also the worst degenerates. In his development the occultist transmutes the scorpion first to the serpent and then to the eagle, in that way preserving the highest expression of the Scorpio power. The constellation is one of the most fascinating in the heavens, with its great tail running across the sky. It is a very powerful sign, either for good or for bad, being capable of the greatest beauty or the most heartless cruelty. It makes surgeons to cut for the love of cutting, and vitalizes martyrs who die for their ideals. It is a thinking, intellectual, scientific sign; argumentized, analytical and, when trained, a highly spiritual sign.

It can be briefly considered with the aid of the following keywords:
Cold, Mute, Moist, Broken, Watery, Unfortunate, Phlegmatic, Strong, Feminine, Southern, Autumnal, Obeying, Nocturnal, Long ascension, Northern Fall of the moon, Fixed Detriment of Venus, Fruitful.

General Characteristics:
Active, Hypnotic, Secretive, Malicious, Sometimes deceitful, Experimentative, Cruel until transmuted, Strong will, Courageous, Fond of education, Hypocritical, Rather gloomy, Fraudulent, Sanguine temperament, Black magic.

Physical Appearances:
Strong, Sometimes corpulent, Usually angular, Hook-nosed, High cheek bones, Deep eyes, Middle size, Dark complexion, Brown curly hair, Thick neck and legs, Short body, Hairy and coarse, Dusky complexion, Bony.

Health:
On account of the position of Mars, Scorpio is subject more or less to fevers also to brain trouble. Violent insanity is sometimes found under this sign, but not often. Eccentricities are common under this sign and these eccentricities sometimes become obsessions. Scorpio people usually neglect and abuse their bodies.
Its diseases are:
Confirmed melancholia. Violent forms of venereal disease. Obstructions in the intestinal canals. All forms of disease and accidents in generative system, Danger from poisonings and excessive drinking, dope, or vice of similar nature.

Domestic Problems:
Scorpio is not particularly fortunate in domestic problems because of Mars which usually prevents harmonious domestic understanding. Scorpio is the least fruitful of the watery signs because of its being ruled by the fire planet, and its secretive morose temperament with love of study and being alone does not add greatly to its matrimonial and domestic possibilities.

Countries under Influence of Scorpio:
Judea, Upper Bavaria, Maritana, Barbary, Catalonia (in Spain), Morocco, Norway, Kingdom of Fei, West Silesia, Part of Italy.

Cities Under Its Dominion;
Valenti, Messini, Franckfort-on-Ober, Vienna, Gaunt, Urbine.

Colors:
Red, Brown, Brick color, Black.

According to Ptolemy, the bright stars in the front of the body of Scorpio have the influence of Mars and partly of Saturn. The three in the body itself, the middle of which is called Antares and is ruddy and luminous, are similar to Mars and moderately to Jupiter. The stars in the joint of the tail are like Saturn and Venus, and those in the sting are like Mercury and Mars. The nebulae is like Mars and the Moon.

According to Agrippa and Francis Barrett: of the Twelve Orders of Blessed Spirits, Scorpio rules the Arch-angels; of the Twelve Angels over the Twelve Signs, Scorpio is ruled by Barbiel of the Twelve Tribes, Benjamen; of the Twelve Prophets, Obadiah; of the Twelve Apostles, Phillip; of the twelve months, October 20th to November 20th; of the twelve herbs, mugwort; of the twelve stones, amethyst; of the twelve principal parts of the body, the generative system; of the Twelve Degrees of the Damned and of Devils, the sifters, triers and accusers.

SPIRITUAL HEALING

How far should a healer go in his attempt to reconstruct the physical body of a suffering patient? Is the exercise of occult force in healing permissible? How are we going to judge accurately the needs of patients? These are very important questions, as healing is one of the most prominent phases of occult work. The ancient Rosicrucian Order formed for the purpose of healing the sick, and the eighteenth degree of Freemasonry stands for the exercising of the power of the Great Physician.

We may safely say that healing is a constructive work but certain elements are necessary before it is safe for the occult student to exert his powers in that direction. The average occult and metaphysical healer does more harm than good.

The realization of the existence of a cure often encourages intemperance, thoughtlessness and carelessness in the soul of the average individual; consequently, the doctrine of forgiveness, the power of consciousness over karma and similar ideas are not, generally speaking, safe concepts to give to the world, because these teachings fail to dwell upon the most important point of all—prevention. An ounce of prevention is worth a pound of cure in every case, and occultists who are always teaching ways to escape from dilemma rather than ways to keep out of trouble are not doing the work of the Elder Brothers in the world.

Before a person attempts to become a healer, he or she must be in a position to answer several questions which the average psycho-therapist knows absolutely nothing about. First of all: Am I or am I not a thorough anatomist and physicist? A scientific education is as important to an occult healer as it is to the student of materna medica.

Occult healing is not faith healing. Occult healing is scientific depending upon an accurate knowledge of universal law and the knowledge of how to manipulate these laws until they break up various etheric and astral combinations in the bodies of man. The occult physician knows every bone and muscle of the body, while the average so-called "healer" knows little if anything concerning the constitution of man.

It is possible that such persons will secure results, but they are not healers. They are mediums who must accept conditions as external powers dictate, and they are not healers who manipulate these powers at will.

The second requisite is: An occult healer must be able to analyze the cause of ailment, tracing it, if necessary, back seven or eight incarnations to find out why the patient is suffering today. Most healers try to heal everybody and, in this way, again do more harm than good. It is just as much of a detriment for some people to the well as it is for others to be sick. Health and sickness are problems to be solved by the ego itself and when outside intelligences seek to solve these problems, the result is detriment rather than advantage to the consciousness.

Around us there are many healers who know nothing of natural law do not know whether the patient deserves the sickness or not. They try to heal every ailment, sometimes battling straight in the face of karma, natural law, and the plan of the evolution of that consciousness. Such a course is hopelessly detrimental and many people who have been thus healed of their ailments have wasted their entire incarnation for they have not learned to be any better or stronger themselves.

The third qualification of a healer is that they should realize the source of their power and know that this power is given them to use in accordance with the plan of being. When they attempt to exert their will power over the plan, they destroy their usefulness as healers.

The old doctrine used to be: "Come, and be saved. Lean on the Lord and let other people do it." The average so-called healing case is just a metaphysical expression of this idea. What good is there for a healer to concentrate for perfect digestion over an individual who is living an unbalanced, intemperate life and whose every action causes the ailment which he is seeking to relieve himself of? The average person who comes to a healer for help should be given a bath, a dose of good common sense, and sent back to clean up. They come with twenty-five years of accumulation of mental, physical, and spiritual filth, looking for miracles, when what they need is soap and water inside and out. There is no greater expression of bunkum in occultism than on the healing side. In the hands of the great Initiate or the authorized representative of a great spiritual work, or a disciple who has seen the plan of being, healing is a very miraculous thing, for all of his efforts are to swing the patient in line with natural law and assist him to assist himself.

Out in front of the average healer's office you can find them lined up chilblains, gout, locomotor ataxia, tumors, scrofula, eczema, dropsy, scabbies and barber's itch. They come with their tales of woe when all that most of them need is to clean up. If the healer does do anything for them, they just turn around and get sick again. It is a thankless, hopeless, helpless, job because the healer is as foolish as the patient. Occult healing should only be resorted to under two conditions. First, when all common-sense methods have failed. Second, when the disease is of an occult nature such as obsession, attacks from black magicians, etc. To be sure, occult methods will help all diseases, but the first requisite of occultism is that the individual himself should make a conscientious effort, and under general conditions they get well when they make this and do not need healing.

To encourage individuals to believe that the Lord decreed them perfect health is foolish. They may enjoy perfect health when they behave themselves, otherwise they will not. The Lord decrees that as well. A healer who makes an automatic profession out of his work is a curse to occult science. When he lays his hands on Smith, chants mantrams over Jones, and shivers over Brown, he is a disgrace to himself. To be sure, these people will immediately feel better, or at least a percentage will, for most people's ailments are in their heads.

The law of karma is slighted, natural law is set askew, because an ignorant healer thinks a person ought to get well when the Lords of Karma have worked twenty thousand years trying to get the patient into a position where he has to do something for himself. An ignorant person with a little psychic ability comes along and heals them of something that they never earned the right to get well from. Cults and creeds which preach peace, health, and happiness as the result of inertia or somebody else's effort are not spiritual, sensible, rational, or worthy of any consideration.

THE FLOWERS THAT BLOOM IN THE SPRING, TRA-LA.

A dear friend of our has two little children whom she is raising like little wildflowers, lilies of the valley and so forth. First, they were creepers, now they are runners, and later they will blossom forth with all the beauty of uncultured wildflowers. They are surely daisies even at this point in the game, and the neighbors know them as for-get-me-nots. Like flowers they do not bathe, but unlike flowers they do not stand out in the rain. She neither corrects them nor bends the youthful twig, but is letting God take care of them. The reward for this is that they are positively the greatest nuisance of their size in ten counties. When one tries to correct them, the mother goes into hysterics, claiming that they are God's perfect children and are without sin. They throw tin cans at the cat, rub soap on the windows, fall into the cistern and play marbles on your roof. They cuss like troopers and little Willie, aged five, have already touched the depth of the smoker's degeneracy. These two little wildflowers with a daffy-dill for a mother, spent a day a little while ago in setting fire to an automobile, ringing doorbells and stealing the Sunday newspapers. They are the examples of those sweet, simple children who grow up like little blossoms on a poison ivy vine.

Such is the story of a large percent of our population who grow up in spite of their parents rather than because of them. Well, they are blooming flowers now alright and promise to be in the penitentiary before they become of age. They have no manners, no civility, and they run around in ragged clothes which are in themselves sufficient to build only shiftlessness in their souls. The mother spends her days getting over her nights and sends them off to play in somebody else's yard. Such is the sad drama of most homes.

FEBRUARY 1924

THE CONSTANT THINGS
By a Prison Poet

FAME and wealth may come and go,
The lights of splendor flicker low
And sometimes die; but the simpler things—
The sitting-room where the laughter rings,
The mother's smile and her cheerful song—
Are seldom swayed by the moving throng.
These are constant! The man may lose
The place he holds and the world may choose
To flatter the skill of a younger hand,
But the walls of home for him shall stand;
And if he has builded his life for them
He shall still have friends—though the world condemn.
The great may sometimes lonely be
But he has glorious company
Who comes at night to his dwelling place
Where his boys and girls may romp and race;
There—though bitter his fight and grim—
Are loving hearts who believe in him.
He has friends for the night and day,
For die mountain climb or the level way,
Who writes his life in the smiles of those
Who watch for him at the journey's close.
Of all life's friendships these few are
Beyond the sham of the world to mar.

EDITORIALS

THE PHILOSOPHY OF THE ABSOLUTE

THERE are two kinds of people in the world, people with a vision and people without a vision. Those people with a "vision" who claim to have surrounded the Absolute are those without a vision. So first of all, let us take up an argument in defense of the Absolute. If any human creature knows all there is to know, the Absolute is not very wise because the more we hear about Him from His disciples among men, the more foolish traits, the more idiosyncrasies, and more lopsidedness we find attributed to Him. The man who says "I know all there is to know" is made either a fool out of God or an egotist out of himself.

We have a large group of people who are personal friends of the Infinite, have been properly introduced to the Unknowable and spend their weekends (heads) in conflab with the Definitionless Abstract. There are several types of people who know this Absolute. Some of them are inclusive and some of them are exclusive. We have a certain amount of patience for the inclusive absoluter, but the exclusive absoluter excludes the Absolute. It is this certain group of people who are not even willing to know what God knows, and have long left such ordinary ignoramuses as the Father, Son and Holy Ghost far in the rear. They speed by the cosmic Logos in their twelve-cylinder Rolls-Rough with a "Ta! Ta" to the Universal Creation. They glide by eighty-two thousand hierarchies of Devas, Chohans, Mahachohans and Rishis without even condescending to consider them, they step from star to star leaving a thin trail of blue smoke behind them from the exhaust, of their intercosmic velocipede (said tail stream is now called the Milky Way). They are headed for the Footstool of All There Is, dissolved in All That Is Not. They are true Star-Rovers (with apologies to Jack London). The gods of their fellowmen are pigmies unworthy of notice; they have found that which is not, yet is and ever shall be; their mind is dissolved into unison with the cosmic void, and they have attuned their body and consciousness to the low-pressure area of the Absolute.

They no longer worry as to what they shall eat, nor what they shall wear, nor how they shall speak, nor in whatsoever manner they shall perpetuate themselves or propel their personality. Their minds are on the mystic ethers of the divine Is-ness-naught else will interest them nor fill the aching void between their ears. They are the living contradictors of visible and tangible things; they have made the solidity of nature a vacuum, while they have asphalted the Absolute and made of the Abstract a solid concrete deity as brainless as they are. Now let us take a careful analysis of the mental caliber of the Star-Rover and find who composes these seers and sages who have left creation to its own destruction and sailed to salvation on the pinions of their mentality (mostly opinions.) We will analyze the stock which flavors of the divine wisdom of ages, like onions flavor soup, those people who have become tired of terrestrial things and who consider the universe to be the divine failure and they the successes.

One of our leading absoluters, who has shaken hands with a non-existing entity and has defined the depth of Is-Not, is Mrs. Patricia Murphy whose husband runs the local barbershop. Mrs. Murphy was born with a vision. She does not know the occipital frontalis muscle from the Latin word for broom handle, but in spite of this, she has the vision; she has not the slightest idea of what God has ever done, but she knows Him personally. She has told a number of her friends that she has traced French pastry back to the first outpouring and is quite confident that the Absolute's gray whiskers are made of icing. This is her total idea of the Absolute. She does not know the meaning of any of the episodes that surround her in life; she has been careful not to consider them for fear that she might be enveloped in the veil of Maya and lose her personal touch with the abstract. Her idea of the Absolute is a large round dark hole, for she has absolutely nothing in her own brain to fill it with. But she admits that there is such a hole and by so doing becomes "saved."

The second member of this celestial trinity we are considering in our little spasm is Gluck McFag, a well-known disciple of things vacuumized. He has come into the light by realizing that there is not any and by so doing has proved that there is. This is a little problem in celestial mathematics based upon the fact that if you have something, it isn't while if you lose it, it comes back. (Undoubtedly Pythagoras would have enjoyed this system). In other words, we glorify God by proving that His manifestations are foolishness, we worship Him as an Individual who spends all His time making mistakes and filling the universe with a series of unnecessary nonentities that through them, we might learn how good He is (another mathematical problem with apologies to Euclid.) But let us return to this error of the mortal mind commonly known as Gluck McFag. According to all the lights of absolute reasoning, Gluck does not exist at all and not being himself is capable of being blended into the eternal Vacuum. Socrates, we believe, attempted to solve the problem in the same way, but finally got so twisted up that he took a hemlock so he could have another brain a little later. He lost the brain he had trying to find a round hole in the center of a depthless opening.

Gluck is our leading haberdasher and necktie vender. He sells collar buttons, arch supporters and imported suspenders with great ease and fluency and is considered a leading light in the affairs of earth. He is not a very highly educated man.

One day a friend came up to him and said, "Gluck, give us your definition of the Absolute," whereupon he opened the front door and threw his chest out and with great gusto gave a scintillating description of Henry J. Ain't, commonly known as the Absolute. "The Absolute," says Gluck, "is that ever existing emptiness surrounded by its own outpouring, all of which are unreal. The center of this emptiness is in the middle and around the edge while it is bordered by its own commencement." Whereupon said friend was deeply impressed.

"What does it look like?" he asked then.

"In order to see it," was the answer, "you must close your eyes in a dark room and look at the inside of the lids."

Is it intelligent?" asked the friend.

"No. no," said Gluck, "intelligence is all illusionary. If it had the power of reason, it would be false. If it could see, it would be unreal."

"Oh-h-h! I think I grasp its import. In other words, it is, but it isn't. "Ah-h-h," answered Gluck, "your powers of erudition are in perfect line with the reality of things. I talk with the Absolute every night."

"How do you do it?" marveled the friend.

"Why I come into the realization that what is, is not and what's left afterwards is." Said friend was duly impressed, bought a five-cent collar button, and called it a day.

The crowning glory of our trinity of unrealities is Professor Alpha Episolom the one who has impregnated the community with this divine misunderstanding. He is the branch of mistletoe which hangs above the arch of spiritual wisdom, the original discovery of the Absolute. Someone came along and out absoluted him, whereupon he blossomed forth with the super-absolute, which is the dot in the center of the hole in the middle of the blank. If anyone out-supers him, he will probably discover the absolute-absolute which has not been bothered with yet, being the hole in the center of the dot, which is the center of the vacuum surrounded by the blank of the previous chapter. Prof. Episolom has a falling upper plate and a celluloid collar. When he moves, like Mark Twain, he travels in a cigar box. Prof. Episolom is the one who can tell you all about something which he admits does not exist and is the only real thing because it does not exist. We think our friend Diogenes must have been looking for this a while ago, but we understand his light went out somewhere along the line.

Professor will bring you into union with Isn'tness if you will cross his palm with Is, the exchange of Is being absolutely important to the realization of Isn't. Prof. Episolom is the keeper of the vernacular at the lower end of which we start on our choice journey to the upper end which is resting upon a hypothetical vacuum. Prof. Episolom is in a position to express himself upon the reality of things because he has learned to know the folly of knowledge and his first great instruction is that to think is excessively dangerous to the realization of the plan because if pursued this path will speedily separate you from him which would result in a decline in his finance. Prof. Episolom is a master of abstraction, but the greatest abstraction which he is capable of doing is to abstract money from a sealed pocketbook.

Now what is the philosophy of the true Absolute? Let us analyze this problem in a rational, sensible manner. Every time an individual has an idea these days, he forms a new religion. Every time he has two ideas, it splits up and fights itself, so nothing reasonable is ever arrived at. The Absolute is not a new discovery, and the existence of the Supreme Unformed as the hypothetical base of formation is accepted in every religion of the world. Undoubtedly there is an absolute cause, the perfect base of impermanence from which all things came and to which they shall return, therein completing the gamut of their existence. The abstract is the divine Alma, the definitionless base of all definable things. From the invisible Cause-all pour the shadow shapes of effects which play out in the world of mortality the divine chess game of the Infinite.

Why were these sparks projected into the matter? Why is the universe peopled with great Hierarchies of evolving individualities, which Spencer called the infinite diversities of unity? Is not this the battle-field upon which man learns to know one little stage, one little step in his ultimate growth? Who then knows the Absolute in fullness saves Him, who is the master of the gamut of His manifestations? Who shall know the reality save the Reality itself?

There is an absolute God, the changeless base of ever-changing expression, neither male nor female nor both, neither high nor low nor both. This infinite Cause-all, this self-knowing One, who yet recognizes Himself only through His manifestation, his One is the Absolute. He is to man absolutely unattainable for between Him and man's consciousness there is a void, a gap, which eighty-two thousand hierarchies of celestial beings cannot span. The gods of solar systems and the gods of cosmic schemes themselves know not the Light nor the source thereof.

The doctrine of the Absolute is a true one, but it is one of those truths which is worthless at this stage of evolution. There is no constructive application for it, for there is no sense of consciousness in the soul of man that is capable of even knowing the hem of Its garment, let alone to grasp Its magnificence.

If someone told you they had a billion pennies and another told you they had five billion pennies, what picture would you have in your mind? All you could say is that one had more than another. Man is incapable of mentally differentiating between a million, a billion, a trillion, a septillion, or a quintillion. It is just "a lot more," that is all. When we try to realize that in this Kosmos of ours there are more solar systems, universes, chains, globes, and spheres than there are atoms in the bodies of creation then it looks rather big. They are not counted by octillions they are counted by hundred octillions of octillions and many times that. The Milky Way is made up of universes many times larger than our own, each tiny spark a chain containing limitless evolving atoms. What child is there born of earth capable of expressing or knowing or imagining the qualities of the limitless Intelligence that governs these things? The human mind is absolutely incapable of attempting the struggle.

To try to define the Absolute is to defile It and to deny It. The dreaming savior, saint or sage is unworthy even to whisper it. Gods themselves dare not breathe it, for even His Eldest Sons have never lifted the hem of His mantle. And yet there are people who might be respectable burglars (which would be infinitely superior to being disreputable bunglers which they are at the present time), who rave about that of which they know not, and cast lots for garments that Gods dare not dream of. With the puny intelligence of a grain of sand, they seek to show the stuff that gods are made of.

It is a foolish waste of time and if persisted in will inevitably result in insanity, for the brain is not capable of juggling such tremendous units of intelligence.

There is but one path by which the Absolute may be reached and that is by following the winding stairs of human progress, upward and upward, until finally it achieves union with its source of being. The labors of man in this world period are not to produce gods but to produce human beings and the student of the Absolute would be far better off if he would try to be a credit to the human race instead of spending his time trying to discredit the Unknowable. He does the best he can but he cannot find in the universe that which he is not, therefore the Absolute becomes full of whims and fancies placed there by those who seek to know Him but could only reflect from His subtle shield their own souls.

The world needs people to be truly human, to learn how to master and express the truly concrete qualities which we are here to build. We must have the dreamer and the sage but he must dream dreams to serve his brother man and not try to build with his own feeble imagination a creature which even gods dare not to imagine. Our modern thought is wandering from the field of practical things into the vistas of impracticality. If we are to attain the acme of this race, let us realize that, to be perfect human beings is the ultimate of our goal and that godhood is not the perfection of human beings.

The most glorious concept in the world today is the concept of the perfect man. That dream is attainable. By labors it may be made practical, by conscientious living it becomes a reality, and if people who spend their time quoting the is-ness of Am would leave their intellectual stimulants alone and go out into the world to manifest the is-ness of their own spiritual consciousness by being cleaner, better and truer than their brother man, the Absolute would be perfectly able to take care of Itself. A hundred million years from now, with his greatest effort, man will only be a shade closer to the Infinite. But that shade is everything, for in eternity time is dissolved in works.

And still the Absolute remains veiled in the mantle of His own obscurity, untouched, unfathomed, and undreamed of by those who call His name but do not know His spirit. He slumbers in the infinite void of being, the baseless All. In Him, the worlds spin and move while man dwells as an atom in His formless body. Worlds and universes are but cells in His endless being and no man shall ever know Him, for He is wrapt in the robes of His own omnipotence. 'Tis blasphemy to strive to rend this garment, a blasphemy which gods dare not assail; but man, puny in his own strength but great in his egotism, assails to do that which gods do fear and as a fool to walk the path where wise men dare not tread. He could walk to the ends of Chaos and yet the sweeping folds of the Infinite would remain concealed. His duty is not to unveil the Absolute but to nourish and feed one little spark within his own soul. That labor is too great for him, why then should he assail the Wheel from which the Sparks are born? As he cannot temper the steel of his own spirit, why should he attempt to wield the sledgehammers of Vulcan? His own character is more than he can govern, why then should he seek to govern the Infinite? His modesty is his strongest virtue and those who assail to storm the temple of the Absolute are shorn of their virginity and are gowned in the robes of egotism.

Let the Absolute slumber in its death-like stillness, let the Unknowable remain unmoved in His meditations, for His meditations are the universes and worlds dropping as pearls from His lips. Let the servant be found among men to carry on the work of keeping these pearls in sanctity and reverence, worrying not of their source. For how shall man, with a mind of matter, carry the thoughts of eternity and live? Close down the veil lest passing through too soon the Flame should destroy all. Teach man to live, to love, to labor and to grow; teach him to better fulfill the labors of the lesser and leave in the hands of the Infinite that which He alone can know and master.

These thoughtless words of things we know not of brand us only fools, the lightness of our tone as we speak of nature's deepest mystery proves us unworthy of the trust. For the Absolute is in all, is all, will be all that ever shall be. Gods, men, and worlds are whispered words from His mouth wrapped in the veils of matter. No mortal eye shall gaze upon its depth but as the presence of this being draws ever nearer man shall sink into a depthness sleep and there be one with the Father of all whom he may not know but in whose arms, he shall never cease to be.

GENERAL GRUMP

THE scene of this little narrative is in an old soldier's home and its leading character is an old Civil War veteran who has for years been known as General Grump. His pension indicates the fact that he was never higher than a private in the rear ranks, but his imperious temperament, his bossitive ways, and his grumpitive personality has gained for him the name and title which he now bears. He has been in the Soldier's Home for many years, stamping around and complaining—something is the matter all the time. We must try and draw a picture of General Grump for you.

He is about five-foot-ten high and five-foot-ten wide; he has small beady black eyes set under heavy over-hanging brows; he slouches when he walks, and can scarcely open his mouth without profanity issuing forth. He stamps his cane, and his white chin-whiskers stand straight up when anyone around him has anything cheerful to say. His favorite expression is:

"This is a helluva world!" He is always taking the joy out of life for the rest of the inmates and those quiet, peaceable old folks who like to gather around the checkerboard or play solitaire are eternally disturbed by the General who stalks about, pounding on the floor with his cane, cussing everyone in particular and life in general.

Everything seems to have gone wrong with the General; he is the most abused man that ever lived and admits it; he has always suffered from tough luck and now, as his eighty-first year draws to a close, we find him with a mean disposition as the only product of his life, with various forms of profanity and tough luck tales as the by-products.

In other words, General Grump is a born grouch, his grandfather had been a grouch before him, and his father, Silas, had been known as Hard Cider for years, his name so changed to suit his temperament. General Grump kicks at the beans, swears at the bread, and cusses the service until he bids fair to outgrouch ten generations of ancestors.

So, he is the hero of our little life-drama.

One day after rising from the table and passing out onto the steps that led down to the driveway, General Grump saw a carriage winding up past the stacked muskets which ornamented the front door of the Soldier's Home. There were two people in the carriage, but only one of them is of especial interest to us and that is Uncle Ben. Of course, you do not know Uncle Ben, so we will have to go into details here as well.

Uncle Ben had been a captain in the Civil War and in that war, he had lost one arm, one leg, and both eyes, and in the years since he had gone his way the best he could. Uncle Ben had not seen the world since 1863 and now, more than eighty years old, he was coming to the Soldier's Home when the death of his only child had left him no home in the world. With his crutch and cane and the assistance of his companion, a county official, Uncle Ben slowly climbed the steps and entered the office of the Home where, in due form and time, he was established. Thus entered the most interesting inmate of the Soldier's Home.

It was several days after this that Uncle Ben and General Grump met, both sitting in broken down easy chairs on the porch.

"This is a helluva life," grunted General Grump, "it looks like rain. It has looked like rain for the last two weeks; wish to hell it'd rain!"

"Does it look like rain?" asked Uncle Ben, "you know I haven't seen a cloud since they gathered over Gettysburg and that was a long time ago."

"I told you it was a helluva life," answered General Grump, his brows contracting and the corners of his mouth going down.

"I don't know," answered Uncle Ben, "I ain't had a lot of trouble in my time. I can't say it's so bad. I have learned many things in these years of darkness and many things that I have not seen, I have felt. Now you, sir, I cannot see you, but I know you have a kindly face."

"Well, if you do, you're the first feller that ever did," answered General Grump. "All the world looks kindly to me. In all the years that I have hobbled through life, broken and lame, I have always heard kind words, there has always been someone to help, and the world has been good to me. And life hasn't been so hard, either. You know, even though I lost my eyes and one hand, I used to get work. They were always willing to help me, I've been very fortunate. I have been rich in the love of my children, who stayed with me and loved me until they, too, were called. Indeed, I have been very fortunate all these years."

"Uh-h! I haven't been fortunate," answered General Grump, "treated me like hell!"

"Are you blind too?" asked Uncle Ben.

"Nope."

"Then how fortunate you have been and how thankful you should be that you went through that great war. You have been able to see your loved ones. I could only know mine when I ran this hand over their faces. You should be very happy."

"Aw, hell!" "Did you lose your arms or legs?"

"Nope."

"You were not injured, then?"

"Hell, no. I wish they'd killed me."

"I suppose it is wrong," said the kindly old man softly, "to be jealous, but somehow, brother, I envy you. You can see the world and I cannot, you can walk around, and I cannot, you can work, and I cannot. I suppose it is human that I should envy you. There is only one thing about you I do not envy and that is your voice. That does not sound pleasant. I fear you are not happy. You have all that God gave you, and I was broken before the work was well begun, but let me tell you, brother, I have been content. While the world outside means nothing to me, I live in a different world, a world of make-believe, a world I have made for myself. Wherever I go, the sun is shining, though others tell me it rains; whoever I meet is smiling, though others tell me they weep. All the world is such a wonderful place and I, all these years behind my prison walls, have never been able to reach it, but I have made a go out of it and everything seems good. In the silence of my life, I have thought, for I have had few companions but my thoughts and the voices of my children. During all these years when sleeping and waking, all was dark, I have dreamed, and I have dreamed the infinite dreams. These darkened eyes have seen things that mortal eyes shall never see; this broken form has come closer to living than those who have all. Brother, do not be despondent. You have so much to make you glad, you have so much more than I have that it ill behooves that I should cheer you. And yet, let me tell you this:

"We live in a world of our own making, and this world that I have made is just as real to me as it is to you. Through all these years, I have never lost sight of the goodness of things. On that bloody field of Gettysburg where the bursting shrapnel closed my eyes forever, I saw many things. I then saw the uselessness of hate, the fruitlessness of discord; I saw that man, not God, made sorrow; and if he made sorrow, he could make joy too. Listen, brother, through all these years of darkness, I can still sing the songs I used to know."

And then the old man's voice broke out in a tune of long ago, an old plantation song, the song of the farmer and the workmen that sounded through our nation in the sixties. His voice was thin and cracked and, true, there was not much tune, but there was a great joy in the voice.

"See? I can sing as I used to," and Uncle Ben's eyeless face broke into a merry smile. "I can remember how they used to sing those when I was a boy. How glad I am that I have memory, for I have little else! I suppose God has been good to me and while others' memories fail them, the scenes of my youth grow clearer every day and I can see the blue sky and the singing birds." The old man's hand reached out and fumbled for the hand of the other.

"Brother, be glad and smile with me! Our time is but a little while. The world will smile with you, brother, if you will, but smile too." The old man's face lighted up with something akin to inspiration, and his very presence seemed to breathe light and truth.

General Grump was silent. He could not help but think back in his own life and see how much joy he had had, how much more he had had than this one who sat beside him.

"Are you really happy?" he asked.

"Happy?" asked the old man, "why shouldn't I be happy? I have been happy in the realization of duty well done, I have been happy in the love of a faithful wife, I have been happy in the love of my children, I have been happy in the love of my God, and for many years past I have been happy in the happiness of others. I can do little for my fellow man, but I have tried to make him happy, to make him forget his cares and fears in the happiness of real living, in the happiness of just being where he can hear the voice of other things."

General Grump tilted his hat on his head and looked at Uncle Ben for some minutes. "How long have you been blind?" he asked.

"Fifty-three years, I have been blind as I am today, for one shell did it all." "Were you never down on the world?"

"Oh, yes," and Uncle Ben smiled sweetly. "After it happened, I thought there was nothing left to live for, but one day I found that I hadn't lost anything that could compare with the thing I gained."

The General looked at him for several minutes and as he gazed into the radiating face of the old man whose sightless eyes stared out into eternity, General Grump heaved a little sigh and the corners of his mouth came up.

"I guess I've been a fool for some time," he muttered, and he looked down at his hands. "I've got both of 'em" and at his feet, "I have them too. And my eyes. And here I've been moping all these years."

"Life is a wonderful thing," answered the old man beside him. "We seldom learn to live it until it is nearly done."

"That's the hell of it," answered General Grump, stamping on the porch with his cane. "Yes, sir, that's the hell of it!" And getting up, he stumped off in irate rage.

BROTHERS OF THE SHINING ROBE - VIII
CHAPTER EIGHT
The Return From Glasgow

Three days after my arrival in Glasgow, my work completed, though possibly not as satisfactorily as might have been desired, I boarded a night train to London. I was the only one in the compartment and, as the efforts of the previous days had been heavily exhaustive, I perched my feet upon the seat across and sought to catch a few winks as the train roared through the night. Somehow, I have never slept very well on trains and this particular evening was no exception to the rule. I fidgeted and tossed, trying to find a comfortable position while each rut and groove in the track registered throughout my whole nervous system like the blows of a sledge-hammer. One foot went to sleep, I got up and stretched, then the other one ceased to function. There crept over me a wave of decidedly undesirable and far from spiritual thoughts, dealing generally with the principles of misery and especially that phase of it, which applied to riding in British coaches.

About half-past two in the morning, I could not keep my eyes open for a moment longer, I felt things around me getting more and more distant in spite of my every effort to remain attuned to them, and at last with a heavy lurch I sank in the corner of the seat into a troubled sleep. I do not know how long I remained in tins condition, but it could not have been very long before I became innately conscious of the fact that someone had opened the window. A breath of cold air, laden with that ever-present scent of Scottish moorlands, was blown in across my face. I felt dulled from head to foot and, do what I would, I could not seem to regain sufficient control over myself to move or even cry out.

Suddenly, as I lay there in this lethargy, the train struck an unusually severe rut. It seemed that the car-track must have been tied up in a figure eight. It threw me off the seat and down into the narrow foot-space of the compartment. This thoroughly awakened me, and I sat up, two feelings uppermost in my mind. The first was of anger against the rut and the second was an appreciation of the fact that it had brought me out of this stupor over which I apparently had no control. I sat up straight and determined to remain awake the rest of the night, but I had hardly made the resolution before I felt my head dropping and the fixed objects in the little compartment started to be going round and round, tying themselves into elaborate bowknots,

"Here, here," I said to myself, "this won't do!" I knew enough of things occult to realize that an influence was being exerted against something or someone, and that either through design or accident I was receiving a series of narcotic rays from somewhere in the universe. Even though the realization was firmly fixed in my mind, it just seemed that I could not stand up, nor could I move, and slowly the power to think was leaving me.

With a Herculean effort I rose to my feet, though I seemed to float rather than to walk; I swayed for a second with the lurching of the car and then fell in a crumpled heap, half on the seat, half on the floor of the compartment. As I fell, darkness reached up around me, and the power of think or to even know that I existed slowly departed from me.

Just when it seemed the last flickering light was dying out a great flaming bubble burst around me, filling the entire environment with gleaming pink and crimson flashes, and at the same instant a voice spoke in my ear:

"Pull yourself together, man."

Then I was grabbed by the nape of the neck and yanked to my feet by a hand which I could not see because of the bleared condition of my senses; an arm braced me and held me for a second, the door of the compartment was opened, and I was hurled from the train out into the night. I struck a soft dirt embankment where, stunned, and bruised, I rolled to the bottom and lay face downward in a thicket of branches. I remember faintly the flashing light, the streaming, flaming smoke of the locomotive and the rumble of the cars, then all grew dark around me.

When I came to myself, I was lying in the spare bedroom of a small English manor house, aching from head to foot and so dizzy that I could not look at any object without it spinning round and round like some gigantic pin-wheel.

The room was empty and, as I learned afterwards, my nurse, an elderly Welsh woman, had gone out to prepare some barley gruel for one who seemed in such a critical condition.

As I lay looking upward at pink and white baby roses on the wallpaper, trying to piece together the incidents of the previous day's experience, the well-known form of the aged Hindoo adept appeared beside me. I recognized him, yet in some way he was changed. The long flowing gray robe which I so loved to see him wear had given place to a clean-cut modern military uniform. His head, so long graced by the turban with its streamer of silk, now carried a military helmet with a long horse-hair plume down the back. But the eyes and face remained the same.

"You have had another very close call," he murmured as he stood beside me for a second. Fifteen minutes after I threw you from that coach last night, the entire car was burned up by an unexplainable fire in which wood and metals together were melted into a shapeless mass. No hand lighted that fire, it just burned out of nothingness, and the tongues of flame leaped from stick to stick, fed by the vital body of an unseen presence. In black magic, there is a law, and that law decrees that all who stand between evil, and the accomplishment of its power must be bought off, frightened off, or killed off. They have tried to buy you but to no avail, they have sought to incriminate you, but you stand firm as a thorn in the flesh of tradition. Having failed to attain victory through either the power of the first or of haunting fear, the black ray resorts to destruction in order to silence the power which must some time destroy it. Therefore, I suggest to you that you not only exercise great watchfulness but also surround yourself by the walls of force which you have been taught to build in the temple, that these streamers of injury may not attain their end. A great power was battling with you last night as it has battled with the greatest souls that ever came into the world, a clenching power that strangles out consciousness and leaves nothing behind but lifeless clay- the power of one man's will upon another.

"When a great master of wisdom succumbs, as one occasionally does through egotism or selfishness, the result is a godly intellect gone wrong, a divine fiend, a superhuman devil who, soulless in himself, ensnares the souls of men that light shall never triumph for in the triumph of light is realized the end of the reign of darkness.

"People have a great idea that in virtue alone lies strength, but this is not always true. The bull has neither ideality nor a consciousness of union with light, and yet his rushing blows and the goring of his horns destroy as surely as the bullet. It is the strength of individual omnipotence and the power of one over another that counts. While in the eternal plan of things right always wins, yet in the little world we see around us might rule right with the rod of iron. The one whose mental fingers and streams of spiritual force nearly destroyed you last night was once a great brother, noble and esteemed of men, although today he plays the villain in the drama. He is stronger than you are even, though his powers be evil and yours be good; and were it not that, being true, you are guided and guarded by the Elder Brothers you could not stand for a moment against the power of this demented genius for with the sheer strength of organic quality he could swamp you beyond any hope of retaliation.

"But remember, in your work, three weapons will forever be turned against you and these three you must ever be prepared to meet. First, you will be lured away from the tasks which you have been appointed to perform because the powers of darkness will people the earth with sirens to lure you from your labors. The powers of darkness seldom strike from without but usually play upon weak points in the character of the individual himself and, through the false power which they gain through the knowledge of that weak point, they twist the lives of others to the fulfillment of their own ends. Secondly, if they cannot lure you away through thoughtlessness or false devotion, they will seek to make it worth your while through offers of rewards, promotion, financial increase, or the promise of spiritual power. In other words, if they cannot lead you from it, they will seek to have you sell your labor for selfish ends. And if both these fail, if you have stood strong for right, for truth, for light, then be prepared for the other blow, the one that comes in the dark. When neither soft words nor caresses, this world's goods, or those of another cannot tempt you from your appointed way, then you must be prepared for the last great attempt which will come as the bolt of black magic to destroy that which it can neither buy nor bend and therefore seeks to break.

"In your work this will prove to you a very useful lesson and, while it will be some days before the soreness and pain works itself out of you from the accidents you have passed through, when you are yourself again you will be a better and wiser man."

The Initiate vanished through the checkered pink and white flowers of the wallpaper, leaving me to analyze and digest a great yet little understood reality in nature—that Redbeard was right when he said that nature's law is the survival of the fittest but that in the eternal plan of things each one seeks to become the one who is fit, and evolution is the fitting of oneself to be the fittest.

LIVING PROBLEMS DEPARTMENT

POWER AND DOMINANCE

One of the most difficult things in the world is to possess power without exerting it over another. Apparently, the proof of power lies in domination, but this is not so. The true proof of power is the control of self, all other things are comparatively unimportant. In the present European tangle, many things express themselves and this problem along with others. Mercy and consideration ennoble the victor of every fight, while those who grind down victims show themselves often less than the individuals they oppose. Generosity is the privilege of the strong, it is also their opportunity. When they fail to make the most of this opportunity, they fail to prove victors in the battle. There is no glory in spite, no reward in revenge. Many of the nations involved in the late European war who would have come out of it loved and revered for their noble gallantry sacrificed that reverence and forfeited the esteem of the world when they proved that they were generous victors and gallant, thoughtful over lords.

HOLY WATER

In the ancient tabernacle of the Hebrews was outlined the way of initiation and in the courtyard before the temple gate was the laver of purification, a great bronze bowl in which the priests performed their absolutions before entering the holy place. There is positively no sarcasm intended but we just want to remind some people of the exact position of that bowl as it stands before the temple steps, a yawning menace to the poise of many of our students of the mystical. The old adage was that cleanliness is next to godliness therefore it seems that the mystery of that mighty laver must become a part of the esoteric instructions to students. It is possible to over bathe, but it is not commonly done except by fanatical individuals. All things can be carried to an extreme but there are two kinds of baths man must find a way to take. He must be initiated by fire and water. He must learn the value of the sun bath, which is his physical initiation of fire, and the old family tub bath fashioned after the laver of purification.

RELIGIOUS CLEAN-UPS

Every so often we hear of the churches and religious organizations launching a campaign against dance halls, theatres, picture shows and various similar things. While there is no doubt that there is a certain class of improper amusement, we beg to call the attention of the religious people to a truth much more fundamental than the one they are seeking to emphasize. It is basically this: that the morale of a nation depends upon the finer spiritual truths which should be implanted by the religious organizations of the world. If the "drives" which ecclesiastical orders are launching upon the world were turned right back into the church, they would do a great deal more good. Some of the worst of those whom they attack are shrouded with serenity and protected by the enfolding arms of religion. While the religious organizations are fussing and stewing among themselves as to who is greatest, splitting up over trivials, and etc., they are forcing people out of the church. Many of those whom they now brand as lost souls were forced into their present position by the heartlessness of religion and the injustice of creedal theology, which preaches forgiveness and compassion but shows none of it to the sinners of the world. The first clean-up which theology should advocate should begin with the washing of the inside of the cup for while religion dickers and bargains, plays favoritism to some and condemns many, it can never meet the crying need of a world in spiritual pain. The church has no right to condemn vices in others while its own heart is full of vipers and thieves who pray upon the Sabbath and go out robbing the widows and the fatherless on Monday morning.

THE MAN WHO FOUND GOD

THERE is a story told of a great scientist who built a unique laboratory far from the sight of man where he installed mighty instruments and many wonderous mechanical contrivances, all to achieve a single end—to create an instrument wherewith he might span the chasm 'twixt man and God. The years went by, and the scientist labored tirelessly upon the child of his dream. Wheels and levers were slowly placed and after many years, the great shape of a looming mechanical mystery rose from the floor of the laboratory as the completed result.

As a young man, the scientist had commenced his labors. Many years had passed, years of consecration to a single end, years of concentration upon a single work. He had never lived in the world of men since a disappointment of his early life which had broken his trust in his fellow man and the moving events of earth meant little to him, his great machine meant all. So, we find the snow of an ever-gathering winter upon his bowed head, long lines and furrows mark his face, and his piercing eyes sink ever deeper beneath the massive brows and tawny lashes; his body is bent, and frail and long purple veins show out upon his hands. For him this span of earth is nearly done, yet in his soul is the same flame of youth which had inspired him in the ages gone, the same indomitable will had never been broken for within him burned the determination to perfect a machine which would connect spirit and matter, to finish his great work whereby the veil should be rent and mystic nature give up her secrets.

His laboratory was a great domed room built like an astronomical observatory. In the ceiling were a number of trapdoors, while the entire room revolved by pulleys, counterweight and bearing. He had but to press a button and the floor rose some dozen feet, carrying with it the great machine; he need but pull a lever and countless windows in the dorm opened at prismatic angles, casting gleams of light upon the almost shapeless mass of wheels; he had but to turn a knob upon the wall and the great machine itself swayed back and forth to any angle, balanced upon gigantic steel rockers.

Each day brought the moment of victory closer, each day the fire of triumph flashed stronger in the aged man's eyes and the cold blood rushed faster through his veins until at last the great day came! The last wheel was in place, the final bearing was tested, and the great machine stood a mammoth dream of a man who gives his all to learn that which he knows not. The great scientist sent into the world of men and drew around him the mightiest minds of the time that they might gather in the vaulted room to see and hear the marvel of a life's labor. They came from all over the country; with hoary heads and weighty brows, with dignity and age, they gathered to see the fruitage of a life work. Twelve in all there were; great astronomers, great physicists, masters of logic and philosophy, they gathered from their several ways at the foot of this mighty instrument.

The time of the experiment was at midnight and, as the clock struck twelve, they all gathered in the domed room with its levers and its wondrous mechanism. The old scientist came and, in his face with the exultation of youth, told of the mystery he had conceived.

"When I open those great shutters in the ceiling, each of the prismatic panes shall gather in the light of the stars, the light of the planets, of suns and moons; the intelligences that rule them shall be concentrated tonight upon these sensitized plates, built like the sense centers of the human organism. Here is an ear as fine as that of any man, threads so delicate that only a microscope can show them, an organ which can hear all things; here are vocal cords of slender steel and catgut wherein sounds of infinite may be reproduced; here are eyes of metals and fiber as perfect as any organ of human sense; and here, gentlemen, is the masterpiece of all, a brain of precious metal, with every nerve and sinew, with every force and power. I have built a god, an oracle of matter which is capable of using the light brain of the infinite, one who shall speak to us, inspired by the rays of planets and the stars. This brain will register the thoughts of God, these lips shall speak His will, these ears shall hear His infinite melody, these eyes shall see His wonders. Seventy years I have been building this machine, far more perfect than anybody built by man, and tonight I shall quicken it with the ray of a hundred million stars, of suns, globes, and universes, by concentrating their endless light through these prisms in the roof, and finally reflecting them all upon this gigantic sounding-board wherein shall be given out the mystery of creation. This chair is where I shall sit to work the tuning forks and coils that each thought of the Infinite mind shall vibrate through this brain. "Marvelous," murmured the group of scientists gathered around.

"Marvelous, but impossible."

"No, no! It is not impossible!" cried the old man vehemently. "Gentlemen, give me just this night and I will prove that it is not impossible! Gentlemen, you have little trouble to expect from me, if this machine shall fail, I shall kill myself! I have lived alone to create it; with its failure I shall die. But it shall not fail! By all the laws of natural dynamics, by all the laws of science, of invention, of mechanics, of electricity and of nature's subtle forces, it shall not fail!

"Now gentlemen," and he calmed himself with a mighty effort, "we will raise the machine." He pressed the button on the wall.

A shudder ran through the floor of the building and, almost imperceptibly, the floor moved upward. The scientists gazed around in amazement. The entire laboratory was upon a gigantic elevator which carried a work room, instrument, and men, upward into the dome of the observatory.

Finally, some dozen feet from the dome the progress of the moving floor was stayed and then with delicate astronomical instruments the scientist arranged his mighty machine, tilting it upon its massive rockers until all pointed to a single ray which was to be the keynote of the machine—the planet Saturn.

"Now, gentlemen, will you please be seated?" and the scientist waved his hand to a circle of twelve leather easy chairs which surrounded the instrument. "I am going to ask you to please remain silent during this test for fear that the vibration of your voices might derange the currents.

The wise and learned took their seats. The gray-browed philosophers leaped back in their chairs, their gaunt frames at rest but their minds tensely centered upon the great experiment.

"If it succeeds," breathed one, "both past and future shall unite in blessing the inventor."

The inventor gave one last look at the great creature of steel and wire -the child of his hopes, the creation of his dreams, the supreme achievement of his life, and then pressed a tiny button on the wall. The great electric arc-lights went out, and the observatory was enveloped in total darkness, darkness which seemed peopled with mystic shapes and thrilled with a stillness that was audible. Nothing but the low breathing of the watchers and an occasional slight movement in one of the chairs told that a living creature was anywhere in that still room.

Suddenly there came a grating sound and the whole room was flooded with a strange, blue-white light filled with rainbow colors and dancing, flinging, swirling sparks of iridescent hue. The great prisms in the ceiling had been thrown in place and a hundred million stars sent their tiny rays down into the room. A gasp went round the circle in the easy chairs. "Marvelous! Marvelous!"

This opaline light bathed the machine in a weird and unnatural glow and revealed the wizard of genius standing by its side, his eyes turned upward to the millions of sparks reflected upon the prisms in the ceiling and between which the dark blue of the sky appeared as a piece of plush, jeweled with diamonds. Slowly he turned the mighty arm of the crank and the prisms moved one after the other until the light focused into a little spot no larger than a ten-cent piece, one gigantic finger of concentrated power. This was turned upon a sensitive organ of steel and silken wire which glowed and gleamed like the mighty Kohinoor.

The professor sat down, his hand on the tuning fork and coil, and his eyes fastened to the fine dials before him, which quivered like the nerves of a racehorse. The air was filled with a droning, moaning sound which seemed like the rush of mighty bodies through the sky. Something oppressed the eardrums of those sitting around and a faintness of nausea stole over them; but still, sturdy searchers that they were to whom life meant nothing and knowledge everything, they remained in their chairs, gazing at the strangest sight man has ever witnessed. A gigantic mad man, a genius possessed of insanity, that dared to build lips of steel for God to talk with!

As the professor sat there, his hand upon the dials, a great chill came over him, he seemed wrapt in a damp blanket and began to shiver in spite of himself. But his eyes never left the tiny spot of light, varicolored and ever-changing, seeming to hiss and sputter as it struck the discs.

"I shall soon know all," he kept muttering to himself, "the mystery shall be unveiled to me."

Suddenly the light ray seemed to pass through the discs and spread like a phosphorescent glow all over the great machine. The blazing eye of steel seemed to blink at him and the nerve wires to twitch.

"I shall win! I shall win!" breathed the scientist. "At last, man shall know! At last, the infinite shall be attained! The mystery shall be solved!"

As he spoke, the glow of light seemed to condense itself into a ball, opal-like in its formation, its color and shape ever-changing, its position ever-moving. It hung swaying, twisting, and turning in the very center of the great machine. Then there unfolded from it like mighty arms two streamers of winglike force which poured out as flaming fins from the sides of this shapeless globe.

The scientist gazed in awe and amazement at the strange phenomena unfolding itself before him. He wanted to call the attention of the other watchers to it for but some unknown reason his tongue refused to speak. All he could do was point his finger and gasp. The minutes passed and there slowly formed itself out of the flaming mist a great opaline figure many times larger than a human being, a great glorious figure surrounded by a halo of light and wings of steely force. Only the head seemed well defined and was formed out of the great ball. The robes and draperies streamed off into nothingness while the fingers were hazy streams of flame pointing first in this way and in that. A great roaring rumble filled the air, and the eardrums of the old scientist seemed ready to burst. He could not, however, keep his eyes from the shining face, so terrible yet so magnificent, beautiful yet relentless in every part of its being. Great streaming eyes of living fire gazed out serenely upon the face of the aged man and yet the serenity itself was terrifying.

"Are you God?" gasped the old man. "Had I but known what you were, I fear I would not have dared call you!" The great figure shook its head, and a voice sounded in the man's soul, words which lips could not frame.

"No, I am not God. I am the least of His messengers. It is who has been appointed to unveil to you the mysteries you have waited seventy years to learn. Since time began, you have sought the mysteries that are so carefully hidden by merciful Deity who conceal His own power that man may not die from His flame. Man, flutters around the throne of Light like the moth around the candle-flame until finally, singed and battered, he falls to rise no more. I stand here as guardian of the earth for you have launched upon it a power which could bum it to the core, could throw the planets from their several orbits and twist creation into a ruined mass. But this is not the privilege of mortal man.

Therefore, these rays of light, I receive them to myself lest passing me they should destroy you."

"Who are you?" moaned the scientist. "I am the Lord of the Light Devas. Look." And his great flaming hand closed over the discs of steel and celluloid, crumpling them to pieces. 'Tis better that these should perish than that man should lose this ray which could slay across the universe in the hands of the foolish and yet can raise the dead. Let this thing of steel perish and man live. As for you, sir, come, I would show you something."

Beckoning to the aged man, the flaming specter rose and pointed along the ray of light that led to the prisms in the ceiling.

This golden ray seemed to form stairs as they ascended.

"Where am I going?" asked the professor.

"Into cosmos upon the ladder you have formed," answered the guide. Draperies of many subtle substances seemed to brush the face of the scientist, lights danced in the ethers about him, swaying figures surrounded him, and far off the plants in the sky gazed down with the same great faces as the one of his guides, only greater and more noble. Crisscross currents which were themselves words and sentences of living fire connected the globes together like cords passing through beads to make a necklace of the whole.

"Is this God?" asked the scientist in awe.

"No, it is not," answered the Deva. "Do you see this great blue haze in which these things float in endless pageantry?"

"Yes," answered the scientist, "is that God?"

The Great One shook his head, "'Tis but the hem of His garment," he answered. "Do you hear this strange song of wild fantastic symphony, mighty roars and tender cadences, heavy rumbles, and soft purring's as of the flutter of a bird's wing? Great seething comets and tails of vrillic power, these make up the creations of the Uncreated, these are the least of the Great, the unimportant of the Mighty."

"How, then, can I gather His power into my machine?" asked the scientist.

"You cannot," answered the Shining One. "You but take one single sound and upon a string of steel seek to hear the harmonies for which all nature alone is not a complete sounding-board."

"Then I have worked in vain," muttered the scientist.

"No," answered the Great One, "you have only found the way. Many substances must sound in harmony before God talks to man. Spirit, mind, and matter are alone, organs of His speech, the eyes of His vision, the ears of His understanding. Long has science failed in that on earth they seek the things of heaven; in steel, stone, and stick they have sought the God, which rests alone in the infinite. Come with me and I will answer your riddle, the riddle of all living things, the riddle of the Eternal Future which no man knoweth, of the ultimate, which is concealed, the completion as yet veiled by the density of mortal thought."

The Shining One passed slowly on and behind him walked the professor, searching and seeking with a new light and deeper understanding the answer to the Riddle.

* * *

About an hour had passed. The light still shone down from the ceiling, but the passing of the orbs of night had moved it from the dial. The waiting scientists moved uneasily in their chairs.

"Isn't it about time something happened?" muttered one under his breath.

"It seems to me it is," answered his companion in an undertone.

At last, one bolder than the rest spoke, saying, "Professor, have we not waited long enough?"

But no answer sounded.

"Professor!" he called again. Still no sound.

One of the watchers reached into his pocket and, drawing out a match, struck it and held it aloft. It gleamed on the mighty instrument and also upon the figure of the scientist who sat in the chair, his head upon his chest.

"Why he has gone to sleep!" exclaimed one, and rising to his feet he fumbled around until he found the light button which he pressed, flooding the room with brilliance. "Poor man, he was all tired out of his experiment." He leaned over and touched the professor's forehead, then sharply drew back his hand. Then he placed his ear to the aged man's heart. Rising, he spoke solemnly to the other eleven.

"The inventor is dead. He died on the night when his supreme achievement was to be given to the world, when man through a tiring of steel should learn to know his God."

As he spoke, there came a humming, droning sound—the wheels in the machine were moving. The great lips of steel opened and a voice, deep and terrible, spoke:

"I see, I see, I see—No! No! No!"

At the same instant, the machine was galvanized by a bolt of electricity. When it had cooled again, it was welded into a solid block. No wheel or piston could be moved.

THE DANCE OF THE DEVAS

ACCORDING to a legend that is as old as the rock-hewn temples of the Himalayas there is far up on the side of Mount Everest a cave hollowed out of the solid rock of the mountain. Its pillars and columns are of living stones, their surfaces chiseled into wondrous flowers and arabesques. This ancient temple is a mystic maze of passageways twisting in and out from unknown depths back again into eternity. None ever seemed to know how old this temple is but it was called the Shrine of the Devas. The average mortal never learns of its existence, and even the devout Hindoo may search his life through and never learn of its existence. It has one duty, one labor to perform—it is the temple of Temptation where the Eastern Initiates, seeking the life of immortality, pass the test of the astral world.

The entrance of this temple is built like the human ear and far into the earth, its passageways twist and turn like the labyrinth of the human ear. Upon its walls are traced slender filaments like the fine threads of the auditory nerve and to drop a single pin in the depth of that cave is to produce a thundering roar, so perfect are the acoustics.

Many have heard of Diocletian's Ear, where the emperor sat in a cave of stone to listen to the whisperings of his prisoners. But this cave in the heart of India is more wondrous far than this ear of a Roman emperor, for it is the cave of the Devas, the Sound Creatures of eternity. One at a time the appointed Children of Light enter into this cave to learn of immortality, to pass from mortal tribulation to the tranquility of omnipotence.

Some years ago, a truly great one passed through the Ear of the Devas, and we will follow his wanderings among its carved pillars and terraced sculptures. Three figures approached the door, a massive pivot of stone, which swung away when they pressed upon it. Two were old men dressed in yellow robes, their heads shaven, and upon their foreheads the mark of the illuminated. The third was a youth who walked in silence and deep asceticism between the two, in the great repose of the fourth step. Without a sound the two priests stepped aside, allowing him to enter, and then they separated, one going to the right and the other to the left, resting on each side of the cave entrance was a large flat stone. Here each took his seat, twisting his feet up underneath him and crossing his palms upon his lap; then slowly the eyeballs of each turned upward, eyelids drooping, and the priests entered into meditation for strength, peace, and power to the wanderer.

In the meantime, the youth was entering the darkened cave. It was not totally black, but a very faint phosphorescent glow was emitted by the rocks, just enough that he might not stumble against the pillars nor fall by missing the steps. Around and around wound the candidate, through the labyrinth of the rock-hewn ear, his bare feet making but little sound, and even this becoming a faint rumble in the taut stillness of the cave.

At last, he reached the end of the spiral where this great twisting nautilus of stone ended in a small circular chamber from which arches ran in all directions. In this chamber was a great tree carved from the solid stone of the mountain. Under this tree with its branching a wealth of stone-carved leaves was a smooth rock and upon this the candidate seated himself to await the pleasure of his God.

As he sat there, there poured forth from the subterranean arches streams of shining gas which wreathed and twisted in the phosphorescent darkness. As these streamers came closer, the lights resolved themselves into glorious creatures in swaying draperies, great eyes gazed at the candidate, great forms came forth, demon shapes whose bloodshot eyes gazed at him in blinking terror. Slowly, these forms swayed back and forth to a great rhythmic heating, like the pulsing of a human heart. Back and forth they swayed in endless glory, passing round and round the seated figure, performing in the mystic ethers of this subterranean vault the Dance of the Devas. These forms kept beckoning to him and from their lips poured forth great streams of music, seeking to lull the soul of the candidate.

Slowly a subtle dream-trance stole over him, and he felt himself being drawn from his rocky couch to join in that endless chant and mystic dance. With a great effort he drew himself back, crying out, "I take my refuge in Buddha!" Still the figures called him and the music as of a thousand stringed instrument and peals like those of mighty organs echoed and re-echoed through the Ear of the Gods. Deafened by the sound, his head singing and his body torn, the candidate swayed in his meditation and sought to launch himself into the endless rhythm of the Devas' Dance. And then, with a mighty effort, he drew back his mind upon Buddhi and remained in meditation, saying:

"All these are the great unreality — they shall not lead me from my appointed task. Man, who serves these Devas and joins in the Dance shall never attain Nirvana, nor by opposing them shall he destroy them, but only through the realization of the Divine Presence."

From out the carved arches poured another stream of mystic beings who floated about like the beautiful Undines in the ethers of the ocean. Streams and rays of light poured from them, and they twisted through the air like winged creatures from other worlds. They wound themselves around the figure of the meditating aspirant; they twined their arms about him, seeking to lead him from his meditation. Through half-closed lips, the youth replied, "All these are of the world of illusion; you shall not tempt me, Devas of the Flame Being."

This whispered, they cried out, and through the subtle essences of the cave, their voices sounded as music in his ears. But still he remained in silence, the silence of deep contemplation upon the Body of Brahma. Then they're issued from the mystic corridors a trooping band of fiends, great seething creatures of demon proportions with the heads of beasts and of dragons and the crawling forms of reptiles and snakes. These, too, surrounded him and dashed at him, leering, and screaming. The chill of fear crept into the heart of the candidate and when it did so, these great slimy forms grew greater and stronger. He sought to leave the cave and to escape these terrifying creatures that raised flaming fingers to destroy him. Then came the thought of his work, and he remained.

"Thou to art creatures of Maya. What have I to do with you? How can you harm me if I am at peace with myself? I have naught to fear of you." And closing his eyes, the youth returned to his deep meditation in which these seething forms vanished forever, and he became lighted by his Buddha.

It was the strangest scene that man ever looked upon, in the Cave of the Labyrinth. On a tiny altar of stone, under the shade of a tree of solid granite, sat the yellow-robed priest, his legs crossed, and his hands folded. Around him were three circles of supernatural beings. The first swayed and moved as they passed in an endless circle to the right, the second danced their weird dance to the left, while the third worked back and forward and as flaming fiends attacked the body of the candidate. This was the Dance of the Devas when the great Beings from other worlds tested the courage of the candidate's soul.

Slowly he sank into ever deeper meditation until even the realization of eternity was obliterated from his soul and alone in the great Ever-Existing the candidate saw nothing, heard nothing, felt nothing. And there he remained while they danced their weird dance. Slowly there radiated from him a glow of light that grew ever-stronger until it lighted the very carved arches with its presence. Then like mists the phantom forms dissolved into the shadows and in their place, there entered from the corridor a great stream of yellow-robed figures.

A new door had opened and from the realms of Shidda-Loka the saints had come to bless the new-born Buddha and his working. Slowly they passed in endless file, a swaying mystery of phantom forms, until they too vanished in the gloom of the cave. Then through the darkness great faces appeared, many times the size of human face, the Great Ones of the seven worlds gazed upon the Initiate. Impelled by an inner urge which he could not understand, the youth rose, ascended the altar, and passed slowly outward through the spirals of the Ear.

At the gate sat the two priests, still in meditation. With his hands folded, the newly awakened one passed onward and outward into the worlds of his activity, worlds that were no longer his because he had unveiled them. So, the priest was again in the world but not of it, for the veil of Maya had been torn away while the Devas danced in the Labyrinth of the Ear.

QUESTION AND ANSWER DEPARTMENT

Where and what are we when a sleep?

Ans. We are exactly the same asleep as when awake. We work in exactly the same degree of helpfulness asleep as when awake. Those who cannot function consciously in the plane of sleep remain in their astral body, suspended over their physical body in the shape of a globe.

What is it that reincarnates?

Ans. The thing that reincarnates in man is the Ego which assumes form after form, these forms being built around centers of consciousness which are called permanent atoms carried in the brain, the heart, the lower body, and in the solar plexus, the centers of our four present bodies. These bodies come into form through the elements and ether, and the physical body is drawn around by attraction.

Must Karma created here always be worked out on this plane?

Ans. Karma created here is worked out on one of two planes—the lower plane or the astral.

Has every person now living on earth been reincarnated?

Ans. No one can exist who has not been before. We are just exactly what we have made ourselves in lives we have lived before.

What is the cause of walking in the sleep?

Ans. A partial division of bodies in which the lower side of the body is partly in control while the higher vehicle is partly out.

Can one incarnate into a different race of people?

Ans. The average individual reincarnates into a higher race of people.

Can a man live forever if he will not sin?

Ans. If man does not sin, he will turn to stone. Sin produces experiences. What we call sin and suffering is one of our greatest friends. We sin and break a natural law, if we did not suffer, we would soon find ourselves destroyed and never know it. We can live forever if we absolutely harmonize ourselves with all the planes of nature, but it cannot be all in one place. People who live forever would get tired of it as they get tired of dying today. You must be reminded that we live forever now, we never die. We just do not realize it because we have not had enough knowledge to see it. We have to evolve the intelligence to realize that we already have what we are looking for.

What happens when God rests?

Ans. When God rests, all life and spirit, and the matter which is working through it, is withdrawn into Him. Man, having no vehicle of expression capable of remaining conscious at that rate of vibration, which is God, sleeps also and does not come into manifestation again until the universal reawakening.

Explain sex.

Ans. Sex manifests through all the regions of nature as the two polarities of one nature.

What was the first cause of evil among men and women?

Ans. Perversion. Perversion is the natural result of inexperience. Man is working with vehicles and powers which he cannot understand, and contending with laws which he breaks (thinks he breaks, but the law breaks the man instead of his breaking the law.) Man made his first mistake through crystallization, through the abuse of his powers and continues to make those mistakes and will continue until he ceases to abuse natural powers. The first and last mistake is the result of ignorance, and ignorance itself is now a crime. Ignorance and the inability of complete manifestation through the vehicle is so-called evil. Man is like a little child; he will have to learn through his mistakes, keep stumbling and falling on his nose until he learns to walk.

THE HOMAGE

CIVILIZATION, with its spreading power, dissolves into itself as quicksilver the wild places of the world. Where mighty forests once raised crested tops, gloomy buildings, chimneys, and iron girders now dark narrow cobbled ways where the natural grandeur of things has been swallowed up in the sordidness of human concept. Here and there, however, are still spots where the devastating hand of man has not rested, where the sound of the axe, the cries of the woodmen, and the rumbling of logs has not broken the primeval stillness. One by one the savage denizens of the wild, the beasts untamed, have slunk away into these untrodden places, into the Rocky Mountains and lonely crags where they gaze out with great furtive eyes at the hand of civilization which, as it devastates the primeval wilderness, strangles out their lives.

In a certain land where there is a mighty range of mountains which raise their rough and wooded sides like great supplicating arms to the skies. The barrenness of these hills is clothed with the verdant garment of tree and shrub. Mighty straggling monarchs of the forest toss their branches upward as though to grasp in their shaky fingers the clouds that hover over them. A narrow trail winds up to these mountains, barely a footpath; here and there, leads over loose rocks and broken boulders and from stone to stone across some waterfall that descends like a stream of crystal from the snow peaks far above. There is no silence in that wood for there is ever a swishing, ever a rippling, ever a sighing, as from the mountains pour the streams of water or through the tree-tops the wind whispers its message to any ears that are there to hear.

Up this narrow path climbs an occasional hunter for the deer still peer shyly out from the thickets or spring from rock to rock and amid the scrub growth that clothes the walls that rise on either hand. Here too the mountain lion lurks and at night his shining eyes gaze from the darkness at the campfire of the hunter. Here also are wolves and foxes and in the lower valleys dwell coyotes that howl at the gathering shadows as the shades of evening fall. Mayhaps an awkward bear will cross the path and waddle along on his short, ungainly legs. It is the joy place of the hunter, who, with the glee of the sportsman, slays to prove the merit of his aim.

There are many stories told of those mountains, many legends which the mind of the ancient Red Man fashioned, and the mind of the jesting white man perpetuates. But there is one legend that is the strangest of all, the story of the Old Man of the Mountain. It is said that somewhere up in those hills there lived a hermit who had dwelt there many days. As far back as the old hunters could remember, the story was told of how one, tired of the world and its shams, had crept away from all living things of men to go and live in the mountains, among the crags whose lofty peaks touched the sky. Once in a great while, someone saw him far in the distance as he stood mirrored in some mountain lake or in sharp outline against the sky. They knew him as the Old Man of the Mountain, the hermit of the mighty peaks. Some said he was good, some that he was strange and cruel, but all loved to tell of him, to guess, and to speculate.

Once, in the course of human events, there climbed up the mountain path that wound in and out along the rugged sides of the hills a whistling youth. Over his shoulder was slung a rifle, a cartridge belt was around his waist, and on his back, he carried a pack. He was going into the hills to hunt, with the enthusiasm of youth he would slay the lion and the bear, the deer and the wolves whose howling's he had heard from the valleys below.

Round and round the path wound. The hours went by, the gloom of evening fell, and still the hunter was far from the crest of the mighty hill where little scrub pines shown out from the ever-encircling band of snow. The chill of the mountain was in the air, the valley was long since dark and tiny twinkling lights below showed the abode of men. Still the glow of daylight was on the mountain peak and as the youth stood there in the semi twilight, the silence was broken by a crackling sound as of the breaking of twigs and the swishing of branches.

Looking quickly around, the youth saw standing before him a mighty stag. His great arched antlers had a span of many feet, and his noble head was raised to catch the passing warning of the atmosphere. Two large mild eyes gazed at the youth who, in the frenzy of the hunter, reached for his gun and drawing it rapidly to his shoulder gazed along the cold steel sights toward the heart of the stag. Just as his finger was closing upon the trigger, a hand was laid upon his arm. The youth started, the gun slipped from his already nervous fingers, and he turned in amazement to gaze into the face of a strange being.

As he turned, he gave a start for such a figure few men have seen. The face bore the marks of great age and the snowy locks that bordered it were whiter far than the mountain tops that had stood there since eternity. The figure of the old man, for such it was, was draped from head to foot in a cowl of gray cloth and he carried a great wooden staff in his hand cut from the limb of a dead tree. His eyes, however, were the wonder of the picture. Two kindly, twinkling eyes that could register even the faintest shade of emotion, one moment gleaming with the joy and youth of life and the next dimmed by the tears of sorrow, gazed into the face of the hunter. The old man's hand was resting lightly upon his shoulder and his sweet old face held a soft rebuke.

"You—you—" began the youth, "are you not the Old Man of the Mountain?"

The stranger nodded his head and a voice, mellowed by years of goodness, answered softly and kindly,

"Yes, I am the hermit who lives in these hills. But why do you shoot my stag?"

"Your stag?" exclaimed the boy hunter, "how does it that you own the beast?"

"In this world," the old man answered, "proper use warrants ownership, and those who use God's creatures well have the first claim upon them." The old man held out his hand to the stag and the great beast, though viewing the hunter askance, slowly came across the little clearing and rubbed his soft face against the old man's hand. The hermit put his arm around the neck of the stag and spoke to it in soft sweet tones. Just a few sighing sounds, like a pitiful cry, the old man made, but the beast seemed to understand, its soft nose was turned upward and its eyes looked at him with a tenderness of expression which moved even the hunter.

The old man turned to the youth, "Do you still dispute my ownership?" he asked, "do you still doubt that he is mine and I am his?"

"What were the words you used?" asked the youth in surprise, "how did you talk to him?"

"I spoke in the words of the forest and the trees," he answered. "That is his language. He hears the voice of fear in the crackling of the twigs and the stealthy footsteps of the hunter; he hears life and love in the voice of the waterfall and the soft swaying of leafy branch. These are the sounds of his language and during these many years in the mountains, I have learned to talk with the tongue of beast and bird; yes, I have even learned to talk with the trees and flowers who hear my voice and shelter me with their love and protection. Listen."

The old man breathed out a soft stirring sound like the breath of dawn in the treetops and from the shrubs and bushes around an answer came, the same soft, stirring sound and voices seemed to whisper.

"They all know me, they all love me, for I have lived here eighty years and never once have I injured God's creatures. When I want food, they bring it to me of the ripe fruits of their store. The little squirrels bring me nuts from their harvest, while the trees give me of their fruit, and from their own dried leaves they form a shelter which guards me in the chill of winter. You have come into these hills like the spirit of man oft times comes into the world—to slay and to hate. Not that you really care, for in your soul you do not loathe the beasts, but to you, their souls mean no more than a drop of water from yonder stream. But I have learned to look upon with love even the drops of water, for each one has a message; I have lived up here so long that the trees and birds and flowers are one with me in spirit. I love them all and truly they love me. Come, young hunter, lay your gun aside for a while, for in my eyes, and in the eyes of my children of the forest, that gun means hate and death. You need not fear, leave it here, and I will bring you back for its anon."

The youth lay down his rifle and taking the hand which, the old man held out to him, followed him away from the path and into the depth of the great green forest wrapped in evening shades. Mighty trunks rose up about him and failing leaves descended like a gentle rain upon him as he passed. Suddenly, the old man stopped.

"Look," he said. From the side of a tall tree a big gray squirrel came and stood pertly gazing for a few seconds then vanished like a little flash of dusky shadow" to appear a second later carrying in his teeth a ripe hazel nut. Scampering down the rough trunk he climbed up the hermit's gray robe and as the old man opened his mouth, the little gray squirrel placed therein the hazel nut, then hopping onto the old man's shoulder, sat up there, his little beady eyes darting first in this way and then in that. The hermit took the nut from his mouth and held it out to the hunter.

"See how they care for me? But it is no more tenderly than I have cared for them." He spoke a few soft words to the squirrel, which darted away like some little tree sprite into the darkness of the gathering night. He had barely vanished when the youth suddenly jumped back in fear and amazement. Before them on the road stood a great wolf, his longue lolling out and great tusks bared. A growling howl broke from the beast.

"He does not know you," the old man explained, "for whenever he sees men, they throw something at him, whenever he meets them, he expects the flash of flame that pours from their rifles. Therefore, he hates them even as they hate him. But come, you are perfectly safe."

Then he stepped up to the wolf and, bending slightly, placed his hand between the beast's teeth. The wolf drew back its head and licked the kindly hand.

"This," explained the hermit, "has its price. If you essayed this feat, your hand would pay the price and probably your life."

"But what have you done for the beasts that they should so love you?"

"I have been true to them. In the cold winter nights, I have sheltered their young in my little cabin, I have fed the babies that the hunters left parentless, and in the spring, I have loosened them into the world. Many years ago, a hunter climbed these hills and slew the sire of this wolf, another slew its mother and three little cubs; three howling fighting, spitting little handfuls of flesh, were left in my hands. I nourished them and guarded them, and they played with my mountain lions and romped about with the bear cubs that I have in my cabin. The springtime came, and they went their way, strong enough to protect themselves. This is one of them, the other two mayhaps we shall see also unless the hunters have slain them."

Then they went on further along the path of nature's miracles. The great stag walked behind them, his arched antlers breaking the tree branches as he passed.

"Look here," the old man spoke, pointing to a crutch in a tree just a little ways ahead. "In this nest are four little birds. Yesterday the sound of a gun was heard in these mountains, there was a fluttering of wings, and with a screeching cry the mother bird fell downward from this nest. There was a great whirr of wings and with a hoarse cry of rage, the father bird flew straight into the face of the hunters. Another shot was fired and he, too, was laid low without even a fighting chance. Now hear the cries in the trees."

The old man climbed up onto the broken stump and from the encircling arms of a dead pine he drew a nest, in it, several little shrilling specks of life with ugly featherless bodies and great gaping beaks.

"I shall take these too with me to my cabin, and drop by drop I will feed them as I have long ago learned to do. Their mother and father are gone, slain by one of my races; but among the beasts and birds I have tried to redeem my people and to prove to them that in the heart of man there is still a generous spirit."

His soft hand cuddled the tiny birds in their nest and with soft cries and little shrill notes, he sought to quiet them. In a few moments the cries from the nest ceased and, sheltered by the old man's love, the little hungry birds rested until he could procure them food. The youth marveled at the sight, for he had never supposed that there could be among the worlds of men one who so loved dumb creatures. The old hermit pointed ahead through a little ravine that opened before them and there the hunter saw the peaked roof of a tiny cabin surrounded by little fir trees and with an old tile for a chimney.

A quaint, picturesque building of logs but poorly matched, still this simple structure was enthroned in a frame more beautiful than words can describe. Down below the valley spread out beneath the endless grandeur of the rolling hills, by the side of it the melting stream ran, while behind it, up and up, rose the peaks of the snow-capped mountains. This, indeed, was a home in the heart of nature. About the house could be seen a number of animals. A wildcat cub rolled around in the sunlight, and an old bear was asleep with his nose between his paws, his tail just a tiny stump that wiggled mechanically as he felt in his sleep the presence of his friend. Birds were roosting in the trees nearby and within a dozen feet of the cabin were two score bird nests for it seemed the little creatures of the air desired to come and build their nests of twigs around the cabin door.

The old man invited the youth in. They entered and sat upon sawed-off ends of logs which served as stools. The cabin was bare of furnishing save for a rough straw pallet and the only ornament was a wonderful ivory crucifix which hung upon the wall. The room was filled with birds and squirrels and the young hunter stared in astonishment when he saw that a small hummingbird had built its nest in the arms of the crucifix. He then looked about for stove or food, but there was no sign of either.

"So, this is your home?" he murmured, "this is where the Old Man of the Mountain lives?"

"Yes," the hermit answered, "and here he has lived since the day when he realized that his brother man was false, and that the beast was true. In all the world of men, I found never a friend one-half so faithful or one-half so true as these wild beasts that live among the hills. When I look back at the sorrow of my life and the tears come to my eyes, my little birds all gather around me and sing their love songs in my ears; when I am tired, the great stag comes and bends his back that I may ride him; when I am hungry, then from mountains and caves come birds and beasts with food for me. I have given up the world of human things to serve the things which man abuses, to which he has been false. These birds, these little creatures that play around my door, even the wolves, the foxes, and the mountain lions—they are my brothers and I their father and their elder brother. I ease the wounds that heartless hunters make, and they know that while I live in this mountain, they have one friend in the world of men who will never be false. All the time that I have lived here, I have never spoken one harsh word to beast or bird, yet they serve me with perfect faith and perfect trust."

A strange feeling came over the soul of the hunter.

"I shall hunt no more," he murmured, "for I have seen the life and love and light in the souls of these beasts. I shall be true to it.

"That is well," said the old man slowly, and he extended his hand. "Brother, I am proud that you have seen the light which shall some time take from the world the karmic curse that rests upon all who slay their brothers. But night is falling in the mountains and in the air, I hear the cry of the bears and lions; I hear the pitiful wail of dying beasts and I must go my way, so I will now take you back again to where I met you. I am an old man and I have not much longer to stay here, but when I am gone, will you be true to the beasts whom I have

OCCULT QUALITIES OF HERBS

The following article is the introduction of Nicholas Culpeper's "Complete Herbal," a rare old book, written in 1653 and published in London in 1837. It is copied here exactly as it was printed then, with all the peculiarities of punctuation and sentence formation. Although this may sometimes lead to confusion and some difficulty of grasping the meaning, the old-fashioned style of it is so odd and delightfully quaint, it would seem like marring to change a bit of it. Even though the manner of expression of 1653 is not so smoothly flowing and eloquent as in our days of a more polished tongue, still it should enhance rather than detract from the wonderfully deep and beautifully simple truths, written with such great pains and infinite care.

But first, here is a short paragraph or two about the author's life and manner of living, taken from the preface of his book:

"Nicholas Culpeper, the writer of this work, was a son of Nicholas Culpeper, a clergyman, and grandson of Sir Thomas Culpeper, Bart. He was some time a student at the university of Cambridge, and soon after was bound apprentice to an Apothecary. He employed all his leisure hours in the study of Physic and Astrology, which he afterwards professed, and set up business in Spitalfields, next door to the Red Lion, (formerly known as the Halfway House between Islington and Stepney), where he had considerable practice, and was much resorted to for his advice, which he gave to the poor gratis. Astrological Doctors have always been highly respected; and those celebrated Physicians of the early times, whom our Author seems to have particularly studied, Hippocrates, Galen and Avicen, regarded those as homicides who were ignorant of Astrology. Paracelsus, indeed, went farther: he declared, a Physician should be predestinated to the cure of his patient; and the horoscope should be inspected, the plants gathered at the critical moment, etc.

Culpeper was a writer and translator of several Works, the most celebrated of which is his Herbal, 'being an astrologo-physical discourse of the common herbs of the nation; containing a complete Method or Practice of Physic, whereby a Man may preserve his Body in Health, or cure himself when sick, with such things only as grow in England, they being most fit for English Constitutions.'

This celebrated and useful Physician died at his house in Spitalfields, in the year 1654. This book will remain as a lasting monument of his skill and Industry."

"Culpeper's Original Epistle to the Reader

All other Authors that have written of the nature of Herbs, give not a bit of reason why such an Herb was appropriated to such a part of the body, nor why it cured such a disease. Truly, my own body being sickly, brought me easily into a capacity, to know that health was the greatest of all earthly blessings, and truly he was never sick that doth not believe it. Then I considered that all medicines were compounded of Herbs, Roots, Flowers, Seeds, etc., and this first set me to work in studying the nature of Simples, most of which I knew by sight before; and indeed, all the Authors I could read gave me but little satisfaction in this particular, or none at all. I cannot build my faith upon Authors' words, nor believe a thing because they say it, and could wish everybody were of my mind in this, to labor, to be able to give a reason for everything they say or do. They say Reason makes a man differ from a Beast; if that is true, pray what are they that, instead of a reason for their judgment, quote old Authors? Perhaps their authors knew a reason for what they wrote, perhaps they did not; what is that to us? Do we know it? Truly, in writing this work, first, to satisfy myself, I drew out all the virtues of the vulgar or common Herbs, Plants and Trees, &c., out of the best or most approved authors I had, or could get; and having done so, I set myself to study the reason for them. I knew well enough the whole world and everything in it was formed of a composition of contrary elements, and in such a harmony as must needs show the wisdom and power of a great God. I knew as well this creation, though thus composed of contraries, was one united body, and man an epitome of it: I knew those various affections in man, in respect of sickness and health, were caused naturally (though God may have other ends best known to Himself) by the various operations of the Microcosm; and I could not be ignorant that as the cause is so must the cure be; and therefore he that would know the reason for the operation of the Herbs, must look up as high as the stars, astrologically. I always found the disease vary according to the various motions of the stars; and this is enough, one would think, to teach a man by the effect where the cause lies. Then to find out the reason for the operation of Herbs, Plants, etc., by the stars went I; and herein I could find but a few authors, but those as full of nonsense and contradiction as an egg are full of meat. This not being pleasing, and less profitable to me, I consulted with my two brothers, Dr. Reason and Dr. Experience, and took a voyage to visit my mother Nature, by whose advice, together with the help of Dr. Diligence, I at last obtained my desire; and being warned by Mr. Honesty, a stranger in our days, to publish it to the world, I have done it.

But you will say, What need I have written on this subject, seeing so many famous and learned men have written so much of it in the English tongue, much more than I have done?

To this I answer, neither Gerrard nor Parkinson, or any that ever wrote in the like nature, ever gave one wise reason for what they wrote, and so did nothing else but train up young novices in Physio in the school of tradition, and teach them just as a parrot is taught to speak; an Author says so, therefore it is true; and if all that Authors say be true, why do they contradict one another? But in mine, if you view it with the eye of reason, you shall see a reason for everything that is written, whereby you may find the very ground and foundation of Physic. You may know what you do, and wherefore you do it; and this shall call me Father, it being (that I know of) never done in the world before.

I have now but two things to write, and then I have done.

1. What are the profits and benefits of this work is?
2. Instructions in the use of it.

The profit and benefits arising from it, or that may occur to a wise man from it are many, so many that should I sum up all the particulars my epistle would be as big as my book; I shall quote some few general heads.

First, the admirable Harmony of Creation is herein seen, in the influence of Stars upon Herbs and the Body of Man, how one part of the Creation is subservient to another, and all for the use of man, whereby the infinite power and wisdom of God in the Creation appear; and if I do not admire at the simplicity of the ranters, never trust me; who but viewing the Creation can hold such a sottish opinion, as that it was from eternity, when the mysteries of it are so clear to every eye? But that Scripture shall be verified to them, Rom. i.20: "The invisible things of him from the Creation of the World are clearly seen, being understood by the things that are made, even his Eternal Power and Godhead; so that they are without excuse." And a Poet could teach them a better lesson:

"Because out of thy thoughts, God shall not pass,
"His image stamped is on every grass."

This indeed is true, God has stamped His image on every creature, and therefore the abuse of the creature is a great sin; but how much the more do the wisdom and excellency of God appear, if we consider the harmony of the Creation in the virtue and operation of every Herb?

Secondly, Hereby you may now know what infinite knowledge Adam had in his innocence, that by looking upon a creature he was able to give it a name according to its nature; and by knowing that, thou mayest know how great thy fall was, and be humbled for it even in this respect because hereby thou art so ignorant.

Thirdly, Here is the right way for thee to begin at the study of Physic, if thou art minded to begin at the right end, for here thou hast the reason of the whole art. I wrote before in certain Astrological Lectures, which I read, and printed, entitled, "Astrological Judgment of Diseases," what planet caused (as a second cause) every disease, how it might be found out what planet caused it; here thou hast what planet cures it by Sympathy and Antipathy; and this brings me to my last promise, viz:

Instructions for the right use of the book. And herein let me premise a word or two. The Herbs, Plants, &c., are now in the book appropriated to their proper planets. Therefore,

First, Consider what planet causeth the disease; that thou mayest find it in my aforesaid Judgment of Diseases.

Secondly, Consider what part of the body is afflicted by the disease, and whether it lies in the flesh, or blood, or ventricles, or bones.

Thirdly, Consider by what planet the afflicted part of the body is governed: that my Judgment of Diseases will inform you as well.

Fourthly, You may oppose diseases by Herbs of the planet, opposite to the planet that causes them: as diseases of Jupiter by Herbs of Mercury, and the contrary; diseases of the Luminaries by the Herbs of Saturn, and the contrary; diseases of Mars by Herbs of Venus, and the contrary.

Fifthly, There is a way to cure diseases sometimes by Sympathy, and so every planet cures his own disease; as the Sun and Moon by their Herbs cure the Eyes, Saturn the Spleen, Jupiter the Liver, Mars the Gall and diseases of choler, and Venus diseases in the Instruments of Generation.

Nich. Culpeper."

From my House in Spitalfields, next door to the Red Lion, September 5, 1653.

LITTLE CHURCH AMONG THE FLOWERS

IN the years gone by the sturdy Christians of a little town banded themselves together, giving of their labor and the fruits of their toil to the building of a temple wherein to worship God—little wooden church with a quaint old-fashioned steeple that ended in a cross of wrought iron. Its walls were white-washed, its floors were bare, and its altar-piece rough-hewn. In the years that came after, the plain windows of the little old building were supplanted by glorious stained-glass pictures of angels and saints. Originally, the church was surrounded by the quaint little homes of the villagers, but as the years went by, these homes gave place to stores and buildings until at last a great city grew up around the village church. But through the change it remained a quaint little edifice, though towering skyscrapers and the bustle and confusion of a large metropolis grew noisy about. And so today it stands in the midst of a garden of flowers among whose waving heads rises the old tomb-stones of the village churchyard, overgrown with ivy, broken down by age, and mutilated by wind and weather. Trailing creepers had been planted around the church and now its walls were a mass of green leaves and when the season is right a splash of colored flowers, red, white and delicate shades of lavender shine out here and there. The sweet odor of the garden blooms was carried by the wind into the heart of the great city, so it seemed that this little church was an oasis of beauty in the midst of a desert of sordid things. Around it, street cars roared and there echoed about it the boom of the overhead railway; the newsboys howled their wares and the bootblacks, their little boxes in their hands, sat along its ancient wall.

From the great church of the small town, this old building had become a delicate memory in the great town. Many other churches there were, massive and glorious, throwing their arches and spires to the very skies, but somehow this little building still remained the most hallowed spot in that great city. From between its ancient portals, brides and grooms rode away and into its low doorway passed the caskets when the greatest of that city were laid to rest. Every Sunday morning snatches of sacred songs were wafted out of the open windows, or the old hell that called to prayer in 1850 could be heard sending out its peals as in the years gone by.

It was known far and wide as the Little Church among the Flowers, quaint and simple, carrying with it the breath of sweet lavender and those delicate old-world memories that are slowly dying out as the generations go by. Little old ladies, still living in the days of bustle and bonnet, came in each Sunday morning holding their tiny black parasols in hands partly shielded by those fingerless lace mitts that grandmother used to wear. The old couples came trotting in, the Romeos and Juliets of '63, and they remembered the day when their fathers had swung their axes to hew the logs and their mothers' nimble fingers had twisted the yams on the spinning wheel to weave the first curtain that hung in the little village church. They remembered the first minister of that church, the dear old doctor who now lay in the churchyard with morning-glory vines twining over his gravestone.

And everyone remembered and loved that dear old man, whose pulpit still hung in the ante-room of the church, whose tireless fingers themselves had driven the nails that built the pews now blackened with age, and whose tired, careworn yet sweet face had so many times gazed out upon the flock who had gathered in the years gone by. Father Jackson was dead, his successor had also been laid away, and now from a distant place had come a new minister to occupy the pulpit of the Little Church Among the Flowers.

The first Sunday he came to them, the congregation was pleased. Both of those who had gone before him were simple men of simple ways whose kindly message of brotherhood and love had helped to mold the lives of simple faiths and the new minister bid fair to follow in their footsteps. The only difference was that he was very young. As he stood before them, they wondered at his boyish face, but then they wondered at several other things as well.

As he stood on the simple pulpit in his quiet black suit one old lady whispered to her friend, as she touched her eyes with a little black-bordered handkerchief, "The dear minister has suffered much. He looks like my son, who has been gone for so many years." Everyone realized and agreed that this minister was a very strange man, a stranger one than had ever gone before. But as Sunday after Sunday rolled by and his clear, simple message found its way into their hearts, they hung his picture with the other two in the old hallway for in his spirit they seemed to feel the sturdy pioneers of faith who had led them before. Let us try and build for you a picture of the new minister as he stands in the pulpit, the many-colored lights of the stained-glass windows playing upon his slender, intellectual face. Father Huntley was still in his early twenties and his fine face was unmarked by line or blemish; his brow, high and noble, met wavy locks of dark brown hair. His form was very slender, almost that of a wraith, and long slender fingers turned the pages of the ancient Bible, marked and remarked with the old-fashioned writing of the earnest souls of long ago.

This young minister had great dark eyes that seemed to gaze right through everyone they looked upon but nevertheless soft eyes seeming ready to weep all the time. His mouth, finely chiseled, had a slight droop at the corners, which gave an air of sadness to his face. His voice, soft and musical, seemed ever filled with pathos and he looked like one who, though young in years, had suffered deeply and known truly. When Father Huntley told of the simple life of the Master and His apostles there was scarce a dry eye in the church, and then when he spoke of the finer sentiments of life, of love and friendship, of diligence and duty, a thrill went over his congregation. As the Sundays went by the congregation grew larger and larger until each morning dozens who could not enter gathered in the courtyard of the church to listen to the voice which spoke with such strange eloquence and such sincere understanding of life's ever-changing sea.

Three years passed, and the minister had won his way into the hearts of each one of the simple folks who came there to the same pew where their fathers and grandparents had come for the last seventy-five years. His life was above reproach and in the daily performance of his ministerial tasks, he exhibited a spirit almost divine. Be it night or day, when he was called, he was ever ready; always patient, ever kind, he fulfilled the little labors for his flock and sought to lead them in the path of godliness.

When the month of June came around it brought, as it always did, orange blossoms and bridal wreathes and the greatest and noblest of that city came down to the Little Church among the Flowers to be united in life's mysteries by the slender band of gold, but more than that to receive the blessing of Father Huntley who seemed to understand and know these emotions that so swayed their souls. One beautiful morning, many rows of carriages and automobiles drew up before the Little Church among the Flowers. Two of the city's finest families were to be united through the marriage of their children. The little church was gloriously decorated with arches of orange blossoms and lilies, the choir, was singing and the pews were filled with the richest and noblest of the day. The bride, a little society butterfly, was demurely hanging upon the arm of her father, while the groom, an army captain with clanking sword and dress uniform, was surrounded by a number of his brother officers. It was a festive day. Two little flower girls were strewing the aisle of the church with roses and the old-fashioned organ that had so many times pealed out its notes filled the air with the soft notes of the wedding march. At the altar stood the minister, in his hands, the open Bible, its pages turned to the marriage service. In his eyes was the same sad look that so often filled them, and his white hands were as pieces of marble against the pages before him.

Down the aisle the solemn procession wound its way, youth, and age together, celebrating one of life's most solemn mysteries. Before the altar they stopped, then in his clear, musical voice, the minister read the marriage service. There was a deep pathos in his tones as he slowly pronounced the words of the sacred ritual and when he asked if there were any who knew why those two should not be united in the holy bond of matrimony it seemed that his voice caught, then he went on. Placing their hands together he raised one of his own to heaven pronouncing in clear, distinct tones that thrilled through the whole church, "In the name of God the Father, God the Son, and God the Holy Ghost, I pronounce you man and wife."

There was a hush for a moment, a weight seemed in the air, and then the organ broke the heavy silence. In a few seconds, the scene again became one of life and ambition. Congratulations, a few previously prepared sobs from the bride, perfectly timed and romantically performed, showers of rice and old shoes, the honking of automobile horns, cries of congratulations, and a few seconds later the church was empty of its throng and all that remained was the slender, sad-eyed minister, his face illuminated by a golden light which shone down through a yellow pane in the window.

* * *

A heavy cloud holding winter rain hung over the city in whose heart stood the Little Church of the Flowers. The gray light coming through the windowpanes sent weird shadows among the pews and rafted ceiling of the ancient building. The pigeons that nested in the bell tower were circling around the ancient belfry uttering plaintive cries at the approaching storm. At first it seemed that the church was deserted but looking more closely there could be seen a figure sitting alone in the front pew, his hands clasped in prayer and his eyes raised to the great gilded cross that hung over the altar. No word sounded from the lips of the praying man but from his heart poured out a great stream of feeling which seemed to circle round and round the ancient crucifix carved from rock wood and gilded by the now still hand of Father Jackson.

It was the young minister who sat there, dimly outlined in the pale and uncertain light. He sat as he had many times before, seeking solace for an unknown emptiness in the cross he so devoutly served. As he prayed, there came the sound of a swinging door, a gray shaft of light appeared and framed against it stood the figure of a well-built and erect man who passed slowly down the aisle of the church and sank into one of the pews near the minister. Then the visitor saw Father Huntley for the first time. He sat for some minutes studying the face of the minister, then as the prayers seemed ended, he crossed over and touched the minister lightly on the shoulder.

"Reverend sir," he asked, "do you not remember me?" The minister looked up for a second as if undecided, then a smile spread over his face, and he extended his hand.

"Yes, I remember you well. You are Captain Hendricks, whom I married in this little church last year."

"You have a good memory," answered the other, accepting the hand and clasping it warmly.

"Yes," in a faraway voice as though speaking with the words of memory, "I remember it well, one of the most beautiful weddings that was ever held in the Little Church of the Flowers. Surely brother, the blessing of God was upon you that day."

The other man's head drooped, and, to the amazement of the minister, he sank to his knees in the aisle. Father Huntley knew that his visitor was crying, and his long slender hand rested softly on the captain's shoulder as he exerted a slight pressure of sympathy.

"Have things not gone well with you?" he asked.

"Ah, no!" answered the other, as with a tremendous effort he shook off the passing weakness and rose to face the minister. "No, things have not gone well. You remember the little laughing-eyed girl whom I led to the altar?"

"Yes," answered the minister softly, the sad look creeping into his eyes, "I remember her. Has she not been true?"

The young captain shook his head.

"Alas, no. I idolized her, built her into the shrine of my soul, but to her I have always been a plaything. A few days ago, she left me, leaving nothing behind but this little note and a broken heart. In my sorrow there seemed to come back to my mind that strange expression on your face the day you married us, and I have come to ask you, friend, both advice and comfort, for I have need of them. Something tells me you too have suffered deeply and maybe you can give me the strength to go on after the idol of my heart has deserted me."

The minister placed his hand gently on the captain's shoulder and pointed up to the cross over the altar.

"In life, brother," he spoke sincerely, "each must take his cross. I have had mine; you now have yours. In the hours of silence, I am indeed alone, for it seemed I was born with a broken heart. Through years of lonely youth, I wandered. There was none who knew and none who understood so, alone, and heavy-hearted, I renounced the world and all that is in it, or rather shall I say, I gave up that which I had never had and renounced an unreality I had never known. I imagined that the great Master must have felt as I did, so I sought to forget myself by serving others.

Coming to this little church soon after graduating from the theological seminary, I found one here who seemed to know and seemed to understand and the spark which had long been dead, in fact had never been lighted, burst into flame within my heart even as it must have done in yours. I kept an idol in my dreams for many years during my service here as the minister of this church; I wound that idol into my prayers; I saw in it the glory of a Madonna, and the face of saint and martyr seemed not so good as that of the idol in my heart. But mine was broken even as yours has been, so I can comfort and console you in your sorrow by saying there is a sweetness in it all. In losing the world of men one finds the world of God I live no more in the bustle and confusion of life, and, God willing, I will stay here in the Church of the Flowers until some day, I am laid to rest with those who have gone before, among the morning-glory vines and honeysuckle in the little churchyard behind."

As the minister spoke, a strange light was shining in his face.

"I have read of the monks in their meditation, how in the prayer and silence great visions came to them that they painted in crude colors upon the walls of their cells, I have heard how year after with colored inks and ancient parchments they wrote and illuminated words of glory to their God and king. As I walk in the gloom of this old church, I seem to feel a cowl fall about my shoulders and it seems that somewhere in the distant past, in the brown robe of the mendicant I wandered amid the arches and pillars of some ancient monastery. I wandered into this world with the body of a man and the heart of a monk. I sought to leave these gray walls, not of stone but of the soul, and be like other living things in the world without. I saw one who seemed a dream of the ages, a face that might have haunted me had I drawn paintings upon dungeon walls or matched fine blocks of marble into mosaics as did those of old. When the world has been false to you, brother, come here to me. I came into this world for a great lesson, and I have learned it, I can aid you in learning yours as well.

"What lesson came you to learn, reverend sir?" asked the soldier respectfully.

"I came to learn to love as God loves," answered the minister, looking up once again at the massive crucifix. "I learned to love and give that which I loved the most. You think you love, sir, and you weep for that which has left you. I loved but I would have left if the one I had loved had stayed. My romance was short-lived, a few short words, a merry laugh, but it left in my soul a mark which ages of loneliness had made hungry for such a token. I dreamed of that day, I lived for that day, and on Sunday mornings as I spoke the soft words of the Master to my flock, I spoke it to one more than all the rest, the one who seemed to understand. Your romance, sir, has ended even as mine has ended. It seems I had waited a hundred thousand years for that day but to have it slip away, like all things earthly, and leave me alone again with my God. I am not so alone with Him now, for I see and understand better. But when that momentous day was over, when my dream was shattered, I fell at the foot of the yonder altar and would gladly have died there, for there seemed nothing left in life worthwhile. Three whole nights I lay in prayer at the foot of that altar, praying for death, for anything to take away the utter loneliness of my life—but, I had to live—a voice was endlessly whispering, "Go on, go on."

The minister's hands were on the shoulders of the captain and his eyes were gazing into those of the soldiers who felt in his sold the agony of the other.

"You lost your dream after it was realized, I lost mine before. Who shall say which is better? I learned to love and to give up the thing I loved and if you love her well enough, you will send her on her way in peace, realizing that your greatest love, if it he true, rests in her happiness."

"Father, how can you say that?" exclaimed the captain. "How can you say that if I love her best, I will let her go? Do you not realize I live for her alone?"

The minister nodded his head.

"I do," he answered, "that is what I say."

"Alas, father, you have had but little of this world's romance," answered the captain. "But you could not love as I have loved and then stand by while another steals the idol of your dream."

"I have done that and more," answered the minister, "I have stood by and aided in the giving. The laughing, blue-eyed girl to whom I married you last year was the one who had been the idol of my dream. She found happiness in you, and I found happiness in her gladness." He turned quickly and walked silently away. At the door that led to the little rectory, he turned and held out his hand in benediction to the captain.

"Goodbye, brother," he said, smiling softly. "You will go back to your world again, but I shall stay here. When you are sad, come to me, for you will always find one who understands here in the Little Church among the Flowers."

QUESTIONS

Isn't the approaching crisis coming in the form of a world war?

Ans. It will come to man in the form of the effects of the things he has done. My suggestion is this: look around you and see what will be the natural result of the present causations. It will take many forms, as our mistakes take many forms.

ASTROLOGICAL KEYWORDS

Sagittarius is one of the most wonderful of the symbolical signs of the Zodiac, for in it is concealed the key to human aspiration. It is a double sign, one-half of which is composed of a horse and the other half of a human being, and therefore called the Centaur of the Zodiac. The sign symbolizes the mind with its ideals and aspirations rising out of the body of the animal, the liberation of consciousness from the shell of matter. The Archer is shooting his shaft far up among the star and aspiration is the keyword of Sagittarius. Often it is too hot-headed and seeks to go beyond its ability, but like the pilgrim of Longfellow's poem it still cries "Excelsior!" as it carries forward the work of its unfoldment. A short group of keywords makes possible a good general understanding of this sign and its powers, which the student can synthesize at his leisure:

Hot, Dry, Fiery, Choleric, Masculine, Diurnal, Eastern, Common, Bi-corporal, Four-footed, Changeable, Autumnal, Fortunate, Bitter, Half-feral, Southern, Obeying, Speaking, Half-human, Half-mute, Long, Ascension, Detriment of Mercury, Double-bodied.

Day house of Jupiter and exaltation of Dragon's Tail.

General Characteristics:

Sagittarius is generally noted for impetuosity and for its unwillingness to listen to advice and counsel. It is also the champion air-castle builder of the Zodiac and has a great deal of the eternal tomorrow in its make-up. It is subject to brain-storming at times but still one of the best signs in the Zodiac because it is eternally aspiring to the highest and the best. It is:

Active, Intrepid, Generous, Obliging, Jovial, Bright, Hail-fellow-well-met, Usually smiling, A promoting type.

Physical Appearance:

Well-formed, Oval, fleshy face, Generally tall, Long in the legs, Ruddy complexion, Handsome, jovial, Fine clear eyes, Chestnut colored hair, Apt to be bald, Face usually appears looking countenance sunburnt.

Conformity in the length of arms and legs As Jupiter rules this sign, we find in later life that the mental picture that we held of the Greek and Latin god holds good with most Jupiterian types—broad high foreheads, massive eyebrows, and often given to wearing beards.

Health:

Wherever Jupiter is present, our mutual friend, the liver, is in evidence. Jupiter is not always moderate in its appetites consequently its ailments are with us wherever die happygo-lucky Jupiterian spirit prevails. Sagittarius rules the thighs, and those born into this sign are subject to injuries and bruises to those parts of the body. Its diseases are:

Fevers, Gout, Pestilences, Rheumatism.

Overheating of the body through exercise, etc.

This sign is also subject to accidents, falls and danger from drowning;

liability of broken bones, dislocations, and fractures.

Domestic Problems:

Our jovial Jupitarians are usually successful in domestic problems, but Sagittarians will wander and leave all responsibilities behind while they soar to nearby stars. For this reason, they usually find their home missing when they return.

(Continued next month)

GREAT SAYINGS OF JESUS

"Judge not, that ye be not judged."

"He that is faithful in that which is least, is faithful also in much; and he that is unjust in the least, is unjust also in much."

"Where your treasure is, there will your heart be also."

"No man can serve two masters, for either he will hate the one and love the other; or else he will hold to the one, and despise the other. Ye cannot serve God and mammon."

"It is easier for heaven and earth to pass than one tittle of the Law to fail."

"Joy shall be in heaven over one sinner that repenteth more than over ninety and nine just persons which need no repentance."

"Whosoever exalteth himself shall be abased; and he that humbleth himself shall be exalted." He that layeth up treasure for himself is not rich toward God."

"Blessed are they that hear the word of God and keep it."

"Every idle word that men shall speak they shall give account thereof in the day of judgement."

"Beware of false prophets which come to you in sheep's clothing but inwardly they are ravening wolves... Ye shall know them by their fruits."

"When ye stand praying, forgive, if ye have aught against any, that your Father also which is in heaven may forgive you your trespasses."

"Woe unto you, hypocrites; ye who are like unto whited sepulchers which indeed appear beautiful outwardly but are within full of dead men's bones and of all uncleanness. Even so, ye also outwardly appear righteous unto men, but within ye are full of hypocrisy and iniquity. Thou blind ones, cleanse first that which is within the cup that the outside may be clean also."

"What shall it profit a man if he shall gain the whole world and lose his own soul?"

MARCH 1924

VANITY OF REGRET

Nothing in this world of ours
Flows as we would have it flow;
What avail, then, careful hours,
Thought and trouble, tears and woe?
Through the shrouded veil of earth,
Life's rich colors gleaming bright,
Though in truth of little worth,
Yet allure with meteor light.
Life is torture and suspense;
Thought is sorrow— drive it hence!
With no will of mine I came,
With no will depart the same.
All we see—above, around—
Is but built on fairy ground:
All we trust is empty shade
To deceive our reason made.
Tell me not of Paradise,
Or the beams of houris' eyes;
Who the truth of tales can tell,
Cunning priests invent so well?
He who leaves this mortal shore
Quits it to return no more.
In vast life's unbounded tide
They alone content may gain,
Who can good from ill divide,
Or in ignorance abide—
All between is restless pain.
Before thy prescience, power divine
What is this idle sense of mine?
What all the learning of the schools?
What sages, priests, and pedants?—Fools!
The world is thine, from thee it rose,
By thee it ebbs, by thee it flows.
Hence, worldly lore!
By whom is wisdom shown?

The Eternal knows, knows all, and He alone!
—Omar Khayyam.

EDITORIALS

THE ECONOMIC PROBLEM

THE problem of human equality is ever confronting us. The Master Jesus said, "The poor ye have with you always," and technically, this is true. There will never be a time in nature when all things shall be equal. The only equality is when things are equal to themselves. Just as there is childhood, manhood, and old age,—birth, growth and decay—so there are three stages in the progression of consciousness through matter, there are three grand divisions of organic quality in bodies. Two things are necessary for expression in matter and all expression is limited by these two things. First, organic quality; and second, size. Size is the measurement of power, all things being equal; size without high organic quality produces the brute and organic quality without size produces those sensitive individuals who seldom live to great age because the fine-grained quality cannot be supported by a small, undeveloped body. As long as there is a difference in organic quality and size there cannot be equality in mental or social position because man's expression in this world is the direct result of the power which consciousness is exerting over matter. Where the organic quality is low, consciousness is low, and the brain is incapable of fine discriminating thought. Such persons must follow instead of lead, for the very structure of their organism inhibits intelligent leadership. When such individuals do rise to power we have the Marat, the Robespierre, the Napoleon, or the radical who is incapable of reflective thought himself and refuses to credit reflective thought in others.

Man has an impossible golden dream which he has fostered for a long time and that is that he is going to tear down the so-called caste system and that the man with the pick and shovel is going to sit in meditation with the sage while the bricklayer is going to recline in the carven chairs of arrogance. This is a mistaken idea. The desire of the true ethical and social reformer does not rest upon these conditions at all. His cry is for opportunity, for the true philosopher realizes that opportunity is the divine birthright of all living creatures, and he also knows that the modern economic situation does not give every man an honest opportunity. The average reformer, however, becomes bolshevistic.

He is not satisfied with an opportunity but demands affluence as his birthright, and the average soap-box orator along these lines would be more arrogant and despotic than those he condemns if the goddess of finance ever smiled upon him. The sweat-shops, child labor, and similar institutions, are depriving man of his birthright and as such should go, and with them depart the greatest curse of modern civilization; but the abolishment of these things will not equalize human intelligence. The thing it will do is give man an opportunity to unfold himself according to what he is, but he is always limited in two ways. First, by surrounding environments; secondly, by organic quality.

Man's greatest hindrance is not a heartless world, but a useless body. Useful bodies are not built in days or years, but in ages and lives. Organic quality cannot be improved by politics; it can only be improved by man as an individual when he makes the most of every opportunity to improve himself mentally, spiritually, and physically while he lives. There is a caste system in nature. In the universe, there is the upper and the lower set, divided from each other by the ideals and works of life and by the conscientious effort of each individual.

Man must learn to be contented to live in accordance with what he is and yet at the same time be ambitious to improve his lot. The hope of the universe is not in ranting and raving for equal rights, but in the burning of the midnight oil. When we see the laborer come from his labors, tired, surrounded by the crying needs of family and friend, but who sits alone under the light, studying to improve himself, working with tired, chapped fingers roughened with toil to become a man among men, to learn the things which divide ignorance from wisdom, such a one is the hope of salvation, such a one will become in the due course of nature's time a spiritual aristocrat and, naturally, there will come to him his birthright of being a thinker, a doer, and a superior. Then we see his companion in labor, one who does not take the somber course of study and thought but throws bricks at the houses of aristocrats, hating them because their skins are white while his are tanned, their voices soft while his is harsh. He curses and spits at them, suffering in his hate, such a one will never be the thing he longs to because the difference lies in quality and not in the strength of the bull or the beast within.

If you entered two horses in a race, the one a dray such as is used to pull milk wagons and the other a fine Arabian stallion, which would win the race? Just so, it is the same in the race for success. The dray horse is hampered by its own weight; and while it may dash forward madly with all the strength that is in it, it simply cannot race. No matter whether it is dragging a milk wagon or is a pedigreed horse, it is that type and there is no hope for it. But the Arabian stallion, without an effort, outdistances it with ease and grace and leaves it far behind.

Man believes that with the power of his hand, he can rule the world. He cannot. All he can do is tear civilization up by the roots and leave it for another thinker to repair. We will not deny that the poor have cause for dissension just as they had during the French revolution for the mere fact that a man has a fine, executive brain does not prove that he is a humanitarian, a philanthropist, or an honest man, nor does organic quality necessarily indicate virtue. But one thing it always does give, and that is power. It may be that an assassin's bullets will slay a few but in the end the power of mentality wins over the battle of brawn and the only hope for those who are trampled on is to reach mental efficiency by means of which they can intelligently combat conditions.

When we look carefully into the problem of economics, we strike one phase that is well worth our consideration. Those individuals who now spend their time trampling on the poor were, in nearly every case, poorly born themselves. They did not come from homes of wealth, and many of them never went to school. Some of our greatest millionaires today were newsboys without a chance, others shined shoes and started in with a hundred percent less than the average failure starts with. The heel of the capitalism of their day was upon their throats and yet with the sheer force of mental power, indominable will, and perfect faith in themselves, they rose out of the mud and became masters of world affairs. Now, those left behind shake their fists at them, while the energy they use in the railing would lift them also from the rut if it were exerted as their opponents exerted it.

Man must learn to capitalize upon himself; his brain, his heart, and his hand are the most valuable assets he possesses. Incessant effort should be made to increase the efficiency of these assets, for in that alone lies liberation from the rut. When to this is added the realization of limitation, and the gradual unfoldment of powers as the means of liberation from this limitation, we have the man or woman who is going to be a success.

The caste system of the world is as follows:

1. The lowest phase is opposition, materialism, and the battling of beast instincts. In this world, they are the ones chained by ages of thoughtlessness, or recent differentiation from lower races, to the lower physical side of life. Those who dwell in it are chained by like and dislike, by passions and appetites; they deify matter and know no god or consciousness outside of it; they settle their disputes with bullets and sandbags or with fist encounters; they are an ever-muttering horde and in the last analysis are absolutely powerless. Their only

weapon is firebrand or dagger, and these things have no force outside of physical substance, and as true consciousness is independent of substance the most, they can do is destroy their own world. The mere idea that such individuals could rule the universe is beyond reason or logic. They cannot do it, for there is not within their own being's enough self-control to rule themselves. There is no law or logic in them, and as the universe is ruled by law and logic only those who have developed it are capable of governing. They cry out in their agony that they are imposed upon—and they are, for man has not yet gained that consciousness which enables him to be superior without becoming domineering. The reason, however, why they are imposed upon is not necessarily because their opponents are strong but because they themselves are weak. The idea that this problem can be solved without intellectual growth on the part of this great mass is absurd. Their overlords realize that in this ignorance lies the power which they have over them, therefore it seems that every day the higher oppress the lower more severely to prevent them from attaining light. But this oppression should only stimulate those oppressed to greater and more intelligent effort. The world must have those who work with their hands, but these will always have to serve the man who works with his head, while both must bow together before the one who is expressing the qualities of his spirit.

2. The second stage is intellectualism, and it spends most of its time preying upon materialism. These are the minds that juggle the finance of the world, that lead, govern, and direct the mass, and regardless of what they may like or dislike those who would lead or govern must join this second class. The great curse of intellectualism is oppression, for there are very few capable of realizing their power over others with attempting to exert it. This is the main cause of the sorrow of the masses. In other words, man's inhumanity to man. The intellectual individual should appoint himself as guardian and protector of those incapable of functioning on that plane, but instead of so doing he now harnesses them to his chariot and loads their backs with burdens. The only remedy for this is to awaken in him the realization of his responsibilities.

3. The third division is that of the spiritual man, which is the principle of altruism and selflessness. There are but few who have consciously attained this degree. They are the great reformers, the great occultists and thinkers of our world who have realized the oneness of things and have come to an understanding of the fact that while all cannot attain in one life the acme of their ideals, still man should not impose upon the weak but rather should champion them and assist them to a fuller and more adequate position.

We have an idea that we are living in civilized times, but this idea is eternally being shattered by every evident example of barbarism. Voltaire said, "I know I am among men because they are fighting; I know they are civilized because they fight so savagely." Our so called evolved and developed peoples are at each other's throats; our great inventors spend all their time learning how to kill; and competition has been crowned the life of trade. This is purely because man has accepted the science of economics as the worthwhile thing in life. It is undoubtedly the world's most foolish decision.

Man must not deify this problem as he does because, in nature, it holds the least important place. Neither must we reject the economic problem. It is to be neither accepted nor rejected and under no conditions assumed. It is merely here as an examination or test of the consciousness of man; in other words, it exists only to be solved. The wonderful Hindoo race as a nation has never accepted the economic problem as worthy of consideration and of course they did not have to in the of their glory for economics have always been a secondary consideration in the Orient. The modern problem did not confront the ancient races and yet they were far better able to meet it than we are. The Masters did not live in the day when the caste was king. They needed only to seat themselves upon the ground and their people gathered around them; when they wanted a house, they built it where they chose and lived in it, while if they were tired of the bustle of the world, they entered a cave in the hills. If they possessed no sandals, it was perfectly fashionable to go barefoot, and they never met the great inconveniences of modem congestion. As a result of their freedom, we find primitive brotherhood, many examples of which are far more beautiful than the products of our modern ethics.

The Masonic school symbolizes the stages of unfoldment as the three ages of man— youth, maturity, and old age. The ages of the soul are the same. There are in the world today young souls in old bodies and old souls in young bodies. Youth goes out to conquer the world, manhood is content to have sufficient for his needs, while old age renounces the world as an illusion. We may call youth the material man, adultness the intellectual man, old age the spiritual man. Applying the economic problem, we may say: to the material man it is all, to the intellectual man it is a problem, to the spiritual man it is an illusion.

To the ancients, the economic problem was a phase, to the modern mind with its greed and ambition, it is an all-absorbing reality. The young soul starts out on its journey in matter as an egotist and the keynote of its consciousness is to acquire; regardless of cost, it must own, master, and break all other things. This is the key to the economic problem, which in the average mind becomes merely a series of processes for acquirement. The old soul has no economic problem for it has ceased to desire to acquire, for eyes growing dim to material things have begun to see the reality hidden behind the veil. The old soul realizes that we are here to master problems as they are presented by nature, and are never to dally with them but to go straight through to a successful conclusion.

There are over a thousand solutions to the modem economic problem, but when applied, they are all, at best only partial solutions and the great key problem remains unsolved. Many of us would like to wander with Plato and Aristotle over the mountains of eternity, but we are forcibly drawn back again into the world by the economic needs; we are forced to leave our philosophy and go back into the world, both as teachers and pupils, to earn the money for our daily bread. India solved the problem of education in the face of economic difficulties by dividing the life of man into three epochs. For the first twenty-five years, he was supported by his parents and usually graduated from one of the many universities which, in the days of India's glory, made it the most highly educated country in the world. During his youth, provision was made for his life, he was prepared to think for himself in a rational and sensible way; then came the second twenty-five years during which he married and brought up his children, bringing them to a position where they could take care of themselves, and saving up sufficient to provide for his own old age and those dependent on him; then during the third part of his life he retired from the bustle of the commercial world and devoted his entire time to study and philosophy and the solution of life's problems, supported either by that which he had saved or the assistance of his children.

The entire economic problem of the physical universe is an expression of matter and the solution to it can be found in human anatomy where three worlds of consciousness express themselves in the mental, emotional, and physical centers of the body. A civilization based on the lower man would express all the qualities of the animal instincts. For example: a carving from Mexico linking this country with ancient Egypt, accompanied by a marvelous description from the pen of a famous geologist, was presented to a newspaper for publication. It was thrown into the wastebasket while ten columns were given to a murder because the human animal reads only that in which he is interested and, while man is so attuned; he is interested only in the loves, joys, hates and fears of animal consciousness. The same is true for each one of the three planes. We see all things with the eyes built of the organic quality of our vehicles.

In man's anatomy there are four elements—earth, water, fire, and air—carbon, hydrogen, nitrogen and oxygen, mediums through which the universe manifests concretely. In economic problems, there are four elements—land, transportation, exchange, and integrity which are the basis of economics. Land corresponds to the physical body of man or the principle of earth and is the skeleton of economics; the second or water element corresponds to the etheric body of man and in economics is the problem of transportation which consists of the drawing of raw materials to advantageous markets; the third element of fire or medium of exchange is the astral body, with the heart in its center, and the Christ, the sun principle, is its lord, ruling through the metal gold which is at the present time the medium of exchange. The fourth element is air, the mental quality, and in the economic problem, the integrity of the buyer and seller. These four constitute the body of the economic problem. Man tries to solve the problem of this body by placing one part over the other as master, while the intelligent, spiritualized individual realizes that all of these are vehicles for the expression of something else.

There will be no end to the economic difficulties until the quality of the soul rises out of the four elements of body and transmutes the present masters into the servants that they should be. There is no cure-all to apply to any world problem; these great tests of the intelligence of man must be met individually and mastered individually.

Power remains in the hands of those who are able to wield it, whether for good or ill, and the surest way to equalize power is for each human being to prove worthy of that power. When all men have earned the right to think they can think, but there is no glory in attacking the thinker of today save in one way—tire thoughts of the modem thinker are selfish, egotistic, and enslaving. Let the new thinkers, born out of the darkness of their present sorrow, turn not around and oppress the oppressor, which is the temperament of the best, but let them show the superiority which they have gained by being charitable where others were not, by being noble where others were not, by being true where others were false, and in this way fulfill the dictates of true civilization. This universal understanding, based upon the realization of universal need, is the only permanent answer to any great problem.

OUR DEMI-GODS

FOR some apparently unknown reason this year's crop of Initiates is an exceptionally large one, but with the increase of supply there is a tremendous increase in a market valuation and really this time the supply of Initiates greatly exceeds the demand. It must be a grand and glorious feeling to be an Initiate, so far, far above the rest of humanity that only occasionally the world is seen through a rift in the clouds; but we fear it must be rather chilly and lonely up there and the rarified atmosphere must be trying upon the lungs of our enlightened. It may be this mental or spiritual strain that is responsible for some of the peculiar things they do.

There are at the present time a number of high priests of sundry and varied shrines, cults, isms, oxys, etc., who bestow upon you, various initiations for various considerations.

Let me introduce to you the fruitage of one of these marvelous processes—the Right Honorable Ciomedes Sourdough, C. o. D., F. o. B., S. o. S., R. F. D., P. O., R. S. V. P., I. o. U., B. V. D. This individual is an Initiate of the first water, exceptionally brilliant, a member of everything, and a leading authority on a large variety of subjects. He spends quite a percentage of his time preparing for his degrees and the rest of the time getting over them. He admits that he is an Initiate and can show you check book stubs to prove it He bestows initiation himself by the laying on of hands and exhorting the most terribly binding oath to the Lords know what. From all over the surface of the earth, people come to gain wisdom at their feet. Mr. Dubb came from Arkansas, Mr. and Mrs. Simp from Rhode Island, Betty Boob from North Dakota, and Willie Itt from Utah. All of these entered into the occult path under the guidance and guardianship of our much-alphabeted friend, Prof. Sourdough. Professor writes books, meets with an inner circle and is perfectly willing to be admired. But really, this person has read a few good books and is capable of delivering a rational lecture on several subjects, but when a careful analysis is made of him and the acid test applied, he turns green. He would have been a very successful teacher and a great help to humanity if two things had not occurred. First, someone told him he was an Initiate, and secondly, he believed it.

There are several of our leading occult schools that have installed spiritual mimeographs in order to keep up with the ever advancing and unfolding efficiency system, a sort of an occult sausage machine into one end of which are poured perfectly respectable citizens and out the other end of which comes a never-ending stream of overstuffed sausages. A trip to Europe or some distant country is almost certain to result in an initiation, especially if you go to the right parties, and within the last few years thousands of promising students have been turned into self-conceited puppies by a set process of initiation. Briefly, it is as follows.

An individual who does not know tells another individual what he does not care anything about, then amputates one extremity from the bank roll; and this constitutes the essence of the ceremony.

Initiate number one is a dope fiend, an in venerate smoker, and one of his best pictures shows him tenderly embracing one of the vestal virgins of his temple. Number two has been tied up in so many scandalous enterprises that it is absolutely impossible to list them separately, but suspect him of anything you want to and you are sure to hit it. Initiate number three carries a sideline in oil stock. Initiate number four is wanted for bigamy in three states. Initiate number five is wanted on sundry strange charges; while Initiate number six will have to explain several things to the government, which does not care much for him nowadays. Go right straight down the calendar of the Ten Commandments and we can produce, with very little research work, an initiate who is morally if not physically breaking each one of them. And oh, the advice with which they delight the heart of the seeker; and oh, the esoteric instructions which they launch upon an unsuspecting world!

Let us cite some examples of it. In the esoteric instructions to pupils written by one of these deluded individuals we find the following suggestion as a very excellent means of developing clairvoyance (which, by the way, is not a legitimate spiritual aim but is only legitimate as the result of the living of a pure life). But this individual gives the following process for the attainment of this supernatural vision, the unfoldment of soul qualities, and so forth: Take a mirror and hang on your wall so that when you are sitting down the center of the mirror is on a level with your eyes. You are to put a lighted candle on each side of the mirror and then gaze into it until something happens.

This is an exceptional choice piece. What would the shades of the immortals have to say about it? If you look into this mirror long enough, you will see things. One student tried it, became hypnotized by his own eyes, could not look away from the mirror, and finally, frothing at the mouth, fell into convulsions. This is purely the result of the blind leading the blind, but people have done it and are doing it. They sit down every night and gaze in a piece of glass because the person who outlined the instruction claimed to be the one and only true Initiate, the Lord High Mogul of this, that and the other thing, and the Lord Emir Most Everything.

Leaving this one to gaze in his magic mirror, we pass on to the next one. Henry Brown was a promising boy, and a marvelous student of things supernatural; his lectures were clean-cut and interesting, his work was filled with promise and there was no reason to doubt that one of these days in the normal tenor of things he would become at least an Initiate of the lower orders. But this person was talked out of his straight and narrow way by one of those near-initiates who received him into some deep and mysterious order which he "swallowed whole."

He now returns to the field of his labors absolutely useless, honestly believing that he is an Initiate. All that we have now of our once promising possibility is a narrow-minded, highbrow fop who looks down with benign condescension upon the world at large.

And so, it goes wherever we look. Every little while someone comes up to us and points out some long-eared bewhiskered individual, whispering confidentially in our ear, "Sh-h-h! he is an Initiate!" When we mildly ask who told them so, they usually answer, "Oh, he admits it." Of all the occult teachers who have come to the world in later years there are two who admitted before the world that they were just students, hoping with their own pupils that someday they would attain to the divine light. It would not be well to name them here but they were great because they claimed nothing for themselves and only worked silently, quietly, and simply for the good of the cause.

All over the face of the earth, strange individuals are being attacked with illusions, delusions and confusions. The reincarnation of the Holy Ghost is now loose while there are hundreds preaching the one and only Truth, all different. Each one is being sponsored by a Master, and each one starts in by making a liar out of all the rest. And so it goes. We are producing in occultism a generation of delirious demi-gods who will never be of any real good to anybody until they get down off their high horses and come back to earth where they are chained by every possible tie.

If students could only learn to realize that being a good student is as worthy as to be an Initiate and that when they live honestly with themselves, they are far closer to the light than when they put on long robes, chant mantrams, and act like a lot of ten-year-old children on Halloween! They are disgracing the very thing which they should be defending as above human comparison. The greatest insult that the average man can heap upon occult science is to claim to understand it, and least of all to represent it. When Mr. Gottenberg claims to be an Initiate, while his relatives and friends know positively that he has not taken a bath in five years, that he chews tobacco, is seldom sober, and is eternally mixed up in domestic problems, and several similar things, he is not glorifying himself by his claims but is simply making a joke out of the thing he claims to be and is literally if not intentionally advertising the fact to the world that intemperance is the path to mastery and that being a sot is necessary to immortality. The whole thing is a joke, but it is a very crude one, a blasphemous one, and the average self-ordained Initiate is a living lie, both to himself and the great doctrines which he claims to represent. Those who claim nothing do not have to live up to anything in order to be true to their claims, but when they stand before the world as examples of finished products, what happens to our scintillating, Royal Dresden Initiate? Their faults show all the more because they claim to be without them, and they are all the more ridiculous because of their sanctimonious hypocrisy.

It is only one person's opinion, of course, but we admit freely we do not have much use for them. When we see our leading Initiates concentrating upon nice juicy beefsteaks or surrounded by cigarette stubs, we are convinced of one of two things—either that occultism is a joke or else they are. We prefer to think it is the latter. We do not say, necessarily, that they should live any better—that is their problem. But this we do say: if they do not intend to live any better, they have no right to claim to be that which they obviously are not and, in this way, bring reflection against a noble cause.

We are very fond of retiring Initiates who obliterate their presence in bashful reticence, but when they come out with brass bands and a torchlight parade, we are inclined to be a little skeptical. When the world applauds them, we are quite confident that they are no good, but when they applaud themselves; we gird up our garments and depart, for such is not done in better regulated circles. There may be one or two Initiates out of the thousands who claim to be, but we doubt even that percentage. The real Initiates will always be found to be men and women without claims, and we have no knowledge of the fact that they ever bestowed a degree upon anyone.

The average worker in occult lines is only expressing an opinion, and he does not know whether that opinion is so or not. It is his privilege to express that opinion, but it is not his privilege to use the name of the Initiates for the furtherance of said opinion. Such action is forgery.

The Masters do not retaliate against these insults; they remain silent and unknown, in this way proving their mastery, while the pseudo-Initiates spend all their time accepting glory. The true Teachers are willing that they should receive it, but must smile to themselves when they see the self-conceited egotists accepting the laurels of another man's work.

BROTHERS OF THE SHINING ROBE - IX
(Continued)
CHAPTER NINE
Dreams

FOR many days, I lay helpless in my bed, recovering from the cuts and bruises I had received in the unaccountable accident. This enforced rest proved to be of untold value, for it had been many months since I had completely relaxed. The strain and stress of my ever-growing work had been more of a pressure than I had realized, for my struggle to advance and show the way to others and at the same time resist those at my back who would hold me behind had been a fight both ways. So, in my weakened physical state, I had many hours in which to reflect upon the past months that had whirled by so quickly and to also ponder some upon the future.

After a day or two of the most considerate and solicitous nursing, I was restored enough to take more notice of my surroundings and wonder to whom I owed such generous treatment. So far, I had only been dreamily conscious of the presence of someone busily performing their duties and had only seen passing back and forth before my eyes the motherly figure of the old Welsh woman but as soon as I was able to formulate my thoughts and collect my words enough to make myself heard; I began asking questions of my companion. Not that I felt at all worried or anxious, for I was too comfortably at rest, but with the half indifference of semiconsciousness I just lazily questioned her.

She proved to be rather noncommittal, but I soon gathered that I was on the estate of Lady Patricia March, a young noblewoman who lived alone in this small country manor-house with the old Welsh woman as her only companion. When I asked what physician had attended me, the reply was still rather unsatisfactory, but by piecemeal I gathered that there had not been one and that Lady Patricia was herself quite proficient in the art of healing.

During this rather enforced communication, the door opened softly, and a young woman entered the room. I stared wonderingly at her pale, fair face and guessed that she was Patricia, the name so suited one so noble looking.

"How is the patient, Mariah?" she asked the nurse, ignoring my questioning look, and she was gentle-voiced.

From the moment she had entered the door, a calm, soothing restfulness seemed to pervade the room and at the sound of her low-toned voice, I had a sudden desire to sleep. Slowly, a peaceful drowsiness crept over me, and I dropped into a deep, healing slumber.

And this was the beginning of a series of wonderful dreams. Each time I awakened from one of these calm, restful sleeps I could remember a beautiful dream, a dream that seemed to be a wonderful object lesson played out in picture-like detail for my observation. It was as though I took no part in them and yet the central figure in each, who passed through so many adventures, seemed to be my own soul.

* * *

As ray eyes closed sleepily, a thin path stretched out like a ribbon, winding through valleys and over hills, around great masses of broken rock, and through dark forests where singing birds fluttered across the gloomy arches. This road wound through the veil of form and onward and upward to an end that no man knows, for none who have walked that silver thread have come back to tell of the mysteries that lie over the edge of the hills of eternity.

Along this path a pilgrim wound his way, leaning upon a palmer's staff. Every now and again, he would shade his eyes with his hands, searching for the end of that twisting, winding path. For many years he had walked that road and seen its forks where others joined it, tiny paths, mere footways seldom walked. Were they? But the pilgrim knew that all these narrow ways led to the Mighty Road for which he was searching, the one that had no name or parting and wound onward into the very sky itself.

On and on the pilgrim went, stopping now and again at some wayside shrine where he knelt in prayer. Over the top of mighty mountains, through the depths of valleys bordered by towering cliffs and broken crags, the pilgrim journeyed, and at last one afternoon as the sun was sinking, a ball of flaming light amid the fleecy clouds of the west, he reached the foot of a lofty cliff. Here he saw a fine, white path winding along its mighty sides to the very top. He stopped and gazed in awe, then fell upon his knees, for instead of ending on the mountain top the winding road kept right on—up, up, into the heavens it twisted and wound like a mighty spiral thread. The pilgrim fancied that it passed from star to star until finally lost in the infinitude of eternity.

Eagerly, he pressed onward, longing to travel that mystic way leading upward to the heavens. Slowly, the shadows grew around him as he entered another grove of sacred trees. A chill weighed upon the wanderer's heart; those mighty ones of the forest that rose above him seemed like great ghosts or priests of old standing in silent adoration, reaching their branches heavenward in silent prayer. As he listened, the swaying of the wind among their leafy crests seemed like the chant of a mystic choir and a great stillness entered his being. Moving on, scarce breathing, he finally reached a mighty arch of white stone which barred his way. The road passed under the arch with its gates of iron and seemed to end in a wondrous white chapel that nestled like some jewel of snowy crystal amidst the dark carbon of the forest.

As the pilgrim stopped before this gate, wondering how he could go on, a low creaking sound was heard and the massive portal swung open as though moved by unseen hands and a great inspiration drew him onward, leading him through, and up the marble steps that led to the mystic chapel. The door of this swung open also, and in awe and reverence, the pilgrim entered and stared around.

He stood in a circular chamber, all finished in pure white marble; the floor of inlaid stones and mosaic seemed like trodden snow, and from it rose pillars of pure Carrara which upheld the mighty dome. Before him rose a shrine and under the shrine a little doorway scarce higher than his waist and through this open portal, the palmer saw the path continuing.

"What place is this?" he thought as he gazed upon the shrine whose soft white curtains were closed, concealing he knew not what. As if in answer, a voice replied:

"This is the Shrine of the Bleeding Heart." The pilgrim turned and behind him stood an old man, his white hair encircled by a band of shining gold and his gray beard falling upon the robe he wore. His garment hung from the shoulders and was of the same colorless white as the temple around him.

"What mean you, master?" asked the pilgrim, bowing humbly at the feet of the aged man.

"This" answered the Shining One, "is the Place of Tribulation. Many there are who walk the way of silver light that you have come, but few have passed beyond this point. Before you the winding path which marks the way of immortal life goes upward to the feet of the divine, but he who would walk it must find the key that is hidden in this chapel. See the door that is open before you, how small it is and how low? Like the eye of the needle is this pathway and none may pass, save those who bow. You now stand at the doorway of immortality for those who pass this portal go on into the infinite and are of earth no more. Come, let me show you the shrine."

The aged man led the mortal one across the room and as they came near, the silken curtains parted, and a great ray of glorious light blinded the seeker. As he grew accustomed to the brilliance and dared to gaze into the mystic recess he saw, quivering and pulsating in the sacred niche, a living heart from which poured streamers of golden light.

"Master, what is that?" asked the pilgrim in awe.

"That, my son, is the Bleeding Heart, the Guardian of the Sacred Doorway. None shall pass this point save they be anointed with the drops of blood that pour from this mystic shrine. You cannot approach the door, for the light will blind you. So, this guardian stands; and to you, oh man of earth, if left the riddle, how to pass this mystic shrine."

The pilgrim sought to press forward, but the light drove him back and the great glowing, pulsating Heart seemed to grow greater as he sought to near the Infinite.

"Master, I cannot pass! Where shall I find the key to this mystery?"

The old one shook his head. "That is for you to know and not mine to disclose," he answered kindly.

As the wanderer stood, his head bowed in sorrow that his path should end thus, a strange dizziness came over him and the room swayed and rocked, things grew dim about him, and the old man's face seemed to swim in a sea of light. Slowly shadows fell, the white temple faded away, the mountain with the path into the stars dissolved, and the pilgrim found himself standing upon the same endless road that stretched for miles before him and was lost in the shadows behind.

"What way shall I go now to reach the Light?" he murmured, gazing around in sorrow.

From somewhere, a voice seemed to whisper: "Go on, go on." And slowly he began again that endless wandering to the very furthermost part of creation, praying that he might again find the point where the road passed into the stars. His torn, bleeding feet leaving their tracks of blood upon the path, the pilgrim wandered on, and at last fell for a moment's rest beside another wayside shrine.

"Is there no end to these wanderings?" he mutely asked, gazing up at the Crucified One hung in the little alcove. From the Dying Figure came the echo of his question: "Is there no end?"

"For years I have walked the way faithfully and truly; each turn of this road whispers that the end is near but when I reach the bend, it stretches out as endless as before. Everywhere I have sought my God and His light, everywhere I find a promise that fades as I approach. Many a night I have seen a wondrous city shine out from the skies on the top of some distant mountain but when I climb its lofty sides and fall exhausted the vision fades away, only to be built again upon some other distant peak. Alone, with none to give a word of cheer, with none to understand——oh God! Must it be forever?" Again, the Figure upon the cross echoed back his words: "Alone with none to give a word of cheer, with none to understand, oh God! Must it be forever?"

As the pilgrim knelt there, his heart broken and bleeding, a tottering form slowly approached the shrine and, falling, stretched weak hands towards the crucifix that it contained. He was an old man, and his raiment was torn and tattered, his face deeply lined with sorrow turned in despair to the cross, and slowly dragging himself along he reached the foot of the tiny shrine.

"This is the end," he murmured. "It seems ages that I have sought, but I can go on no more. And here, brother, when I am gone, lay me to rest—here beneath the crucifix."

The young one turned, and a feeling no mortal man can express filled his soul as he gazed at the dying form. "No, no, my brother!" he cried, "have courage! I too have wandered long and suffered much— I know what you have been through and how the miles seem without an end, for I have walked them as well. But courage, brother, for I see now what I never saw before. Something within me that has cried many a long year is loosened; something whispers that have long been silent. My heart too was broken but as the iron fingers closed upon it, a new world opened to me, for out of it escaped a gleam of light that shows me the way of the wise. Come, brother, let me help you and we shall yet find the light—for see round yonder curve a gleam of light appears. I am sure that this indeed is the end of the way."

The old man looked, and a new hope filled his eyes. "Indeed, I see it also!" he whispered, "come, let us go on."

He rose and his tottering steps seemed strengthened for a moment as he pressed forward towards the light, but just as he reached the curve, with his hands outstretched, he fell forward upon his face and lay still. The pilgrim himself, rushing towards that gleam, stopped and wavered for a second and then turned back to the form that held out a hand weakly.

"No, brother, I will not leave you. I have suffered as you have suffered and will stay with you, for well, I remember the agony I went through when none would stop."

Reaching the side of the old man he knelt down and, lifting the aged head upon his knee, tried to sooth the sufferer, unheeding the fact that but a moment before he had himself been dying of a broken heart. As he knelt there, he did not see that the great trees around him with their massive pillars were slowly turning white; he did not realize that the swaying branches that linked overhead were turning into a dome of marble; but as he knelt the figure before him slowly faded away and with a cry of amazement, the pilgrim rose to his feet and gazed around. He was again in the temple, but this time alone. He looked towards the Shrine of Bleeding Heart. It was empty. The little door below it was open before him and a voice seemed to tell him to go on. Reaching the little gate, he knelt down, and bowing in humility, passed through. Before him, the path led up to the stars and, with hands crossed upon his breast, he started up a path that seemed like jewels and diamonds, glistening in a spiritual sun.

Gazing down at his garments, he found that they were not those that he had been wearing but were of white. Obeying an impulse, he raised his hands to look at them. They were covered with blood, and twisting and gleaming between his fingers was the Bleeding Heart which had been on the shrine while behind him stretched a fine thread of blood that marked the path he had been walking.

A voice said: "That is the key."

(To be continued)

THE WINE OF LIFE

NEAR the close of the 11th century at Nishapur, in Khorasan, there lived a poet-philosopher — Omar Khayyam. Little is known of his private life and history, but today the verses of Omar the Rubaiyat, live as they have never lived before. He was the first great writer of Persia and has been read and studied through all these hundreds of years in his native land, but it does seem like a strange twisting of Fate that he should be so alive in this ultra-modern world of ours and that his piquant, old-world philosophy should ring so true today. However, there is probably no more widely misunderstood writer in all the annals of literature than Omar, for the peculiar phraseology of his work is very deceiving, and his meaning is usually directly contrary to the statement made. But a careful analysis of his writing will show the observant thinker that in every case there is a deep underlying meaning that bespeaks of great philosophical understanding. Nor did his genius stop at verse making, for he was the foremost mathematician and scientific astronomer of his day and much of the calendar system we use now was brought to its present state by his efforts. And it does not seem fitting that one who so lived the life of a sage and mystic should have written light and meaningless things.

But that is the way of the world, they only see with the eyes they have. It is just the same with our Bible: the historians read it as history; the imaginative read it as romance; the astrologers read it as astrology; the alchemists read it as alchemical; and the materialists—well, to them all the spiritual scripture of the world is just so much useless tommyrot, consequently they condemn, destroy, and paint darkly everything of such nature with which they come in contact. And that is just why most of the ancient books of a religious nature were written as they were, in allegory, hidden from the eyes of those who are not ready to know.

Reading the following verses of the Rubaiyat through the eyes of the rank materialist, what have we? Waste not your Hour, nor in the vain pursuit Of This and That endeavor and dispute;

Better be jocund with the fruitful Grape than sadness after none, or bitter, Fruit.

For "Is" and "Is-Not" though with Rule and Line, And "Up-and-down" by Logic I define,

Of all that one should care to fathom; I Was never deep in anything but—Wine. Come, fill the Cup, and in the fire of Spring Your winter-garment of Repentance fling:

The Bird of Time has but a little way To flutter, and the Bird is on the Wing.

Just the rambling fantasies of a drunkard, nothing more nor less than beautiful poetry about drink and intoxication. And that is what the average individual sees. Others say, no, no, there is something deeper behind it, and so lay it aside. They are willing to believe that it is inspired perhaps, but how and why, or what it really means, is nothing at all to them. However, it is a known fact that Omar talked a great deal more of his wine than he drank of it, and though his entire philosophy is centered around the brimming cup, he means something else.

The Rubaiyat is a conversation or soliloquy delivered by the human soul to its divine spirit, referring to the body as the Clay Cup, in some instances as the Loaf of Bread, and to the life in man as the Red Wine:

Here with a Loaf of Bread beneath the Bough, A Flask of Wine, a Book of Verse—and Thou Beside me singing in the Wilderness and Wilderness is Paradise now.

For thousands of years the juice of the grape has been used to represent the life essence in man because it is the closest thing in nature to human blood and it contains the sun's vitalizing rays in a greater amount than anything else for the sun is the base of its fermentation. And as the human brain with its many convolutions resembles a bunch of grapes, it is called the Bough or Grape, while this essence or spiritual life of man is in the brain centers and is therefore the Juice of the Grape.

And so, Omar says that the Wine of Life is all there is and all else is a lie. Speaking of his search for some other thing worthwhile and the uselessness of it all, he says:

Myself when young did eagerly frequent Doctor and Saint and heard great argument.

About it and about: but evermore come out by the same door wherein I went.

Why, all the Saints and Sages who discuss'd Of the Two Worlds so learnedly are thrust Like foolish Prophets forth; their Words to scorn, are scatter'd, and their Mouths are stopt with Dust.

And who has not heard, as he did, the saints and sages discussing? We have a number of them right in this city. They gather on the street corners and in halls, shouting in all directions. One will say: Ectoplasm is the base of all things. Another will answer: No, it is protoplasm! Then: You, fool! it is ectoplasm! And they rip, and rant, and roar. It was this that Omar enjoyed and said of them: "They are foolish prophets" and "In the end their mouths are stopped with dust." And it is true, for that is the end of all; the ranters and roarers die hard but there is only one ending—death stops it all.

And so, Omar preferred not to speculate upon the beginning nor the hereafter, he deals not with where we came from, where we are going and why, but only with what we are doing today. His sentiments are, "If I do that which is good today, tomorrow will take care of itself; if I made a mistake yesterday, it does no good to worry about it now."

Strange, is it not? That of the myriads who Before us pass'd the door of Darkness though. Not one returns to tell us of the Road, which to discover we must travel too. Alike for those who for To-day prepare, and those that after some To-morrow stare, a Muezzin from the Tower of Darkness cries "Fools, your reward is neither Here nor There."

Ah, my Beloved, fill the cup that clears To-day of past Regret and future Fears: To-morrow!— Why, To-morrow I may be Myself with Yesterday's Sev'n Thousand Years. Ah, make the most of what we yet may spend. Before we too into the Dust descend; Dust into Dust, and under Dust to Re, Sans Wine, sans Song, sans Singer, and, sans End! And of the hopelessness of human destiny, he speaks: into this Universe, and Why not knowing, Nor Whence, like Water willy-nilly flowing; And out of it, as Wind along the Waste, I know not Whither, willy-nilly blowing. What, without asking, hither hurried Whence? And, without asking, whither hurried hence! Oh, many a Cup of this forbidden Wine Must drown the memory of that insolence! Up from Earth's Center through the Seventh Gate I rose, and on the Throne of Saturn sate, And many a Knot unravell'd by the Road; But not the Master-Knot of Human Fate. There was a Door to which I found no key; There was the Veil through which I could not see; Some little talk of Me and Thee There was, and then no more of Thee and Me. Earth could not answer; nor the Seas that mourn in flowing Purple, of their Lord forlorn; Nor rolling Heaven, with all his Signs reveal'd. And hidden by the sleeve of night and morn.

Omar realized that all living things are Pieces on a great Gameboard, all moved by a Mystic Player in the way that they should go. This Mysterious Player is the spirit of man, and the Checkerboard is Life and the Pieces on the board are the living problems which confront us. And we are the mystery of every game we play; but most of us get so wrapped up in our game that we become enslaved to our own selves instead of being masters of the chessboard.

We are no other than a moving row Of Magic Shadow-shapes that come and go Round with this Sun-illumin'd Lantern held In Midnight by the Master of the Show;

Impotent Pieces of the Game He plays Upon this Checker-board of Nights and Days; Hither and thither moves, and checks, and slays, And one by one back in the Closet lays.

The Ball no question makes of Ayes and Noes but Right or Left as strikes the Player goes; And He that toss'd you down into the Field, He knows about it all—He knows — HE knows!

The Moving Finger writes; and having writ, moves on: nor all your Piety nor Wit Shall lure it back to cancel half a Line, Nor all your Tears wash out a Word of it.

And that inverted Bowl they call the Sky, Whereunder crawling coop'd we live and die, Lift not your hands to It for help—for It As impotently rolls as you or I.

And as though to lessen or counteract the utter hopelessness of this, he brings the power of human individuality to bear:

I sent my Soul through the Invisible, Some letter of that After-life to spell: And by and by my Soul return'd to me, And answer'd "I Myself am Heav'n and Hell."

Heav'n but the Vision of Fulfill'd Desire, And Hell but the Shadow of a Soul on fire, Cast on the Darkness into which Ourselves, So late emerg'd from, shall so soon expire.

And then of the responsibility of the soul, perhaps a hint of Re-incarnation, he writes the following, and gives the urge to live in the To-day and drink the ever-present Wine of Life:

Yesterday this Day's Madness did prepare To-morrow's Silence, Triumph, or Despair: Drink! For you know not whence you came, Drink! For you know not why you go, nor where.

And so the entire philosophy of the Rubaiyat twines round the Vine of Life and the key to the whole is in learning how to drink this mystic Wine. When man lives properly and is vitalized by this life, the food he eats and the sun he absorbs, he gathers into his being a spiritual essence, extracting it from all of the base elements that constitute his bodies. And this essence of life is the basis of all energy, and the whole secret of this mystic wine is in the conservation of energy and its expression through creative channels. Wherever energy is used, it should produce something equal to the amount expended, and if man would only realize this, he would be less likely to waste the precious motive power of life in riotous living for he would know that when he expends it constructively, he would gain constructively and when he uses it destructively, he loses twice as much. A person who gets violently angry and cannot restrain himself is intoxicated by this life energy and the essence is fermented through perversion.

It is when this energy is turned upward into the brain that it becomes creative, and when turned downward into the generative system in perversion that it becomes destructive. When this subtle substance, the Wine of Life, vitalizes the brain and all the energies ate turned into the upper room, then man truly drinks of the fruit of the vine, and partakes of the substances he has transmuted. And Omar says if you are living on this fruit of the vine, you have secured all this world has to give, symbolizing the great life-giving qualities of the wine:

The Grape that can with Logic absolute The Two-and-Seventy jarring Sects confute: The sovereign Alchemist that in a trice Life's leaden metal into Gold transmute:

Why, be this Juice the growth of God, who dare Blaspheme the twisted tendril as a Snare? A blessing, we should use it, should we not? And if a Curse, why, then, who set it there?

I must abjure the Balm of Life, I must, scared by some After-reckoning ta'en on trust, or lured with Hope of some Diviner Drink, to fill the Cup, when crumbled into Dust.

Oh, threats of Hell and hopes of Paradise! One thing, at least, is certain. This Life flies: One thing is certain, and the rest is Lies; The Flower that once has blown forever dies.

And so, this transmutation of the life energies is the greatest alchemical mystery the world has ever known. If the Cup is empty, there is no philosophy, and the argument between sage and seer means nothing. The path that the individual walks through years and lives of experience, the growth, the gains by practical labor, mental, spiritual, and physical, are the basis of the Wisdom

Teachings, and there is no other way.

Omar says that life is Wine poured into a Jug and that a broken Jug is of no use to anyone, for there is nothing in it. And we have with us and all around those broken jugs, walking about with nothing in them but ashes. Inside they are cremated by the fires of desire, hate and fear, and the flames of passion, burned out. The Vine is dead, and all that remains is just an urn filled with ashes.

And so, if you will read Omar Khayyam's beautiful verses, taking the human soul as the vine, the bread as the bodies, the wine as the blood or life-giver, and Omar as the spirit, you will find something very useful. The bunch of grapes as the brain has been the symbol of life for ages for in it is contained the life forces which make possible every expression of energy man has. And mastery and initiation are the complete control of it and the turning of it into the development of the spiritual organism. It is suffering, sorrow, philosophy, art, science, and study which gradually attain to that end, but the greatest means known to man are purification and balance. Purification of life and motive turns this energy from all destructive application and the absolute poise of mastery prevents its expansion into useless pursuits. All depends upon the individual; when he lives the life, he shall know the doctrine.

There are many, many more wonderful and deeply mystic truths brought out in this beautiful classic and in this article, we have only touched a few of them lightly. While lack of space prevents going into it verse by verse and giving it the interpretation, it deserves, still this brief summary will give some idea of the great import of this deeply religious poem.

The whole work is based upon the knowledge of man's duty to the life forces within him. And death means that this energy is gone, and therefore Omar says that whoever has inverted the Cup is dead; and so, ends the poem with these verses:

Yon rising Moon that looks for us again—How oft hereafter will she wax and wane; How oft hereafter rising look for us Through this same Garden—and for one in vain! And when like her, oh Saki, you will pass Among the Guests Star-scatter'd on the Grass,

And in your blissful errand reach the spot Where I made One—turn down an empty Glass!

LIVING PROBLEMS DEPARTMENT

CORRECT BREATHING

Man's lower bodies receive nourishment and vitalizing power in three general ways. First, through the direct rays of the sun passing in through the crown of the head or the spleen; secondly, through food from which he extracts the vital element; and third, from breathing by which he oxygenizes his bodies. Oxygen is absolutely necessary to the unfoldment of man's consciousness. The average individual has no idea either of its importance or of how to do it, thus he overlooks a valuable opportunity for health. Everyone should sleep in well-ventilated rooms with the windows open and should spend five or ten minutes every morning in deep breathing. The more one breathes, the less one will have to eat until finally it is possible to practically maintain oneself on oxygen. Man, only uses about one third of his lung capacity; he should at least double the quantity of his inhalation. The corresponding out-going breath frees the body from carbon dioxide, the great death dealing element in man. If he breathes twice as much, he can divide his ill health and subtract one-half.

FURTHER LIGHT ON THE HEALTH PROBLEM

When suffering from the following ailments, do not go to a doctor, just knock your head against a wall. If your corns ache, it is not nature's fault; leather shoes would bring corns out on a bootjack; and as a very powerful nerve center is in the sole of each foot and leather shoes prohibit the feet from breathing, do not be surprised if you are sick. Any gentleman who wears a tight-fitting hat must not be surprised if he develops a furless pate for you cannot strangle hair roots and have them live any more than you could go into an air-tight room for several hours and come out alive. Any of our dear lady friends who insist upon walking around on stilts (French heels) are subjecting themselves to over forty diseases, including spinal ailments, kidney trouble, nervousness, general lassitude, paralysis, stomach trouble and nearly every known form of disease except accidents and those are not strictly excluded as a person can twist their ankles on high heels without Half trying. Yesterday we passed down the street behind a pair of two and a half inch heels and the ankles above were rolling like chips in a heavy sea while the party above the ankles has been wondering why she has had a general debility for years. Any man who makes a chimney out of himself has no right to be healthy and will not be and those of our dear friends who insist upon their nice juicy beefsteaks should be tickled to death when uric acid gets them because they have been inviting it to come. The mystery is not that we do not live longer; the mystery is we live at all. If we continue to wear tight-fitting clothes which will not allow the body to breathe, we will keep right on having all the diseases that medical science has differentiated and some more they have not found yet. So mote be.

THE ETERNAL EXCUSE

When it is gently hinted to an individual that he is not living up to the best that is in him, could be doing better, etc., there is one excuse that will almost always come back to you—well, I am doing about as well as you are—I am as honest as the next fellow—or similar expressions. Man is eternally excusing his own weaknesses by pointing out similar short-comings in his companions. He considers this to be a clinching argument, while in reality it is no argument at all. The virtue of sin cannot be proved by its mere existence, neither can our short-comings be sanctioned because our brother man expresses them as well. Many times, we go out to put a slick deal over on our brother, excusing ourselves by saying, "he'll do it to me if I don't get to him first." All these things are excuses to cover human weakness. Man should strive to attain the best and allow no comparison to deter him from attaining individual mastery. His duty is not to be just as good as the world but to be perfect and he must attend to the accomplishment of this end.

QUESTION AND ANSWER DEPARTMENT

Please name some occult literature that is good to study.

Ans. "The Brother of the Third Degree" by Garver; "The Dweller on Two Planets" by Philos; "Miriam of the Mystic Brotherhood" by Howard; "The Romance of Two Worlds" by Barabas; "The Sorrows of Satan" and "Life Everlasting" by Marie Corelli are as good fiction as can be secured on the subject. The writings of Jacob Boehme, Andrew Jackson Davis and Emanuel Swedenborg are excellent from the mystic standpoint: Sibley, Raphael, William Lilley and Nicholas Culpeper are good in astrology. "The Secret Doctrine," "Isis Unveiled" and "The Key to Theosophy" by Madame Blavatsky; "The Cosmo Conception" by Max Heindel are of the best occult works of modern times. Spencer, Huxley and Plato lead in scientific research and philosophy, while H. G. Wells has written an excellent history of the world.

When can we know that past debt has been paid?

Ans. When we met with an unpleasant problem and master it. We never have to pay the same debt twice. If it still bothers us, we have not met it.

How can we change our environment?

Ans. Our environment is created within ourselves and if we would see harmony, we must build harmony within, for we see all the world through our own eyes, our own failings, likes and dislikes.

Why does the Lord's prayer say: "Lead us not into temptation?" Is this not a blasphemy?

Ans. This part of the Prayer is directed to the lower emotions, asking in the name of the divine that they lead us not into temptation. It is not addressed to God, but to the lower man in the name of God.

When should we be guided by our intuition?

Ans. When we have proved by experience that our spiritual natures have unfolded to that degree that they guide us in the way that leads to constructive acts. If we do not purify the bodies and make the glass clean, we can never be sure where inspirations come from.

Can we get anything we want by wishing for it?

Ans. Yes, if we wish to work.

Why are we born with so many imperfections?

Ans. Because when we finished our last visit here, there were many little things and a few great ones that we had not completed. There were many things which we did wrong and for them we are suffering. We start at this time where we left off before.

What is the best way to free oneself from the clutches of a hypnotist?

Ans. There is only one possible way, and that is the developing of a positive willpower and making it stronger than that of the operator. Outside aid is only a crutch and the victory over his enemy of mental freedom is only possible through the divine help of the God in man, the individual consciousness within.

How long and how often should one fast and pray for spiritual growth?

Ans. Next time you decide to do this, take a vacation, roll up your sleeves and go to work to help someone who needs something and fast in your spare time. In your fasting, let your lower emotions starve for lack of nourishment and let your prayer be a life lived well twenty-four hours a day.

Is the anthropoid a degenerate human, or a highly evolved animal?

Ans. Neither. He is the result of the inability of a certain percentage of the last life-wave to advance to human consciousness.

What effect has cremation on the spirit?

Ans. Cremation about three days after death, immediately destroying the body, severs the last tie between the higher organisms and its form and in that way frees the spiritual bodies to go on with their work.

(To Be Continued)

THE MAN WHO LAUGHED

ON sunny Sicily beneath the towering height of Mount Etna, under whose mystic pile, so legend tells, the Vulcans hammer out the weapons of Jove on the anvil of the gods, there lies a little village. Sicily is dotted with many lovely little hamlets, looking like bright nosegays set in frames of green and brown. One of these little villages nestles close in the arms of Etna, and many of its buildings reflect the whims of the volcano. Far above it, a little dot on the mountain, one can see the great observatory and below rolls the blue waters of the Mediterranean. A picturesque little town it is, just as the mind of the dreamer loves to create and as in imagination, the homely old-fashioned peasant life is still lived.

On a wall built from the rocks of the flaming mountain sat a native guide who looked not unlike a brigand, and was dressed in accordance with his personality. His ears were pierced and in them hung heavy golden rings, his hair was controlled within the bonds of a red bandanna handkerchief, and his drooping black mustache was carefully and fiercely combed, adding a swagger note to his eccentric figure. Beside him stood George Washington. By way of explanation, we may add that George W. was a long-eared, tired looking Sicilian donkey who would always lie down when you wanted him to stand up and stand up when you wanted him to lie down. Washington and his master were part of the natural scenery of the village and strangers passing through on their ride around the island were shown the village church, the cave of the saints nearby, and George Washington. Leonardo, the guide, had a peculiar distinction; he spoke the best English for miles around and therefore was always watching for an opportunity to commercialize his intelligence. At the time our story opens, he had Henry Thornton at his mercy. Thornton was a man with a past, not the kind that men are ashamed of, but the kind that some men are broken by. It is said that the world is filled with heartless men, but this is not essentially the case, and careful investigation will prove that the heart of a man breaks just as easily as the heart of a woman. But a man hides it more carefully and receives little sympathy for the ache that the world does not see.

Thornton was one of those men who could neither conceal nor forget, and he carried his sorrow with him wherever he went, his mind was always obsessed with one thought, and he lived entirely in the years that were past.

The tale of woe of this man was a long one, and also an old one. It fills the lives of thousands all over the world, for there are none who can hurt us as much as those we love and trust. It was simply the story of one who cared and another who simply played, and with the carelessness of a child, broke a human heart.

That was years ago, in the days of lace and lavender, and the thoughtless one had lain asleep these many years in a little village cemetery. All the world had forgotten to save one, all the world had forgiven save one; but even as the gray shadows began to fall on the life of Henry Thornton, he remembered. His handsome face would cloud, and his jaw set tighter than he vainly sought for something upon which to wreck his venom, a poison long brewing in a heart that hated happiness because it was not happy too.

As Thornton stood beside the guide, leaning over the old wall, his eyes fell upon a little garden some twenty feet below him, a pretty place filled with rustic chairs and tables where the town folk came to sup their sour wine and tell the stories of the day. It was deserted save for a few children playing in a corner and one figure that sat huddled in a brown robe at one of the tables. The children were playing some strange game and every few minutes they would tumble over each other in a mad whirl of bare arms and legs and the Sicilian dust rose in a cloud about the scene. The figure at the table raised his head, and a long peal of deep-throated laughter sounded up to the two men above. Thornton's face had been composed but as this merry sound broke upon his ears, his jaw set, his eyes became slits, and he hissed out three words with all the bile of years of acidity.

"Damn that man!"

The guide looked at the American in amazement and then followed his eyes to the little scene below. He quickly crossed himself, but made no audible reply, although he murmured something under his breath.

Thornton continued to gaze at the little group, and then feeling that he must make a confidant of someone, he turned to Leonardo:

"Come sit down on this wall. I want to tell you something—I will explain my attitude, for it must seem very strange to you."

"Si, Signior," answered the guide, and with a look at his mule, he seated himself upon the wall, perfectly willing to let the American talk as long as his pay went on.

Thornton took out a cigarette case and gave the Italian a smoke, then closing the case, sat gazing at it for several seconds, and then turned it so the guide could see the little oil painted miniature beautifully done by some master's hand upon an inlay of purest ivory.

The Sicilian looked at the face for several seconds and then, raising his eyes and opening his hands, he muttered, "She is a beautiful face."

"Yes, she was beautiful in the days gone by," answered Thornton staring out into the distant haze that hung over the Mediterranean, "beautiful but thoughtless; she played with hearts as children play with dolls, and mine was broken in the game. That was nearly forty years ago in America's sunny southland where beauty is nature's order and gallantry her decree—Oh, God, that I could forget like others do!—but I cannot—I have gone from one end of the earth to the other, but ever that face haunts me. I have never laughed since that day unless it was in a mad delirium. I have taken the path of forgetfulness, but there is no peace; in the opium smoke she haunts me, in drink she dances in my wine-glass, breaking my heart again and again as she did that day. My hair turned white in just a few short months, and I have lived in sorrow and sadness these many years. That is why I hate to see people happy—why should they be so when I am not? Did God send me into this world to wander my life in agony? When I see these children playing in happiness and hear the glad laughter, I go insane to think of the years of loneliness I have come through, how I might have listened to the laughter of my own children, and in my old age been peaceful in the realization of life's dream. That, sir, is why I hate people that laugh, and revile the God who gave me the heart to love and then doomed it to be broken—Bah! there he laughing again!—Oh, damn that man—I shall go mad if he does not stop!—I would give all I own to be he this day, just so that I could laugh."

"Surely, Signior, you are jesting. You do not mean to say that you would like to change places with Fra Angeleco, the old man who sits down there at the table? Surely you jest."

"No, Leonardo, I am in deadly earnest. I would give all I own if I could laugh as he laughs today."

"Signior, you have told me a story, now let me tell you one—the story of the old man who sits there at the table, laughing at the children who play around his feet. May I tell it to you?"

"Yes, go ahead, I do not care when I get back to the hotel, I would not be sorry if I never did."

"All right, Signior, I shall proceed. It was—let me see," and the Sicilian counted on his fingers, "three, four, five, six, — yes, six years ago, that Antonio had his little market in Ademo. He had a beautiful little farm up on the side of Etna—you see where that black streak is? Well, Antonio's farm was just a little to the right of that heap of boulders. Signior, that was in the year of the eruption—down the sides of our mountain, the lava came in a great fiery stream and

Antonio was in the market-place at the time. Like a madman he rushed home, but when he got there all he saw was a great fissure in the earth, with Sulphur fumes rising from its depths. All in a few seconds—his wife whom he adored, his mother whom he worshipped, and his five little children whom he cherished more than life itself were swallowed up by the flaming mountain. Well, Signior, we saw little of Antonio for many months! He wandered like a madman among the hills, and even the brigands grew afraid of him. He climbed among the rocks, wild-eyed and crazy. But at last, he grew quiet again, and feeling that he had nothing left to live for, he climbed up yonder hill to the little monastery. There, he took holy orders and gave his life to the service of Christ and the Blessed Virgin. Antonio vanished from the world and there appeared in his place Fra Angeleco who has lived ever since to try and help others."

"Did he really go through all that?" asked Thornton in amazement.

"Si, Signior, and much more in his heart that no man shall ever know."

"And yet he can laugh! Oh, how I envy such a man as that! Why did God give him courage to laugh and me only the weakness to cry? Leonardo, I am more jealous of that man than of any other living thing in the universe—I would give anything to be as happy."

"Surely, Signior, you do not mean that? You are not jealous of poor Fra Angeleco?"

"Yes, I am jealous of him; he is able to laugh and forget."

"He cannot help laughing, Signior, nor can he help forget. The good God has taken his mind away from him: the poor father has been madding these many years. Surely you are not jealous of a babbling idiot, nor would you curse a man whose sorrow has taken away his mind? In this world, Signior, it is well to be careful whom we envy, for those who laugh often are sadder than those who cry."

THE HOMAGE - II
CHAPTER TWO
(Continued from last month)

It was about four years after when the youth went again up into the mountains, four years of sunshine and of rain, four years that changed the affairs of man but left the mountains just the same. The green grass, the lofty pines and the great belts of whitened snow had apparently not changed at all.

One morning as the sun arose a strange scene confronted the eye. Over the mountain there hung a great, gray cloud which twisted, turned, and seethed in a million ever-changing folds. The whole atmosphere in the mountains was hushed and still, and a great leaden silence hung over nature. Hunters and trappers whispered that never before in all the years they had lived among the hills had they ever seen such a strange mystery before. As the day wore on, the dark cloud became deeper, a low moan broke out. From the heavens, it rose and fell with the passing of the winds, a great sighing sound as that of the dying. Each tree seemed to pick it up, reverberate and echo it from their crests and branches. Little shrubs and bushes seemed also to bow their heads while the arms of the lofty pines hung drear and dismal in the steely light. Up among the rocks great groaning sounds came and masses of boulder and dirt became thundering avalanches upon the mountain sides. The snow upon the crest turned gray and everything seemed to hang in awe and suspense during nature's agitation.

That day the youth was impelled to climb again that mountain and so he wound in and out along the little path and, following intuitional guidance, branched off from it and after a short walk reached the point where the valley began, and the mountain peaks left off. There among the rocks, half hidden by the darkness, stood the little cabin as he had seen it before. But now everything seemed different. He shrank back in wonder for coming out of the mountains, out of the very earth itself, out of the skies, and up out of the waters of the river that flowed by the door, a great stream was coming—a stream of living creatures. Stately stags and meek-eyed does, surrounded by their young, broke through the forests in silent majesty, great lumbering bears came also, not one but many. The air was filled with the humming, droning of the wings of birds and even the steely light was shadowed by the multitude of their wings.

From the forest came the wolves and foxes and in the little pool by the cabin door fishes of many colors gathered, swimming to and fro, so many that the water seemed one living mass. Then it seemed that the great heads of the pine trees were bowed, their branches bent low, and from the mountain tops a great cloud of leaves and fine pine needles descended like a rain upon the cabin. All nature was united in a strange sad song, even the very earth itself seemed joined in a sobbing melody.

In awe and fear, the youth crept to the cabin door and gazed within. There on his pallet of straw lay the Old Man of the Mountain, his hands folded upon his breast, his white beard spread upon his cowl, and his eyes closed. Without entering in, the youth knew the tragedy. The hermit was dead. At the foot of the rough wooden pallet stood the great arched-antlered stag, his head down so that his soft nose rested on the edge of the couch. In the hollow of the old man's arms sat the little gray squirrel, trying to force a hazel nut between the cold white lips. The little birds were shrilly crying as they circled around his head and the great wolf lay like a watchdog before the body of the one, he loved. The soft scent of the forest came in through the door which stood ajar, for in the old cabin that door was never closed. Little baby birds in their nest cried for the hand which could feed them no more.

A thin stream of tears poured over the youth's face as he gazed upon the scene. Nature knew it had lost its truest friend. In all the world that taunted, one alone had loved them; in a world that slew and hated and thoughtlessly robbed them of their right to live, they had found one who understood. And now the cold fingers of eternal night had closed his eyes and the chilly voice of the mountain peaks had whispered in his ear. Who could they go to now when their friend was dead? Soon again, the rude hand of the huntsman would have no sweet voice to offset it. The beasts knew this and were sad.

The youth stood for several seconds, unable to take his eyes off the scene. A great something welled up in his soul and he remembered the promise he had made—his promise to be true to the furred and feathered friends. He passed slowly through the cabin door. The great wolf looked at him but did not move—just a low howl like a groan of despair broke from the beast's throat.

As he touched the still cold form of the hermit, the little squirrel raised his eyes, beady bright eyes like sparks of fire, and two tiny paws reached out to cover the face of the master he had loved. The youth stroked the little beast's shiny body as it lay stretched out across the form of the hermit and, biting his lip to hold in check the pain of his soul, the hunter of the days gone by stepped again to the door of the cabin and gazed out. He started back from sheer amazement—such a sight as met his vision had never before confronted a man, nor probably ever will again.

As far as the eyes could reach in every direction, the mountains and valleys were alive. Each tree branch bore its weight of feathery life, in each glade and opening stood some stately beast, not hundreds nor thousands, but it seemed all nature was gathered there. The mighty gray clouds over the mountains rumbled and moaned and lurid flashes of lightening rent their hazy depths. A gentle rain was pouring down, pattering among the leaves, and the youth, looking at the form on the couch, murmured, "Indeed blessed are the dead that the rain raineth upon."

A voice within him spoke, saying, "When has such homage been done to a living man? Has the emperor or king had such a cortege as this? Many great ladies and grand men march in the funerals of the great, many there are who come and pay respects to a nation's dead, and ofttimes they do not know and do not care, but each one who stands in this great cortege is true to the soul of its being. No sham is here, no pretense. Each one of these beasts, to its very soul, adores the thing it pays its homage to. Each of these little furred and feathered things would gladly die for that one. Each tree and stone would give of its fleeting life the fullest and the utmost. When man has a friend among the beasts and birds, that man is good, for there is no guile in their lives, no subtleness in their adoration."

The youth was overcome and, sinking upon his knees, gazed out at that endless stream of faces—great sorrowing eyes that could not speak but with lowered heads and drooping bodies whispered the emotions of their souls. The great strong trees, even the blades of grass, bent their heads, for the one who loved them all had gone away.

"This is my task," murmured the youth, "and I will fill it. What greater proof has man of the depth of his sincerity than that a ring of faces such as these should pay devotion to him? I am not going back into the valley again, I am going to stay and serve these beasts and birds as the Old Man did." The shades of night fell over the mountain, but they were alight that night with a million fires. A million flaming altars sent up their sacrifices and through the night gleaming coals of fire, the eyes of the silent watchers, row after row, stretched out into an infinity.

The next morning, when the sun rose, there was a new hermit living in the mountains. Under a cross of rocks, the body of the aged man was laid to rest while his spirit interceded before a greater throne for the beasts that he had loved. The great cowl was worn by another, the staff strengthened another's hand.

So, through the years that went rapidly by, in his love for nature, the one who once had slain nursed the wounds that he had made. The birds and beasts learned to know him also and soon they gathered around his door to whisper their secrets in his ear and tell their love stories to his soul. And some there were who slowly learned to forget the other one and to love him anew in the one he had awakened. Down in the village, no man knew what had happened. They did not know that the hermit of the pines was dead, for still his gray cowled figure wandered among the hills. They used to say, "How is it that a man should be willing to live with beasts?" The old hermit had known the secret and the younger one was fast learning it.

And so, the legend says that to this day in the heart of those hills there lives an insane old man, broken by some earthly sorrow, who has given up the benefits of earthly affection to live in the mountains like a beast. They laugh about him in the village, and they lay wagers as to who shall find his bones, but in the same voice they tell you of that wonderful day years ago when the mountains grew dark and the beasts flocked together and the great miracle took place in the hills. That story will never die in the little city at the base of the mountains. In awe, they tell you of the thunder and of the majesty of the lightning. The superstitious cross themselves and say that the Spirit of God Himself walked the hills that day. They never knew nor will they ever know that this was Nature's homage, Nature's only way of showing its reverence and its love for the old hermit in the gray cowl who lived in the little cabin where the valley meets the hills.

THE CHAIR OF DOOM

IT was in the summer palace of the Emperor—where cherry blossoms filled the air, little bridges led across waterways filled with fishes of gold and silver, and little dwarfed fir trees scarce higher than your waist edged the rowed and parked lawns of the summer garden. In the midst of this beauty was a little pagoda where the Emperor used to come and sit and in it was a glorious chair of carved ebony, its back cut to resemble an ancient tree through which flew ho-ho birds with little eyes of gleaming mother-of-pearl. The Emperor used to love to come here and sit in the midst of his summer garden to laugh and smile with nature, but as the years went by and the step of the Emperor grew halt, the cares of state resting heavily upon him, he came less often to his chair in the garden.

One who was close to him and beloved of him came to the Emperor one day and said, "Sire, you have been sad these many days but the sun shines in the sky and the garden is in bloom. Come out once more to the Pagoda of Dreams as you used to do in days gone by."

The Emperor was silent, for his mind went back over the years beyond recall and he dreamed of the hours he had spent in his garden of cherry blossoms. Then leaning on the arm of this one whom he trusted he went into his garden where he had not walked for many years, and there, with but few to attend him or to break the solitude of his thoughts, he sank as a weary pilgrim into his chair in the garden.

For years, none had sat there. The chair was dusty and streaked with age and the glinty eyes of the ho-ho birds had fallen out. But the Emperor did not care, for in the hours he sat upon it he lived in the long ago—in the days when in youth and carelessness he had lived in his garden of dreams. Still the same chrysanthemums raised their many-colored heads and danced in the sun, still the golden fishes leaped in the pools and the white storks with their crimson crests balanced in silent majesty in the watery rills, he heard the same waterfall which had sounded in his ears when he had played his love song in the gardens years before.

And the Emperor was sad, sad with the remembrance of loves, and joys lost forever. So, he sat in his chair, moody and silent, while the glorious sun sank down in the endless West, as his own life was fast sinking in the endless West of eternity. And in this way the Emperor fell asleep, in his garden of cherry blossoms and there he slept forever. When dawn came, they found the spirit gone and the body asleep in the Pagoda of Dreams.

The years went by, and another king sat upon the throne, but none would enter the garden, for it was there the Emperor had gone to sleep. So, a story came down through the ages that told of the Chair of Endless Sleep in the Pagoda of Golden Dreams. It was warned that whoever went into the garden of pleasure would some time go back again and enter the rest eternal in the garden of their dreams. So, the new king never went there for fear that he, too, would fall asleep in the enchanted chair. He had a mighty wall built around the garden that none might enter for he had been told by a reader of the stars that he would go to asleep as his father had in this Pagoda of Dreams. So, he issued orders to all the world that none should go into that garden, and none should ever speak to him of that garden for he had vowed in his soul to live forever as a ruler of his people. Thus, for a hundred years, the old chair stood alone in the garden of wild cherry blossoms and the old king swore a new oath every year to outlive the curse.

Now it seems that there came into this land the foot of the white man, coming as it so often did, not to lift but to rob, not to serve but to pillage. One of these white men learned of the Pagoda of Dreams and the sacred chair that was in it and one night when all was still, he climbed over the high old wall to steal this treasure. Passing through the darkness of the night, amid the little arches and bridges and altars of granite, he finally came to rest at the gate of the Pagoda of.

Dreams. The hinges were rusty and old, the golden lattice work was tarnished and broken, the lanterns that had lighted the garden were but skeletons of wood from which the gay silks had long since rotted, the little fish no longer played in the stream for it was dried and their hones were mixed with the sand. The chrysanthemum beds were filled with weeds and the palms were overgrown with hushes, for none had entered it since the day the Emperor had died.

The American, with his hand on the hilt of a revolver, broke the lock of the pagoda door and passed in where the pale rays of the moon lit dimly entered through the gaping holes of a decaying roof. There, in the center of an inlaid floor, stood the Chair of Doom. It was a broken thing that had once been the resting place of an Emperor, and overgrown with a tangle of weeds and cobwebs where spiders had built their nests in its carvings.

The American stood for several seconds viewing this broken chair, dreaming of the fortune it would bring in the Western world when they knew of its secret history. As he stood there in the night, he heard a footfall behind him. Turning, he saw coming towards him an Oriental robed in a wonderful garment of embroidered chrysanthemums and lotus flowers. This figure walked slowly forward with his hands out-stretched before him. The American looked fixedly at his face and saw that his eyes were closed.

"What can it mean?" he muttered, creeping back into the shadow.

The robed man walked up to the battered gate and then slowly round and round the pagoda, in the same measured tread, with eyes closed and hands extended. At last, the truth flashed into the mind of the American -the figure was that of the ancient Emperor and he was walking in his sleep! The ideas and thoughts of his life had become so fixed in his mind with the dread of the chair of gloom that night after night, when his body was in resistless sleep an unknown and unnamable force drew him into the garden to the Pagoda of Dreams amid the scent of the cherry blossoms.

Slowly the Oriental entered the pagoda and seated himself, eyes still closed, in the Chair of Doom from which none might rise. As he sat there, the American started in surprise, across the floor of the pagoda a strange creature was crawling, its hard shell-like claws grating on the stone! He stood as though fascinated and watched while a gigantic scorpion, like a small crab or lobster, crept slowly towards the seated figure of the sleeping Emperor. With his eyes fixed upon the insect, the American stood as if spell-bound as the thing climbed up the robes of the Oriental as he sat sleeping in the chair.

The moon glided for a second behind a great wall of clouds that had risen from the valley and hung like a shade around the crest of the distant mountains. When it passed from behind the clouds and shed its cold beams again into the Pagoda of Dreams, a strange sight was revealed.

The Emperor lay in the chair where his father had died and on the ground beside him the crushed body of the scorpion. Over the two stood the American, who gazed in astonishment as the light came on. Seeing the dead insect, he shook the quiet form. The body swayed as he shook it and would have fallen from the chair had he not drawn it back. Then, as he looked more closely, he saw on the back of the dead hand two tiny marks, like a pair of lips, where the kiss of the scorpion had fulfilled the ancient prophecy.

"So," murmured the American, "that is the Chair of Doom. Well, I'll leave it forever where it stands in the orchard of cherry blossoms, twice it has fulfilled its pledge." And slowly he passed out from the pagoda and to where the great wall surrounded all.

Suddenly a figure appeared from the darkness, a long, thin, hollow tube was placed to its lips. Then through the night a shaft of tufted steel shot from the mouth of a blowgun. The American turned, swayed for a second, and slowly crumpled up at the foot of the wall, just a few feet from the pagoda.

When morning came, they found the Emperor asleep in the Chair of Doom and by die wall the body of a foreigner, in his back a poisoned dart.

A new law was passed on that land, and a great crew was turned into the garden. For many days and nights, they labored to destroy a superstition. They tore up the bridges and the shrines, filled the stream-beds with dirt, they burned the pagoda and, with it, the Chair of Doom. And now another world stands in that garden of dreams, a wonderful building of brick and stone with an elevator running up and down! The busy purr of an East, awakened by the hand of the West, stands where once the cherry blossoms swayed.

The legend of the Chair of Doom is nearly forgotten but hidden away in the records of a mysterious person is the old story of the Pagoda of Golden Dreams in the enchanted garden of the Emperor.

ASTROLOGICAL KEYWORDS

Capricorn is considered being a very ambitious sign also particularly anxious for worldly honors and social aspiration because it is the natural ruler of the tenth house, which has to do with the public fortune of the native. Capricorn, being ruled by Saturn, is sometimes cold, sarcastic, and suspicious. It is a very long-life sign and under it are born those sprightly old people who swing around at eighty-nine or ninety with the speed and alacrity of youth. Capricorn people usually have two codes of ethics, one for the world and the other for their immediate families; they are gracious and smiling with strangers but often cold and irritable at home. A well-developed Capricorn, however, is a very lovable person, true, faithful, and always willing to help in any way possible.

We find a great deal of loneliness among Capricorn people, especially the old folks. They are often imposed upon by others or at least imagine that they are, therefore, their old age is not always a happy one.

The keywords for Capricorn are:
Cold, Dry, Earthy, Nocturnal, Melancholy, Feminine, Southern, Obeying, Weak, Movable, Cardinal, Tropical, Domestic, Four-footed, Changeable, Unfortunate, Crooked, Hoarse, Night house of Saturn, Exaltation of Mars, Arid, Sign of the winter tropic, Detriment of Moon, Fall of Saturn.

General Characteristics:
There is always something peculiar about Capricorn people. They seem to stand a little different from all others because of certain eccentricities. Their physical appearance always draws attention to them as they are different and while sometimes good mixers are generally poor company until the higher and finer side of their nature is awakened.

The general characteristics are:
Love of social honor, Ambitious, Bound by heredity, Family pride, Sometimes crafty, Usually thrifty, Subtle, Economical, Witty, Changeable, Liable to melancholy, Subject to curious dreams, Usually mystic, Carry the air of veneration, Scientific, Given to boasting, Stubborn but not always strong-willed.

Physical Appearance:
Dry constitution, Slender, Long thin face, Thin hair or beard, Dark hair, Long neck, Narrow chin and breast, Weak knees, Long legs, Voice weak and effeminate, Loose jointed Angular.

If Saturn is posited in Capricorn, it adds to the aged appearance of the body, which, however, is usually much stronger than it appears to be. Young Capricorn people are usually judged older than they are, while very old Capricorn people are judged to be much younger than they are.

Capricorn is subject to diseases of a crystallizing and drying nature, also especially to the ailments listed below:
Sprains, Dislocations, Broken limbs, Melancholia, Hysteria, Cutaneous eruptions, Cold chills, Disorders of the chest and lungs, Dry coughs.

Domestic problems:
Capricorn, being a barren sign, is not always as fortunate in these matters as might be. It is also liable to be broken homes through excessive melancholia

and a Capricorn who does not know better often fills their home with blues and despondency. If they can be made to see the brighter side of life, their home becomes as radiant and cheerful as it once was depressing.

Countries Under the Influence of Capricorn:
Part of India, Saxony, Macedonia, Albania, Thrace, Bulgaria, Part of Greece, Part of West Indies, Mexico.

Cities Under Control of Capricorn:
Mecklenburg, Oxford, Wilma, Cleves, Brandenburgh.

Colors:
Dark brown, Black, Very dark indigo.

Ptolemy says that the fixed stars in the horns of Capricorn are similar in nature to Venus and partly to Mars. The stars in the mouth are like Saturn and partly like Venus. Those in the feet and stomach are the same as Mars and Mercury, while those in the tail are like Saturn and Jupiter. Henry Cornelius Agrippa, listed the following in his tables concerning Capricorn: of the Twelve Orders of Blessed Spirits Capricorn is ruled by the Innocents; of the Twelve Angels over the Twelve Signs, Capricorn is ruled by Hanael; of the Twelve Tribes, Gad; of the Twelve Prophets, Mahum; of the Twelve Apostles, Thomas; of the twelve months, December 20th to January 20th; of the twelve plants, dock; of the twelve stones, chrysoprase's, onyx, moonstone; of the twelve principal members of the body, the knees; of the Twelve Degrees of the Damned, the witches. Capricorn rules lead because of Saturn on its planet.

(Continued from last month)

Countries Under the Influence of Sagittarius:
Arabia-Felix, Moravia, Spain, Dalmatia, Hungary.

Cities Ruled by Sagittarius:
Cologne, Budapest, Avignon.

Colors:
Light green, Olive.

According to Ptolemy, the stars in the point of the arrow of Sagittarius have an influence similar to that of Mars and the Moon. Those in the how and at the grasp of the hand act like Jupiter and Mars. The nebula in the face is like the Sun on Mars. Those in the waist and in the back resemble Jupiter and also Mercury moderately. Those in the feet of Jupiter and Saturn. The four-sided figure in the tail is similar to Venus and, to some degree, to Saturn. Henry Cornelius Agrippa says that of the Twelve Orders of Blessed Spirits, Sagittarius rules the Angels, of the Twelve Angels ruling over the Twelve Signs, it is ruled by Anarchial; of the Twelve Tribes, Napthali; of the Twelve Prophets, Zephaniah; of the Twelve Apostles, James the Elder; of the twelve months, November 20th to December 20th; of the twelve plants, pimpernel; of the twelve stones, hyacinth; of the twelve principal parts of the body, the legs between the thighs and knees; of the Twelve Degrees of the Damned, Sagittarius rules the Tempters and Ensnarers.

QUESTIONS AND ANSWERS
— CONTINUED

Are earthquakes and the sinking of continents natural causes or are they effects of the inharmony among those who inhabit them?

Ans. They are caused by the inharmonious thoughts of those who inhabit the planet. Emotion is attuned to lire, and fire is the cause of all the changes in the earth. Our thoughts affect our bodies as we know. We are the cells of the Body Cosmic, cells with a very bombastic temperament, and we are continually causing aches and pains to our planet. However, all is progression, all is moving and working forward.

Can the mind imagine anything unreal?

Ans. It is impossible for a human mind to create or imagine anything that does not exist somewhere on one of the many planes of nature.

Is the power of communication with the astral spirits a sign of development?

Ans. Not necessarily. Development is a positive step forward while many become conscious of superphysical things through a retrogression. Crystal-gazing, magic mirrors, and all those things are not developments but are degenerations which will destroy us if we continue them.

What did Christ mean when He said "In my Father's house are many mansions?"

Ans. One translation of this paragraph says, "In the Father's house are many resting places" and the "mansions" undoubtedly refer to the different planes of nature where the spiritual consciousness lives and rests in its progression towards perfection.

What is the best cure for an inflamed stomach?

Ans. Fasting, non-irritating diet and a purifying of the entire system are the only means by which treatment of a permanent nature can be carried on.

Is there a healing for sore and aching feet?

Ans. It is amazing what a marked connection there is between a disturbed stomach and sore feet, but if people will keep their general system in good order much foot trouble can be eliminated.

What are the real dangers of psychic development?

Ans. The first great danger is negative development, which results in mediumship and obsession. The second great danger is seeking to unfold spiritual powers before the body has been properly purified to sustain the strain.

What is the meaning of the word "occult" and how is it to be used in connection with spiritual sciences?

Ans. The word "occult" means hidden. An occultist is one who through the powers of reason is trying to lift the veil of allegory from science and religion and find the germ of truth and unity concealed in their diverse, complex, and literal explanations and teachings. The occultist is the eternal seeker, seeking eternal truths.

Who is a mystic and how does he differ from the occultist?

Ans. The mystic is one who is seeking to gain the same truth and lift the same veil by developing the heart side of his nature and to gain by intuition what the occultist searches for by reason. It is the union of these two paths, the mystic and the occult, that gives the seeker the balance that is necessary before the higher initiations are possible. When action of the proper kind is added to this and the student applies his theoretical knowledge, then the eternal triangle is perfected and balanced in man.

What is the true object of all the Wisdom Teachings?

Ans. Their purpose is to show man his true position in the great plan of creation. They explain to the student the responsibilities of life, and, through the knowledge that they give him, prepare him for the Great Work that awaits all when their days of schooling are over.

How should we regard a religion?

Ans. A religion is a phase of truth attuned to the states of consciousness of them who are evolving through it. It is the doctrine, part of a still greater doctrine, to which we are drawn by the faculties we have developed and the spiritual sight we have unfolded within ourselves. It is a changeable point. As we grow in experience and understanding, our religion and religious concepts should broaden with us. Every living being changes, or should change in some way, his religion with each experience and unfoldment which daily life brings; if he does not do this, he is standing still. When we are inclined to look down upon creeds or religions that seem primitive to us, we should remember that they are all steps in a great plan that must be passed through before the Planner can be revealed. When we have passed through and reached a more elevated ideal, our broadened, spiritual intellect should help us to realize the need of all of the other steps, and the fact that a doctrine exists at all on this plane of nature is proof certain that it is helping someone who would fall without the protection and inspiration that it gives, for nature supports nothing any great length of time that is not of use in the plan.

What is a creed?

Ans. Creeds are steps in the unfoldment of religious truth which have on this plane of nature drawn around them forms which we call denominations. Creeds are incarnations of spiritual truth, functioning in ever better vehicles furnished by the consciousness of those souls who are evolving through them.

Which religions are occult?

Ans. All religions have a hidden or esoteric side. The same may be said of all the divisions of a religion. The esoteric doctrine we see in a religion depends upon the esoteric eyes we have developed in our own spiritual natures. They who look through the eyes of form can see only form and in religion only the history of people now dead and countries now unknown; while to them who have evolved the spiritual sight, the life behind the form (the truth behind the allegory), is visible. All religions are steps in the unfoldment of one truth and they only clash when their spiritual ideals are crystallized into material forms.

What is a miracle?

Ans. A miracle is an effect, the cause of which is unknown. The cause, however, must be as great as the effect it produces. If the student wants a miracle to happen to him, he must set in motion causes great enough to produce the desired effect. Our universe is governed by law and order in spite of what many people believe.

Who is God?

Ans. God, as He is now generally understood, man, and the universe are at various stages in the concrete manifestation of the Absolute. The God we know is the individualized part of this Unknowable One, who through the unfolding of consciousness has become the ruling spiritual intelligence of a solar system. Man is eternally making adjustments of bodies within two planes of consciousness without, and God is relatively perfect on a plane of consciousness where

GREAT SAYINGS OF ZOROASTER, THE PERSIAN

"The teacher of evil destroys the lore, he by his teaching destroys the design of life, he prevents the possession of Good Thought from being prized."

"Those men of evil actions who spurn the holy Piety, precious to thy wise one, O Mazda, through their having no part in good Thought, from them Right shrinks back far, as from us shrink the wild beasts of prey."

"Bliss shall flee from them that despise righteousness."

"He that does not restore a loan to the man who lent it steals the thing and robs the man. Ever moment that he holds it unlawfully, he steals it anew."

"Let your ears attend to those who in their deed and utterances hold to Right and to those of Good Thought."

"Teachings address I to maidens marrying and to you bridegrooms giving counsel: Let each of you strive to excel the other in the Right, for it will be a prize for that one."

"Whatever happiness ye look for in union with the Lie shall be taken away from your persons."

"He who sows corn sows righteousness: makes the Religion of Mazda walk, as well as he could do with ten thousand sacrificial formulas."

"Violence must be put down; against cruelty make a stand, ye who would make sure of the reward of the Good Thought through Right."

"Well, is he by whom? That which is his benefit becomes the benefit of anyone else.

APRIL 1924

SELECTED VERSES

Shall any gazer see with mortal eyes,
Or any searcher know by mortal mind?
Veil after veil will lift but there must be Veil upon veil behind.
* * *
Who toil'd a slave may come anew a prince
For gentle worthiness and merit won;
Who rul'd a king may wander earth in rags
For things done and undone,
* * *
Ye suffer for yourselves. None else compels,
None other holds you that ye live and die,
And whirl upon the wheel, and hug and kiss Its spokes of agony.
* * *
This is the doctrine of Karma. Learn!
Only when all the dross of sin is quit,
Only when life dies like a white flame spent
Death dies along with it.
* * *
Enter the path! There is no grief like hate!
No pains like passion, no deceit like sense! Enter the path!
Far hath he gone whose foot Treads down one fond offense.
—Light of Asia.

EDITORIALS

Notice to Subscribers

This number concludes the second magazine subscription of six months, which we offered to our friends and students. Any who have not received six numbers as per their subscription may secure any of the back numbers which they do not have through communication with us. The further development of the magazine cannot be definitely stated at this time, but our subscribers will be informed thereof by a circular letter within thirty days after the receipt of this number of the magazine. We still have a few of the first numbers which we will be glad to supply to those sending in and we ask you all to wait patiently for the next

development in connection with this publication.
Very truly yours, THE EDITOR.

SHALLOW BROOKS ARE NOISY

HAVE you ever stopped to consider how much valuable energy is wasted in tears, repentances and wailings by individuals who follow blind alleys of sorrow, all of which led to oblivion? At a moment when a great crisis presents itself, energy should be conserved; when one who has long meant to us something which words cannot describe is taken away by the hand of death or our illusions are broken by grim reality and people raised upon pedestals have come tumbling down, when we are confronted with problems requiring the coolest calculation and the most discerning reason—about that time we collapse, heart-broken, and howling like a three-year-old child. The salt of life loses its savor, there is a total eclipse of hope and we allow whatever energy remaining to trickle out of us in cold sweats or pour down our faces like a spring freshet in the mountains. As the result of this, we are sick afterwards, all used up, and make the very worst possible decisions on all matters of importance.

Let the emotionless East answer this problem. We may be called cruel and heartless because we do not drench our handkerchief and our neighbor's shoulder when someone dies, but we will find ourselves of a great deal more use in the long run if we are the only person present who has retained even the shadow of self-possession and is capable of issuing the necessary command at the critical moment. Emotion is one of the greatest causes of weakness and inefficiency which at the present time besets the human race and an individual who can remain balanced and self-possessed not only saves the situation but also lengthens his own life many years. The moment of catastrophe should be the moment of conservation, whereas, now, individuals run around in circles perfectly conscious of the fact that they are getting nowhere but feeling that they must give vent to their emotion if the only thing they can do is wring their hands.

Problems which present themselves in our civilization must be met with clean-cut reason and in an efficient, sensible, rational way. You never knew a businessman, long bent over the desk which has transformed itself from his place of business into the casket of his soul, to throw himself upon your neck when you come in to sign an insurance policy, (although you may be the only one who has been in that week), then tell you that he is awfully, awfully, awfully glad to see you, going into ecstasies, from thence into convulsions, to finally end in a cataleptic coma. What usually happens is this: he twists his cigar to the other corner of his mouth, picks up a pen in a slow, disinterested way, dips it in the ink, then sticks it under your nose, grunting, "Sign here and pay the cashier." If similar tactics were to be used in moments of emotion, the individual who followed them would be ostracized from society but would be infinitely more useful than all the mourners put together.

There is a story told about a Chinaman whose house burned down in the middle of the night, he barely escaping with his life to say nothing of his clothes. Sitting in front of the ashes of all he possessed in the world, he turned an old wooden tub over and asked his friends if they had saved his memorandum hook. They answered no and asked him why he was so interested in such a small detail at such a moment. He looked at the ashes for a minute and at the tiny wisp of smoke that still rose from them and then turning to the friends said, "The reason I want my memorandum book is that I may send a message to the American gentlemen who was to dine with me this evening. I must send him my humble apologies and request him to dine with me at a restaurant instead, and my only regret is that after giving my word, I am unable to invite him to my house." The average American whose house catches on fire cries out, and runs up and down, blowing so hard that he fans the flame, and the entire building is consumed.

Emotion is no sign of grief nor pleasure, but only shows that an individual is incapable of controlling their nervous system. The deepest of grief and the greatest of joy find no expression in the physical organism. They are qualities too deep to express. The individual who weeps for you today will forget you tomorrow for they have cried their brains out with their tears, while a simple pressure of the hand, one simple word of realization, marks a friend who will not forget or an incident that is deeply etched into the soul.

Whichever way you turn, efficiency is lost when superficiality comes in. Those things which are tinseled, and gaudy seldom wear, but like the Christmas tree ornaments, find their way to a premature ash-can. On the other hand, simplicity of design, simplicity of habit, simplicity of expression—these things are the mark of strength; they are the mark of endurance; they are the mark of permanence. In art, many lines seldom improve the drawing, while the artist who completes his picture with a few strokes of the pencil creates an expression of mass, unhampered and uncurbed by tiny lines and useless filagree. People rant and rear too much, they weep and cry too much; they sigh and moan to excess, and they over-flow their banks of sentimentalism with too much ease.

As a result, a civilization noted for these excesses is invariably shallow, and as a mass the Aryan race is shallow, especially those among that super-expression of nervous fidgets which we know as "society." The "upper set" of civilization generally is noted for its veneer, its plating, its filagree work and its expression of sentiment, sentimentalism, and superficiality. As a result, year after year, our leaders of society wind in ambulances among the hills and dales of our countryside on the way to sanitariums for nervous wrecks.

There is in America at the present time a subdued something in the air. The atmosphere seems vibrant with suppressed fidgets, and our people as a mass show practically no self-control. They fight like wild cats over non-essentials; mourn like broken-hearted Romeos over their disillusionments; they commit suicide on the spot, not due to any premeditated plan but just because of the fact they had chills running up and down their spines and just had to do something, This condition is becoming so acute with our mode of civilization that unless something is done to steady the nerves, and curb the emotionalism of our peoples we are going to produce a race of super-sensitive, nervous enemies, incapable of anything except vibratory wiggles of their organisms and water-falls of senseless tears.

Wherever you go you can turn masses of people if you can only work upon their emotions, they will follow you like blind sheep over the edge of a cliff if you can work up the animal within them. Reason plays little part in the modern principles of civilization. People are led entirely by their likes and dislikes and flock like children after an intellect who is great enough to sway their sentiments. This is the secret of theology's power through the ages, it is the secret of the power of the politician; it is the secret of modem advertising, in fact, it rules the modern world, that is, the western world.

On the other hand, the stoic easterner, who remains unmoved by all these things, is laughed at by those whose hysterical outbursts mark the only expression of their intelligence. Laughter is very helpful, especially good for the liver, but for an individual weighed down by a tremendous weight of responsibility, even laughter is dangerous; even the gods laugh but not continually. When there are important things to be done, even the energy wasted in laughter must be conserved. It is said that laughter signifies the fact that you are happy, and we are inclined to believe that an individual is in good humor if we can cause his diaphragm to vibrate. But if you have ever gone through an insane asylum and heard the howls of demonical glee from some poor demented soul whose mind is a blank and whose laughter is as empty, in fact emptier than the howling of the wind, you are forced to agree that laughter is not an infallible sign of intelligent humor or enjoyment. From this, we are able to deduct that happiness does not necessarily express itself through explosive means. Happiness is a state seldom found by mortals here below; what we commonly call happiness is really a tickling of the emotional pallet which causes a pleasant sensation to run up and down the nervous system and drive thought and reason still further out of the picture.

And so, individuals, only partly efficient at best, are wasting what little efficiency they do possess by allowing their constitution and temperament to swing back and forth, like an eccentric clock pendulum, between the posts of joy and sorrow. The result is ever increasing deficiency, ever-increasing work for nerve specialists, ever more thoughtlessness, crime, and various forms of thoughtlessness which are crimes. Through all this, the "heathen" remains in stoic peace. Truly, he is happy as all men are, and few live this span of years without sorrow; he has loved and hated like other men and found, as others must find, that it was not a paying proposition. The result is quite evident. He found that he could do more, gain more, and preserve his efficiency to a greater degree by remaining unmoved amidst the moved and calm amidst the storm.

And so the sages of the east have said, "Only he who is balanced in pain and pleasure is fitted for immortality." For only one who is master of others can lead them and those subject to the same weaknesses as those they lead are like the blind seeking to help the blind and all falling into the ditch together.

So, we suggest the following to you, or rather, present our emotion platform, which may be briefly summed up as follows:

1. Do not mourn for that which is lost, for the more you mourn, the more you lose.

2. Do not weep because you are weak, because you get weaker if you weep.

3. Do not wring your hands or wave them in the air, if you do, you will not have enough strength to walk with later.

4. When you are happy, do not laugh; figure out the joke and you will probably find it is not very funny after all.

5. When you think that loud laughter is a symbol of intelligence and affability, remember that some inmates of the lunatic asylum laugh all the time.

6. Do not weep because you are ruined, for you are ruining your nervous system also when you do.

7. Do not walk around in circles, you will never get any further than yourself if you do.

8. Do not love anybody too much, if you do, do not show it too much, it will give them an advantage over you. When you have found the "one ideal,"

do not swear you will get down on your knees and die for them; get up on your feet and work for them and call it a day.

MENTAL ATTITUDE AS THE BASIS OF EFFICIENCY

GREAT corporations and industrial enterprises are beginning to realize more and more the part that mental attitude plays in business efficiency. They are realizing the value of the contended employee, and that the goodwill of their own servants plays no little part in the success of an enterprise. In days gone by the employee was looked upon as a necessary inconvenience, as a menial who must do as he is told or be fired, while those who were underlings forever stood with the sword of Damocles over their heads, living in awe of the boss and in momentary expectation of being fired, abject slaves of a commercial system which gave them no place. If they sought to rebel against this system, it meant unemployment, suffering and even starvation.

This day of tyranny, however, is over, for industry discovered that those who work through fear are only eye servants and that the sourness and hatred which was showered upon industry by those who were as cogs in its wheels inhibited the output, diminished the efficiency, and left the officials of the corporation without friends or even the respect of their employees. In the days past the employer did not care what his help did think of him, but he is now beginning to realize that the attitude of his office force, and of his industrial workers, must be taken into consideration and form one of the keynotes of an enterprise.

So today we find the cooperative plan in which the servant is consulted by his own master, in which he is given a living wage, in which he is given a voice in the running of the enterprise. Such a system increases the efficiency of the entire and is now the only possible way to prevent a great industrial revolution.

The cheerful worker does three times the work of the over-taxed, under-paid, grumbling clerk. The smiling face of the employee sells the products of the corporation. It means that there will never be a shortage of labor in that corporation and that its workers, humanely treated and honestly considered, will give the touch of personal sympathy to the enterprise, which personal sympathy has a market value many times the amount of money expended in order to create it.

As this is true in the commercial world, so it is true in every walk of life, and as a man at the present time capitalizes upon the efficiency of his brother man and also realizes that his efficiency is his capital, both in the commercial world and in the world of letters, he is realizing more and more that the proper mental outlook on life is the basis of his ability to meet the problem of daily existence.

The ability to meet problems, the ability to endure hardships, and the ability to labor methodically are expressions of efficiency, and in this day and age of the world not only must a product be sold but, because of the keenness of competition, it must literally sell itself because of its economy and merits. And just as a product must sell itself, so the individual who wishes to be a success in world affairs must learn to sell himself to the world. Before a man can sell an automobile, he must sell himself to the purchaser, before a man will be promoted in the commercial world, he must sell himself to the employer.

Now let us briefly analyze what is meant when we say a person must sell himself. By this is simply meant that he must prove that he is necessary to the development of a certain tiring and literally prove that he is the one best fitted to perform a certain work to attain a certain result or to demonstrate a certain quality. In other words, by selling oneself is meant that a person must convince another of his merits to the extent that the other comes into realization of the fact that the party in question is necessary to the success of the enterprise.

Efficiency sells a man in the commercial world more quickly than anything else and efficiency is fifty percent experience and fifty less in his efforts to regenerate the plan of being.

The second undesirable mental attitude which we wish to discuss is the state of melancholia. We have not only the radical who wishes to blow up everything and get his fingers at the throat of something, but we also have the individual who is just sour and who lives entirely in a realm of failure, gloom, despondency and general dolefulness. These individuals are long-faced, sorrowful persons who spread gloom with their very presence. The world has no place for them because at this time everyone has more troubles than they know what to do with and few wish to discuss those of other people or be forced to shoulder the burdens of any save themselves. For this temperament, there is but one remedy and that is the sunshine cure. They must realize that in spite of the fact that the r mother-in-law cut them out of her will or that they had to pay their brother's funeral expenses, the world cares little but hands the palm of the victor to the face with the smile. The attitude of indifference to responsibility and the lack of interest in the problem at hand is a poor recommendation in modem world affairs. A business takes an interest in the person who takes an interest in that business. The office manager today feels that he has really hired a man when he hires with the personality the good will, and few succeed in enterprises which their hearts are not in. Where their treasure is there will their heart be also the Scripture has stated, and the modern business world of today promotes and distinguishes those whose hearts are in their labors. In spite of petty graft, the whole-hearted one seldom fails if he has energy and the proper mental outlook on life. Under the heading of melancholia, we have the individual who lacks interest, who manifests incessantly those qualities which show that the blood moves slowly in their veins, and the doors of enterprises, both spiritual and material, close upon the drone who does just what he has to and nothing more, who labors with his mind far away, or who is turned from the path of sunshine by every reverse. In this way, you see how the mental attitude and not the skill with the fingers makes and breaks us in the world of affairs.

The third division we will mention under the heading of mental attitudes is the egotist. In the modern world, be it political, sociological, philosophical, or religious, the employer and the fellow-worker throw up his hands and turns away in despair when he finds blooming in a soul the flower of egotism. The great sorrow of the egotist is that he seldom recognizes the fault in himself. He fights the whole world to prove his own position, is blind to his own faults, and has the most helpless mental attitude that there is known. There are always a great number of people to fill positions of little importance, but there has never been a surfeit of great men and great women. The world delegates authority to all who are capable of standing it and egotism is the proof of the lack of control of self. When the world bestows power upon an individual, upon a group of individuals, upon a government, or upon a scheme of things, it does so because that individual has demonstrated the qualities of worthiness or because that organization, government, or scheme of things, has exhibited fitness to be entrusted with responsibility. There is an endless need for people who can carry responsibility without showing it. In this world, the successful manager is the one whose superiority is the least suspected. The idea of the great man on the pedestal is dying out and men today serve men more and more because they recognize in the one, they serve the qualities they themselves do not possess. The successful leader in all walks of life is the one who leads through confidence and not one who demands to be a leader because of the scepter of authority. Therefore, we say that the third mental attitude which destroys the efficiency of individuals in world affairs is egotism. It convinces those who do not know that they know almost everything and causes exhibitions of power which are ever obnoxious to the democratic minds of the twentieth century.

If individuals would trace their own characters carefully and study their own mental attitudes on life—whether the world they live in is bright and cheery or whether it is dark and gloomy with the forebodings of their own soul, whether they accept responsibility or not, whether they exhibit the carelessness of mentality which does not give a rap and many similar things—they will find in their own natures and their outlook on life the reason for the position they occupy in society, whether it be successful or unsuccessful. And for those who are molding characters to be, the natural, human intelligent, cheerful outlook, if cultivated, will give them precedence in the world of men over many older and wiser heads whose views are radical, whose minds are sour, or whose lives are rutted with the crystallization of their own thoughts.

BROTHERS OF THE SHINING ROBE- X
(Continued)
CHAPTER TEN

"The key, the key, the key!" the voice kept saying. From everywhere die word could be traced, half seen, half read, and heard by ears that were not of this earth. Suddenly a great star of light appeared before the pilgrim, growing larger and brighter, seeming to spin, dance and twist, and at last exploded into thousands of streamers of colored light.

I felt myself falling, down, down, down, through an abyss of darkness, where not even stars lighted the sky of eternity. Suddenly the fall stopped, and opening my eyes I found myself looking straight up at a filagree pattern of pink flowers that decorated the ceiling over my head. I felt weak and faint and for several seconds could not move. Then turning slightly, I made the rather startling discovery, that I could move, for in some subconscious way I did not feel that the body I had was connected with me.

The morning sun was shining in at the window, casting its bright reflections about the apartment, and I lay looking up at the ceiling, trying to collect my shattered thoughts and piece out the story since the time I was sent whirling from the train and over the embankment.

As I lay there, a dark shadow began to crawl slowly up the side of the wall. My over-wrought nerves gave way and in spite of myself I gave a cry, for creeping up the wall by my bedside was a great shadowy spider which seemed at least a foot across, having no substance whatsoever and existing only as a shadow upon the wall. My mind recalled the black magic that had been used on me before and so I braced myself against what I felt to be an attack, at the same time sending out a call for the Master as I always did involuntarily in moments of trouble.

The shadow stopped and I could see the vibrant, hairy legs of the spider twist and cross each other as the fine feelers felt over the surface of the wallpaper. At the same time, I felt behind me the presence which I had learned to love beyond life itself—that of the Master. Turning quickly, I looked at him and pointed to the spider, crying, "Save me! For I cannot move out of the bed and this thing is crawling down upon me!"

I recognized the majestic form that stood at the bedside by the eyes rather than anything else, for he was dressed in a military costume of western style and his face was no longer that of a Hindoo, but of a European prince. As I looked pleadingly at him, the Brother of the Shining Robe smiled slightly.

"Here, my son," he said quietly, "is a lesson well worth the price of the terror. What do you think this is?"

"Why," I answered, "I know not, but I presume I am being attacked again as I was before by some hallucination or ethereal creature launched against me by the black brotherhood. The slight smile still played around his lips as he answered, "Do you know what is black magic's greatest weapon?"

"No, master," I answered. "Then I will tell you. It is fear. It makes of strong men cowards, of honest men thieves, and of Christians demons, of gods, devils who inhabit the filmy fastnesses of hell. Know you not that black magic deals with the element of fear and much of the evil in the world is based upon the fear of the unknown, which is most often harmless until we people it with demons of our own creation? The creeping creature that you see upon the wall, that shadowy thing which you feel is the blow of black magic, is like indeed black magic itself—but a shadow of the real. "Look." And he pointed towards the window.

Rising a with painful effort on one elbow, I gazed towards the aperture where the bright morning sun was shining through the spotless pane, and there on the window-pane was a black spider, a little larger than a fly, and I realized why the smile had lurked around those lips. The sun shining in through the window had caused the gigantic shadow of the little insect to be cast upon the wall beside my bed. With a sigh of relief, yet a feeling of sheepishness, I sank back upon the couch.

"Yes," continued the old man, "darkness is but a shadow of the real. Evil is like yon little spider, until the reflections of the human mind casts a shadow many times as large upon the walls of the soul. You are safe at this time. No further attempt will be made against you until you are able to be up and start again on your mission. It is then that you need to worry. You are too strongly protected here for them to come, but as you go out into the world again, and you are weakened by contact with the multitudes, and your spirit is broken by the rebuffs of the world, then will black magic become again a vital factor in your effort to succeed."

The master vanished as he had come, but I had not noticed that during the latter part of our conversation the door of the room had opened, the tall, slim form of Miss March, with her pale and highly arched brow, had been standing in the doorway of the room. I knew she had not seen the Master but she must have heard me talking to him and seen the gestures that I had made while he was present.

"To whom were you talking?" she asked as she entered the room and closed the door softly behind her.

Realizing the instructions, I had received concerning the secrecy of the adepts, I remained silent. She repeated her question, and feeling that I must answer in some way, I replied, "I was talking to my teacher."

She looked for two or three minutes at me in a rather strange way and I could see that she did not understand what I was talking about.

"Why!" she exclaimed, "there was no one here. There is no one here now." "In the last assertion you are quite right, Miss March," I assured her, "but in the first I must beg to differ. In my half-dazed condition, I was badly frightened by the spider on yonder wall and in my nervous extremity I called for help in the only way I knew and was discussing the problem when you arrived."

The girl was silent for several seconds.

"You mean there was someone here I could not see?" she inquired. I bowed my head silently in assent.

"Who was it?" she asked.

"I am very sorry, but it is quite impossible for me to answer that question."

"What do you mean?"

"I mean that sacred obligations which I have taken forbid me to discuss the personalities of some people." Miss March laughed slightly.

"Your story amuses me. There is a certain air of mystery in it, and mystery is always fascinating. But come, I want you to tell me the name of this unseen person with whom you were holding conversation."

Again, I shook my head. Miss March looked at me for two or three moments and her face broke out in a pout.

"I do not see what harm it can do, and I am very, very inquisitive. You know I have been a student of herbs, and in my studies, I have come across many statements concerning strange transcendental powers and so forth, but in accordance with the views of the students of today I accepted them only as fables and superstitions of the dark ages. But at last, I find one who claims to know and talk to one of these strange persons who make themselves invisible, and this person—" and she looked straight at me, "refuses to answer even one little question for me."

I felt myself in a rather embarrassing position, but still maintained a dogged silence.

"I think you are just fooling me," she exclaimed, "I think you were talking to yourself, or else you were delirious."

"No, no," I assured her, "what I told you is absolutely true."

She laughed slightly and her thin, pale face seemed rather sardonic with that smile.

"I won't believe any of your stories unless you tell me about this person."

I felt that the young woman, who knew nothing of the power and beauty and magnificence of my master, was deliberately laughing at one whom I adored above life itself and for a moment my judgment left me. I was determined to prove to Miss March that my master really existed and was all that I could claim for him.

I opened my mouth to contradict her, tell her who my master was and where he came from, when suddenly out of the ether formed a human hand which closed over my mouth just as a torrent of words from a befagged, rattle-brained mind was about to expose the position that I held in the work I was doing. Do as I would. I could not speak, for the fingers were like a vice. In a second, I realized my mistake and heard a well-known voice whisper in my ear, "Be discreet."

Without another word, I sank back upon the pillow. As for Miss March, she had seen the hazy outline of the fingers and starting back with a little cry had run from the room.

There was silence for several minutes, then the wind blew closed the door she had left open with a bang, and I was alone with my thoughts and the shadow of the spider which still sunned itself on the wall over the head of my bed.

"Two lessons," I murmured. "Two mistakes. If I cannot do better than this, it was wise for the plan that I should sleep forever." And then the drowsiness of weakness returning, I closed my eyes and knew no more until about two o'clock in the afternoon of the following day.

THE WITCH DOCTOR

THROUGH the jungles a narrow path ran, just a single foot-trail bordered on each side by great ferns with broad, swaying leaves from whose clustered groups rose the round, shaggy-barked trunk of lofty palm trees whose green leaves quivered in the gentle breeze. The sunlight ever penetrated to the foot-path or dried the moist earth from which rose that moldy smell which is ever found where the light of day is excluded. Great streamers of moss, dripping with a slimy ooze, hung swaying from the rotten branches of trees long dead, while here and there a great orchid hung blooming, saturating the atmosphere with a heavy, nauseating fragrance. This is just one view of an immense jungle, an uncultivated and practically unknown area stretching hundreds of miles until finally it reaches the mountains whose snowy crests hover over in strange contrast to the tropical valley beneath.

The sounds were many and as varied as the vegetation. The chattering of monkeys, as they swung from tree to tree or hung by their tails from the gigantic stalks of jungle fern, was ever in the air. Now and then the cry of some gaily plumed bird sounded above their incessant pattering. Other sounds there were too which blended themselves into an endless symphony and were only audible as a faint rumble—the roaring of lions, the crying and laughing of hyenas or the shrill trumpet of the mighty elephant. All these awoke the echoes of the jungle, for this was the tropic primeval.

Suddenly the swaying ferns along the narrow path parted and into an open glade, arched over with palm leaves, strode Gomo the Medicine Man, the much feared and respected fetish doctor, in all the glory of primitive power. Gomo was all of six and a half feet tall with a body perfect according to primitive perfection. Great muscles and sinews like those of an ox shown out through the ebony skin, giving a sense of power and majesty to the gigantic figure. Gomo wore around him the skin of a lion; its shaggy mane covered his chest while the long tail was twisted around his waist as a belt in which was stuck a long-curved knife of some flinty stone. His thick nose and lips were pierced with colored strips of ivory and in his ears hung pendants of crudely pounded metal. The hair was shaven from his head or rather, we should say, scraped their form with the aid of sharp stones, all save a narrow area at the top of the skull where a tiny topknot still remained, bound tightly into a tassel by means of dyed and colored strips of fiber. His face and body were thickly smeared into horrible designs with colored clays and in his hands, he carried his medicine rattle, formed from the skull of an infant. He wore a necklace of human teeth, and his belt was hung with strands of hair from the heads of his victims. On his arm was a mighty shield of rhinoceros leather and in the same hand he held a great club of seasoned wood with a sharp stone lashed to the end.

As Gomo stood in the half light, surrounded by the oozing, decaying vegetation of the tropical jungle, he made a picture difficult to describe and which must be imagined being understood. He stood like a statue, his ears, with the fine sense of the primitive man, listening, listening for the footsteps of an advancing host, a horde of white men who were coming to rob Gomo of his elephant tusks, of his skins and trophies, of his riches and diamonds, and most of all to take from him his power as an invoker of spirits and messenger of the gods.

For many days through the jungles his people had been retreating before the onrush of civilization, before implements of war which Gomo could not understand, before shining sticks of metal that spat out flame and death, before curving blades of steel that gleamed like silver in the sun; before these strange implements of magic of the white man, Gomo seemed powerless. Hour by hour, the jungle that had been his home was torn from him by the evil power of the white man. Not without cost to the invader however, for from among the palm trees, amidst the swaying ferns and mounds of rock, tiny, poisoned arrows flew and little feathered darts, tipped with deadly venom, rained from the blowguns of the natives, shedding death and destruction in all directions. But still, with a power which the natives could not fathom, the oncoming race of another color won inch by inch the slimy ooze which floored this jungle.

Quickly through the underbrush, madly dashed a black form. Staggering forward, he collapsed in a heap at the feet of the mighty Medicine Man.

"Oh, Exalted One!" groaned the form from the ground, whose clay covered body was now streaked with blood, "Oh, mighty Worker of Magic! Save your people, for they are powerless against the fetish of the white man! Even now the mighty chieftain, whose belt is made of the skulls of kings, lies dead in the jungle, struck down by the flaming magic of the white race. One by one, our warriors sink down beside the way; their charms and their incantations are as useless as their shields to protect them from this dreadful magic. Oh, Mighty One, if you do not save us now, there will be none to save! Our arrows fall short of the mark and our stone hammers are powerless. You alone can save us, for you know the will of the gods!"

With a gurgling cry, the figure pitched forward and, rolling over, lay face upward in the path. The bullet of the white man had entered his heart, but, with the same power and courage which marks the beast of the jungle, he had lived for many minutes, whereas a white man would have fallen where he stood.

Gomo gazed down for a moment at the huddled mass at his feet. He saw the mighty muscles of the warrior; he saw the look of fierce hate and determination which still animated the dead man's face, and he realized that the magic of the white race must be great when it could overpower such as this.

Slowly the great witch doctor turned and retraced his steps along the path and finally vanished amidst a great sunburst of palms and ferns that suddenly appeared ahead and into which the trail dissolved. The hours passed, the shadows lengthened in the jungle, and soon the howling cries of sunset sounded upon the air which seemed ever more vital, more mystical, more terrible, as that strange electrical sunset of the jungles shrouded the trees and ferns in ever deepening gloom.

Some three hours after sunset, in the clump of palms and ferns where the path ended, a dull glow arose which tinted the swaying trees and branches with copper hues. It was from a log fire built upon the top of a little mound. Before the fire, like some great gaunt ghost or demon from another world, stood Gomo the fetish doctor, around him the strange utensils of his craft, skulls and human bones, trunks of elephants inscribed with strange and mystic characters, great drums stretched over with human skins, painted and tinted with weird figures. All these and many articles, unnamable and indescribable, were brought into faint relief by the gleaming fire that the Medicine Man had built.

Suddenly the guttural voice broke into a weird chant which sounded not unlike the howling of the wild beasts in the surrounding jungles. Raising his great arms, daubed with colored clays, above his head and swinging the rattle in tune with his incantation, he breathed forth a torrent of strange sounds. The surrounding trees and bushes seemed to shudder at the terrible outburst, their leafy heads tossing as though with a sudden breeze. Unto the gods of the sun, the moon, and the stars, the witch doctor cried; unto the spirits of the dead, he sent forth his lamentations, unto the creatures that dwell in the air, the spirits of the snows, the souls of beasts, plants and flowers, he chanted his strange ritual. His eyes, lined with great circles of white mud, gleamed with a fiery light as he beat upon his chest and trumpeted forth like a mad beast of the jungle or some hairy anthropoid. "If my people are themselves not strong enough to preserve that which is their own and protect their homes from the hand of the foreign devil, let the spirits of nature combine with us, let the birds of the air, the beasts of the field, the creatures of the ether, yes even the rocks themselves rise up with the children of nature against the black magic of the white man!" cried Gome in a voice that echoed and reechoed through the jungle, and picked up by the hills and valleys was carried on and on, none know how far.

As he stood there chanting his ritual, breathing forth his invocations to the elements and his implications against the despoilers of his people, a strange sound broke the stillness. a buzzing, droning sound, and out of the marshes and the swamps, out of the pools where the animals came to drink and those fens where the dripping bushes were ever green with the moisture of the swamp, came hosts of tiny insects. Unnumbered were these poisonous creatures. There came the tsetse fly which spreads the sleeping sickness of death, the malaria mosquito, and a thousand poisonous insects, carrying with them the death of the jungle. In the weird flickering firelight they gleamed, their tiny wings translucent and of a thousand rainbow hues. Swarm upon swarm they gathered, and then along the ground came creeping things, strange beetles with beaks and horns, spiders with a thousand legs, bony land crabs with death in their claws—a great seething, struggling mass pouring from every nook of the jungle gathering ever closer and closer to the twisting, spinning, howling figure of the fetish doctor.

At the foot of the tiny mound upon which he stood, they stopped; while the air around him grew hazy with tiny singing, buzzing insects. Suddenly the great Gomo, he who was robed in the skin of a lion, pointed his finger, gleaming dully with its golden implements, at the tiny path that wound through the jungle.

"Along that trail," he roared in guttural monosyllables, "along that trail come the destroyers of our people. We cannot fight their magic. They come to steal our land and our riches because they are strong, and we are weak and because they have strange magic which we do not know. Our men are weak—they can fight no longer—but the magic of the white men cannot withstand the magic of Gomo, the invoker of the crawling, singing, buzzing things whose army no man can overpower."

Into the fire he threw a handful of strange herbs, mixed with the powdered bones of captive kings. A great cloud of smoke arose and, instead of dissolving, floated like a balloon over the fire, and, slowly becoming less and less distinct, passed along the trail that led into the jungle. Around and about this cloud the insects gathered and in a numberless host, which grew greater as the minutes passed, they swarmed like an army of avenging angels upon the camp of the white man. In a few seconds, all was disorder there. The soldiers built great campfires to drive the insects off, but nothing, it seemed, kept them away. Healthy men sickened and died in a few moments before the onslaught of thousands of insects. The tiny tsetse fly brought a death that sword nor gun could not avert, the great jumping spider was surer than the skill of the white man.

In a few hours, the camp broke and a frightened army began its hasty retreat to the sea, surrounded by a frenzied swarm of tiny insects. They're dead they could not bury but were forced to leave them where they fell, and the great company that started forth with the white man's magic of gun and sword returned just a broken handful of malaria-infected refugees, escaped from the great swamp of the jungle. They had gone forth sane, but they returned insane, broken by the great magic of Gomo the Witch Doctor.

As the white men embarked upon their ships, the great clouds of insects dissolved as though they had never been, disappearing in the jungles, and all that was left of them were little groups that buzzed around the stagnant pools or mildly tortured the mighty beasts of the jungle.

Gomo, the Witch Doctor, stood upon his rock overlooking the great blue ocean and watched the ships embark upon their journey homeward. He had walked along the path dotted with the white man's dead. He even picked up the metal tubes that blazed forth fire and death; but they no longer availed for the hand of the white man was stilled.

"Great was the magic of the white man," murmured Gomo, "with his sticks that belched forth flame and his blades of silver. But greater still is Gomo!" And he beat his chest. "Greater still is the magic of the fetish doctor. They fight with the things they have made, Gomo fights with the spirits of nature."

Note.

This story is taken from an incident that occurred some years ago when an army of white men was invading a certain part of Africa and, according to the best authorities that can be secured on the subject, the story is absolutely and literally true that this race or tribe invoked the insects and the elemental spirits that rule them and launched them upon the invading army. The result was as described.

CONCENTRATION

CONCENTRATION is the key to omnipotence and one who is capable of concentrating his or her mind to a point wherein he becomes able to eliminate life, death and eternity, maintaining only one ideal, one point, or one nucleus of attention—such a one is capable of ruling the earth and overturning the entire plan of civilization. Concentration is the most badly needed factor of the new civilization. The inability to concentrate and the eternal entrance of outside dissenting factors into the radius of mentality, forms the basis of failure and is the greatest thing that stands between the student of nature's mysteries and the attainment of his divine achievement. Without concentration of effort and consecration of life to the ideal, whether material, intellectual, or spiritual, success is impossible in any marked degree. The wandering mind is the curse of our age. It wants to attain a certain end but has not had the courage to exclude other things for the attainment of that end. It has no strength to go against the tide or to balk at its own lower nature. Wishing to attain but without the courage of that wish, the average soul drifts through life, dreaming of success but attaining only failure.

Individuals must have a point, an aim, and an ideal. Those who are successful are the ones who sacrifice everything, life itself, if necessary, to the attainment of that ideal; in spite of opposition and the ever-present human weakness, to live only to attain that ideal to the exclusion of all else. The reward of this mental aim and determination is attainment. It is the secret of commercial success; it is the secret of the scientist and philosopher, and it is also the secret of the power of the World Savior. The accomplishment of the end justifies the use of every honest, conscientious means. It does not justify ill even to produce good, but it does require the complete cooperation of the faculties of the individual.

Fifty percent efficiency is usually sufficient in the business world and is in fact all the employer expects. He expects the office boy to fumble the papers, with his mind on the baseball game, for he lives in just such a world himself. He comes to business in the morning on Monday and all that day he sees pictures of golf links before his eyes; he wakes up with a start to sign a paper, while his mind is tuning in his radio for Havana. This is the way the business world is run usually. Here and there arises one, an expert, who climbs, within a few short years, over the heads of older and apparently wiser men and becomes the marvel of his generation. People wonder how he accomplishes it. The answer invariably is through concentration and consecration. You cannot have your mentality divided between pleasure and labor, between self and service, between your own desire and the needs of the multitudes, and succeed. You must choose one, adhere to it, struggle for the attainment of it, with vigilance as your watchword and labor as the pass-key. The result is success, and in this old world, nothing succeeds like success.

This is especially true among those who take the path of occultism and consecrate their lives to an ideal. Few will understand this ideal, few will appreciate the consecration and still fewer will recognize the end to be attained, but, in spite of this, the student of life's mysteries will never succeed in solving them until he gives himself, his life, and the labors of his hand, to the one end. He may lose much, but the thing that slumps off is the thing, which is impermanent, unreal and unnecessary. Man's needs are few, but his requirements are eternally multiplying and he must learn to sacrifice his desires to the end which he has consecrated himself to. He is usually prepared and willing to make sacrifices but there are usually one or two things which he does not care to sacrifice but feels confident that he shall attain without those things. In this he is wrong but usually does not discover the fact until his hair is gray with age and his heart is broken with suffering.

Whatever your walk of life, whatever your attitude towards life, remember that it is a game which requires the complete attention of the player. Like the game of chess, with its many moves and turnings, if your mind is once taken from it, your opponent will win. Failure is the opponent of Time and a cunning player at the game of life realizes that failure is the result of inattention, the result of lack of confidence in self, the result of a lack of adjustment to a plan in which the individual, as a compound unit, should cooperate completely and entirely to the end which the mentality and soul has decided should govern life. When our hands work against each other, we are as a house divided and must fall, when our lives are split between our whims and our duties, we are a house divided and cannot stand.

Concentration is the answer to the problem. One-pointedness of desire will succeed regardless of the thing which is the aim of life. It is equally the means of success for the merchant, the mechanic, and the seer. The successes of life are those who have sacrificed everything for that success, while the failures of life are those who have failed to cooperate with themselves.

There are many things each one of us wants to do; we want to be Napoleons; we want to be Edisons; we want to achieve the height of public prominence in politics or religion. Every happiness that the world demonstrates we would have our share of. One minute we gaze at the lofty pinnacles upon which stand the forms of the immortals and we wish we stood there also; in the same glance we see the simple happiness and peace of the little cottage, the laughing children, the old hearthstone and long to be there too for our share in the joys of simple things. We see the apparent joy of riches; we see the plaudits of power; each point of the compass carries an attraction which we long to possess. And the youth of today, standing at the parting of the ways, wishes all the joy and none of the sorrow, all the laurels and none of the endeavor. One day he wishes to be great, the next day he gives himself to selfishness and greed. In other words, he is unconsecrated and without concentration.

The sage, standing at the parting of the ways, makes his life decision and swears by all that is holy within him and all that he hopes to be that he will remain firm upon that decision, and if he is too weak to reach the end, you will find him lying somewhere on the path, with his eyes to the front and the same resolve in his soul, even though he could not attain the end. He chose with his eyes open and lived and died upon the strength of that choice. When he chose to walk the path of the World Savior, of the servant of men, he closed his eyes to the path of power; he closed his eyes to the beckoning fingers of greed, he turned, mayhaps with a sigh, from the hearthstone and the children's faces. All these he wanted, but he knew that he could but succeed in one; and so, strong in his decision, he turned his back upon things he wanted, things he thought he needed, and took the trail that led to the highest that his soul conceived of. Many times, again he saw the gloomy shadow of power beckoning to him, promising him all things, many times again he heard the laughter of children's voices and saw in dream and vision the things which he left behind; many times, he was tempted to turn back; many times he half believed he could accomplish all, could have them all; but in his soul, he knew that no human being was great enough to span them all. So, he left them all, to the furtherance of his objective, the thing he had sworn to do.

This is the story of the great capitalists, the great scientists, the world-famed philosophers, and the gods themselves. Surrounded by naggings and hampering's, criticized, and deluged with abuses, tempted upon every turn to forsake a way that shows no progress, they remain true to themselves—and now the world bows humbly at their feet. The price of power is sacrifice, the price of gold is sacrifice, the price of philosophy is sacrifice, the price of mastery is sacrifice—the sacrifice of all else to the attainment of one end. And consecration is that obligation taken to the soul by the soul that it shall attain one fixed, determined, and especially end, and concentration is that attitude of consciousness in which the bodies, mental, emotional, and physical, unite under the direction of the spirit to the accomplishment of that one fixed and especial end.

LIVING PROBLEM S DEPARTMENT

IN this modern age superstitions have left us, only to slink like red-eyed wolves in the gloom which borders the camp-fire of intelligence. To be sure, there are a few voodoo doctors left and I guess our psychologists will be with us always, but thinking people, illuminated by the dazzling brilliancy of Christianity and modem science, pooh-pooh the idea of witches on broomsticks and ghosts that walk at night. Of course, you all know about King Tut, the young Egyptian Pharaoh whose body has been disturbed after thousands of years of rest, and most of you have heard about the curse of King Tut and that singular, shall we say, coincidence of the death of Lord Caravan who was the first to open the tomb. Most of you have laughed around your firesides over the fact that anybody should for a moment suppose that an Egyptian heathen could do cursing more effectively than a Los Angeles taxi-driver. But just after this story got out about King Tut's curse, there began to flood into the museums of the various countries a miscellany of Egyptian relics; Smith, Brown and Jones sent in scarabs their uncles had got in Egypt, fake mummies, and chips of the Sphinx, claiming that they did not care to have such articles in their possession. Of course, this does not demonstrate any superstition or anything like that, it just proves that while people today do not put any faith in those things, they just believe in taking precautions, that's all.

THE YEAR OF HARD LUCK

Another popular superstition that still thrives amidst all our intelligence is that ghastly ghoul, election year. One of the advantages of democratic government seems to be that it goes into convulsions every four years. Farmer Smith says, "Things are tightening up for election." The president of the Real Estate League says, "Things are tightening up for election." When we ask why this, that, and the other thing has gone wrong, why we cannot sell our fresh strawberries for more than half price, etc., the buyer for the Stranded Strawberry Syndicate winks one eye and whispers, "Election year, things are gettin' tight." Bootleg, flypaper, and artificial linoleum are getting higher every day but will go down after election year, we understand. The problem before the house of the unrepresented is: How much is it going to cost you and I to find out which one of the political parties is going to have the pleasure, privilege, and opportunity to live off of us for the next four years, who is going to misrepresent us in congress, who is going to sleep in the senate chair this year? It's a great problem, and while it doesn't mean anything to hardly any of us who gets in, I guess we will have to be patient while things "tighten up for election."

PROGRESSIVENESS IN THE FAR EAST

Most of you have heard of Java, noted for its coffee, its mosquitoes, and for the fact that it is the most densely populated area on the face of the earth.

Leaving Batavia, which is the seat of the Dutch government there, one can travel three hundred miles by a dusty, hopeless train over a road-bed which must have been built by the Corduroy Brothers, to the little town of Djokjakarta, which exists as a sort of a tumor on the railroad track. Stopping at the main hotel one passes into the dining-room for dinner. Three native musicians, playing on nondescript instruments unlisted in any musical catalogue, appeared, seated themselves, tuned up their equipment, and then burst forth into that well-known classic "Yes We Have No Bananas." There was silence for about half a minute, then from among the Americans there burst a howl of laughter and an applause which nearly drowned the effort of the Javanese. Over fifteen thousand miles away, in the heart of a practically unopened country, this reception would have brought tears to the eyes on an optician's window. There is no use talking, the heathens are progressive.

QUESTION AND ANSWER DEPARTMENT

Does justice work through evolution or reincarnation?

Ans. Reincarnation is one phase of the law of evolution. Justice works through all of nature's laws and whichever one is broken—through that, the mistake must be made right.

Is it not better at times to live out desires than to suppress them?

Ans. Absolutely. To be good or spiritual because you have to or afraid not to bring little real growth. The most important thing is to be truly honest with yourself and not try to hide a weakness under affirmations of spirituality. There is always the motive of our goodness to be considered and if it is not up to the action, much of the value of said action is lost.

Do you advise the ceremony of baptism for children?

Ans. It is a matter of a personal solution. If it is liable in any way to help, socially or otherwise, the future of the child, there is no particular harm in baptism, but until it is a ceremony in truth, a spiritual occurrence within the individual when his consciousness is raised by right living, there is no real gain.

Is it right to ask the Elder Brothers for the wisdom of the sages?

Ans. If we ask in a certain way, it is all right. The only safe and sane manner is to prove in our daily lives that we are worthy to represent them. When we do this, the wisdom of the sages will be ours without any other asking. Without this requisite, there can never come true wisdom, anyhow.

What is scientific thinking?

Ans. Scientific thinking is the power to reason in an orderly, consecutive manner without interfering with others' thoughts and not confusing your own.

How may one know when he is using the so-called Divine Mind?

Ans. When his thoughts are in harmony with the divine plan. The divine is neither narrow, creed bound, egotistical, selfish, emotional, temperamental, or harsh in its thoughts and if we are living the life that the divine points out, then we will use or be attuned to the Divine Mind.

Is man a separate creation or evolved from animal creation?

Ans. All kingdoms of life are the results of evolution, each having evolved from the one below it. Man is no exception to the rest of creation.

Can all the laws of inheritance be overcome in one life?

Ans. Yes, they can be overcome as soon as we realize that we have inherited nothing but the opportunity for the fulfillment of causations we ourselves have set in motion.

Will we be promoted to higher forms of life?

Ans. When we have graduated from this. We will not become truly human until the end of this earth period, at which time if we are good and faithful servants, we will be given greater opportunity for hard work.

If God knows that sparrows fall, why is He too busy to help us?

Ans. The main reason why God does not help us more is because God, being the individualized spark of life within ourselves, is not helping itself as it should. The Lord helps those who help themselves.

How can a person best improve his mortal recollection?

Ans. All faculties are developed through exercise. If the memory is poor, use it and it will improve. If you are seeking for spiritual remembrance, develop spirituality by proper living and thinking and the newly exercised organs will serve you if you nourish them.

THE TERROR TREE

FEW have walked upon the Scottish moorlands at night, especially such a night as the one that we describe. A thin, drizzly rain was falling, and the ground underfoot was sogged and muddy. howled among broken rocks and sent the sheets of water swirling in a dozen directions, driving the raindrops against your face like bullets. Now and then a sharp flash of lightning streaked through the sky and lit the moorland with a strange, lurid, electrical light. One of these flashes showed in relief against the bluish radiance of the heavens an old, ruined building which raised gaunt, windowless, turrets to the sky. It was known in the countryside as a haunted place where ghouls walked in the darkness of the night and specter shades of days gone by carried ghost lanterns through the passageways. None lived there for any good, but it was the abode of thieves and vagabonds and outcasts of society. Fiendish crimes had been committed beneath the shadow of its ivy-covered keep. Wanderers upon the moor often strayed there to return no more and the peoples of the town whispered that their bones lay rotting somewhere amid the gray shadows of the haunted castle.

On the night when our story opens a light was seen in one window of the old building and had you been closer you would have seen a figure, enveloped in the folds of a great black cape, carrying in its arms a bundle, creep silently down the old moss-covered stairs, swinging a battered lantern in his hand. On his face was a look of horror, yet grim determination, and the faint glow of the lantern made his strong, aquiline features resemble more than anything else the grinning skull of some old Capuchin monk, long draped in sable cowl, in the catacombs of Rome.

Out into the dark and drear of the storm swept moorland the figure stole. Just as the man descended the steps and crossed the battered drawbridge, which had once spanned the moat, now dry, he stopped for a second and listened. From somewhere in the midst of the gloomy castle a cry sounded, a long, broken wail that rose and fell, and at last died out in a burst of hysterical laughter. The man's face grew pale as death, but shaking off with a terrible effort the spell that the cry had brought upon him, he picked up a spade that lay on the ground by the drawbridge end and slunk like a shadow into the night, his tiny lantern casting gloomy shadows on the ground around him and bringing into strong relief the burden that he carried.

Some three hundred feet he walked in the mud of the moorland and then came to a place by the roadside where, on the side of a hummock of reddish dirt, a dwarfed tree, with gnarled branches and spreading roots, stood firm in spite of the blasts of the storm. Gazing about him as though he expected to find sinister faces gleam at him from the shadows, the man in the cape lay down his burden, and, picking up the spade, started digging frantically in the muddy ooze of the moorland.

The minutes passed rapidly by. Convulsively and nervously the weird figure turned the sod and piled the slimy ooze about him as he furled from the ground a shallow trough some three feet long and a foot or two in width. He desired, it seemed, that the hole should be deep, for even as the lightning flashed about him, he steadily plied the spade. Shuddering, cringing, terrified even by the voice of the wind, the wretched man labored frenziedly. As fast as the hole was dug it filled with water and the task was an arduous one, but in some twenty minutes it was accomplished and with a sigh the cloaked figure stuck the spade in the ground and turned to the bundle wrapped in a dark cloth that lay beside him. Glancing furtively around that none might see, he dropped his burden, with a slight splash, into the water that already half-filled the opening; and then, with frenzied haste, he turned back the mud and ooze to fill the hole.

In half an hour it was done—this thing he had come to do. With a last look around, the strange figure turned from the tree with its gnarled branches and picked his way back through the mud and slime to the gates of the haunted castle. Here, everything was quiet and silent. The cloaked figure threw the spade into the moat where it clanked upon the dry stones at the bottom and then crept back into the passageway where the light of his lantern sent sparkling-eyed lizards and croaking frogs into the distant corners. Up and up the wound along the circular staircase that led to the keep. At last, reaching the loop of this ancient tower, he stopped before a half-closed door. For a moment he swayed undecided and leaned back against the cold stones, his face the picture of agony. Then steeling himself, as it were, for a mighty shock, he turned the lantern low and, allowing the cape to fall from his shoulders, pressed open the door which creaked dismally on rusty hinges and with a half sob passed into the darkened room.

* * *

Many months passed. It was sunshine on the moorland and the dismal barrenness of it seemed even greater than its expanse could be better viewed. Everywhere rough, broken rocks and desert land, and here and there a broken stone or fallen pillar of granite that showed where the Druids of old had built their temples to the god of the winds. Across the moorland, a solitary figure was walking. It was the man who had crept from the enchanted tower on that dark night.

Each day he came. None knew why, none could guess the reason, but day after day he wandered across the moorland to a little mound of reddish dust that raised itself from the rolling land and from whose crest grew a gnarled tree, its shapeless limbs seeming twisted by the agony of the Inferno. For days, this man had never smiled, and all knew a great weight was upon his soul. But none knew what it was, none knew why, in a few short days, a man in the prime of life became a broken wreck, hopeless and lifeless, nursing in his soul a secret sorrow.

At last, he reached the little mound where the tree grew and before him rose the spectral shape—the castle of phantoms. He fell on his knees beside the dwarfed tree. There was silence for a moment, then a great sigh broke from his lips, his shoulders heaved, and a once strong man shed tears of bitter anguish and repentance. He raised his eyes to the heavens, but all he could see was the gloomy torrent of the haunted castle; he turned his eyes to the earth but all he saw there was the heap of reddish dirt; and at last, he turned his eyes upon the tree. For a few seconds he gazed at it and then with a scream of mortal agony he raised his hands before his face and half running, half falling, fled away.

"No, no!" he screamed. "Not that!"

After a few seconds he gained courage and returned again, shaking as with the palsy, and gazed fascinated at the tree which seemed to hypnotize him and from which he could not turn his eyes. He realized that the tree had changed its shape. It was no longer the bush he had visited so many times before. For many weeks, he had noticed the slow change, and now he realized what it meant. The limbs of the tree were becoming like human arms, its branches were fingers stretching out to him, and its gnarled surface was taking the shape of a human body. With a moan, he recognized his sin in the form of the tree.

Tottering and broken, his eyes wild and his steps unsteady, the strong man returned, a slave to his own sin. Yet day by day he had to come there, fascinated. Each time he gazed upon the branches of the tree, he realized with unutterable agony that it was becoming every day more like the thing he had buried.

The people in the village grew frightened at the wild-eyed man who stalked like one marching to his doom through the streets each day. None knew why he went out into the moorland and those who followed him could not understand why any man should lie weeping at the foot of a tree. They could not understand what he knew. From the twisted bark of that dwarfed shrub he could see a face, and the stunted arms, leafless and dead looking, reached out and beckoned to him.

The months passed. At last, it grew more than the human soul could endure—this mystery of the tree that came to life. His crime was ever before his eyes and at last this man decided that if the crime once done was not completed it must be finished now.

* * *

It was another dark and stormy night upon the moorland, again the wind howled through the parapets of that haunted castle as it did on the night when first the stranger with his lantern crept down its moss-grown passageways. Again, the tiny light shown upon the moorland, again the figure with its black cape struggled along, battered by the elements, and drenched by the pouring rain. Again, that expression of terror, again a great determination—and this time the stranger carried in his hand an axe. He was determined to end forever the mad dream by chopping down the enchanted tree that, in his demented mind, was the one witness to his crime. He reached again the knoll of reddish dirt and in spite of himself could not help but stop to gaze at the little tree whose form each day grew more like the child he had buried at its roots. He tried to pray but words would not come, and the silence of the moorland night was only broken by the distant baying of a mighty dog, perchance the howl of a wolf.

Raising the axe, the man hesitated for a second and then, with a muttered word, he brought it down with all his strength upon the trunk of the knotted tree.

For an instant the trunk swayed and to the half-demented man it seemed that its branches twisted themselves in agony. Quickly the man drew out the axe to bring it down again and complete the labor. But as he drew it from the tree, he shrank back with a stifled scream, for down the side of the trunk, from the place where the axe had cut, a thin stream of blood was trickling. For an instant he waited and then something broke within himself—the silence of the moorland was broken by a peal of demoniacal laughter. Casting aside lamp and axe, the strange figure dashed, howling, and screaming, out into the darkness.

This is the story of the Terror Tree. None other knows why the axe was laid to its roots; none other saw what the stranger saw that night on the moorland. But of him no trace was ever found, and it is surmised that, stumbling demented across the boggy wastes, he was swallowed up by the mires and quicksand's of the moor.

THE BREASTPLATE OF THE HIGH PRIEST

THE average student of occultism little realizes the wealth of truth and esoteric knowledge contained within the Bible. For many years, lives possibly, he has studied this great Book only from the or the historical angle. This mistake the world is slowly making right, and there is now coming into the hearts and minds of students a greater desire to understand the mysteries contained within that ancient time, the Book of Seven Seals. The wealth of symbolism it contains is practically boundless, and the only limit to the student of the Bible is that imposed by his own lack of understanding of great cosmic principles.

In this article, we shall briefly consider the Breast Plate of Aaran, the high priest of the Tabernacle, and first of all we shall read the description of it as given in the twenty-eighth chapter of the book of Exodus:

"And thou shalt make the Breast Plate of Judgment with cunning work; after the work of the ephod, thou shalt make it; of gold, of blue, and of purple, and of scarlet, and of fine twined linen, shalt thou make it.

* * *

And thou shalt set in it setting of stones, even four rows of stones; the first row shall be a sardius, a topaz, and a carbuncle: this shall be the first row. And the second row shall be an emerald, a sapphire, and a diamond. And in the third row a ligure, an agate, and an amethyst. And the fourth row a beryl, and an onyx, and a jasper; they shall be set in gold in their enclosings. And the stones shall be with the names of the children of Israel, twelve, according to their names, like the engravings of a signet: everyone with his name shall they be according to the twelve tribes.

* * *

And Aaron shall bear the names of the children of Israel in the Breast Plate of Judgment upon his heart, when he goeth in unto the holy place, for a memorial before the Lord continually. And thou shalt put in the Breast Plate of Judgment the Urim and the Thummim; and they shall be upon Aaron's heart, when he goeth in before the Lord; and Aaron shall bear the judgment of the children of Israel upon his heart before the Lord continually."

When we start to study the mystery of the Breast Plate, we are at the very heart of the wisdom religion, for we can safely say that no student has ever entered the presence of his Lord without the twelve jewels in his spiritual Breast Plate, reflecting the light of the Shekinah's glory. There are two great characters in the study of the Old Testament: Moses, the lawgiver, and Aaron, the high priest. In Moses, we find the development of the mind; to him were given the tablets of the law. In Aaron, we find the spiritual counselor of the ancient Israelites. In many of the great mystery schools, we find the letters A. U. M. used as the symbols of the "lost word." When we realize that Aaron or A represents the heart and Moses or M represents the mind, we can better understand why the word was lost when the U, which in ancient symbology, represents a hook, was removed, and why man must wander upon the surface of the lower worlds until he is able to unify these two great principles within himself.

In the ancient Hebrew there is no U, but instead the letter Vau is used. The meaning of this letter is that of a hook to hang things upon or to fasten things together with. Man standing in the center of the evolutionary scheme like the sacred lily of the ancients, is the Vau or the hook, the letter lost from the word by the death of the builder (the fall of man), the uniting link, who must in himself join his higher and lower natures, the A and the M, in the spiritual marriage of the Sun and Moon.

Most students are acquainted with the literal explanation of the Breast

Plate of Aaron, which symbolizes the mystic path as opposed to the mind path of the Tablets of the Law; so in this article we shall study the Breast Plate only from the spiritual or esoteric angle. First of all, it is important for us to consider the setting in which the twelve sacred stones are placed. The Bible tells us that the Breast Plate was made of gold, of blue, of purple, and of scarlet, and of a fine twined linen. These different materials represent the bodies of man in which are set the stones or centers of his spiritual nature. The twined linen is the purified physical body; the gold is the vital body; the scarlet is the transmuted desire body; the blue is the spirit; the violet, which is a combination of blue, the higher and of red, the lower, represents the link of mind, and is the color of Mercury, which the Rosicrucian student knows is the symbol of The ephod is the covering of the back and breast worn by the priest, and is fastened at the shoulders by two pieces of onyx stone set in gold, representing the two poles of nature; also corresponding to Jachin and Boaz, the pillars of die temple.

The ephod is gathered at the waist by a heavy girdle, which in the case of the priest is of pure white linen, while in that of the high priest it is beautifully embroidered in colors. The Breast Plate is worn upon the front of the ephod fastened by golden cords and chains.

It is well known that the twelve stones represent the twelve signs of the zodiac or the twelve great celestial Hierarchies which focus their influence upon man. In figure No. 1 we see that the stones are divided into four rows of three each. The four rows signify the four elements: earth, fire, air, and water, and

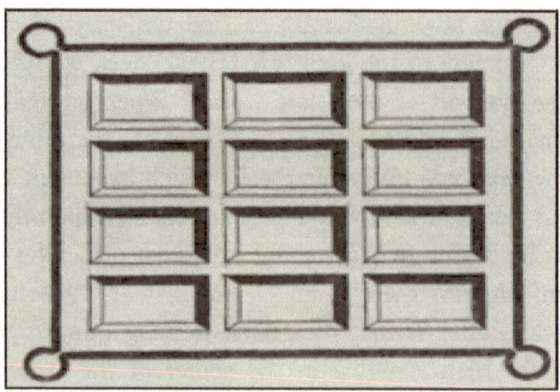

the four Hebrew letters of the sacred name. They also stand for the four basic principles of the human body: hydrogen, oxygen, nitrogen, and carbon. There are three stones abreast which stand for the cardinal, fixed, and mutable signs.

It is said that each of these stones had a name upon it, which agreed with one of the names of the twelve tribes. It is the same in man: each of the twelve stones or centers has a key or rate of vibration which connects it with its external color ray in the cosmos.

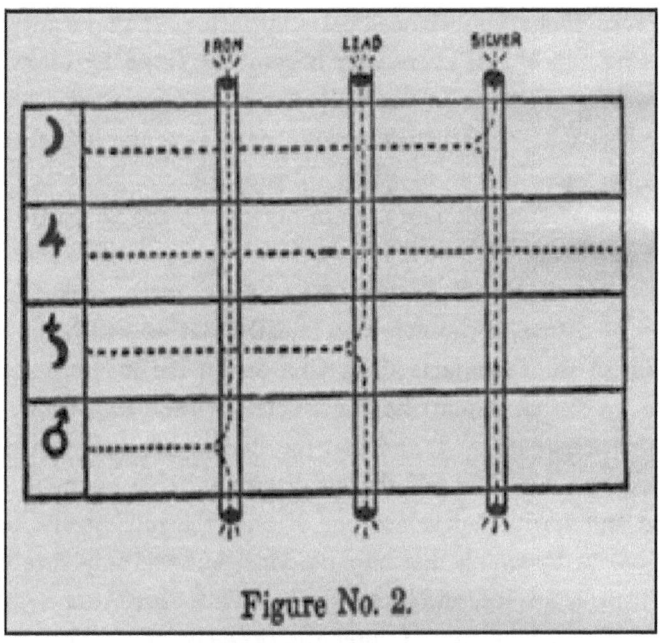

Figure No. 2.

In figure No. 2 we see three poles, one made of iron, one of lead, and one of silver. These form three of the twelve poles which receive celestial rays. The great Hierarchies which are working upon man are surrounding him and this planet at all times with their vibrations and rays. These vibrations can only be received by substances attuned to them. Thus, we see that silver attracts the vibrations of the Moon, while those of Mars, Jupiter and Saturn, although passing through and around the same pole, are not drawn to and exercise no influence upon it. It is the same with Mars, whose vibrations are attracted to iron but not to the other metals; while Jupiter, finding no tin, shows no effect at all, and Saturn is drawn only to lead. It is the same with man: the centers in him of the various rays are like receiving stations; if they are not attuned to their respective currents in the cosmos, the individual does not receive any force through them.

Man is slowly bringing himself into harmony with the various forces of nature, and every time he perfects one of these adjustments, he places another jewel in his Breast Plate. The so called had aspects of a horoscope and the inharmonies of life are nothing more nor less than maladjustments, while evil, so called, is merely good gone astray or misapplied. The planets continue to shed a neutral ray. They were called by the ancients one-eyed gods. These same neutral rays exert either constructive or destructive influences according to the adjustments of the receiving poles. There are very few people who have developed more than one or two jewels in their Breast Plates, and the result is that they are receiving an unbalanced celestial influx. If they continue to play upon single strings, they will eventually become deranged by allowing the stronger powers to become domineering, while the weak grow weaker.

The first duty of the student is to make a mental and spiritual analysis of his character, and instead of going through life doing the things that are easy for him, thus over-developing certain organs, he should do the things in which he is not proficient and, in that way, build up the centers that are now asleep. The twelve stones are all of the same size and shape, and it is not until all of the forces of nature work upon man equally that he will be able to become the high priest of the tabernacle. The first act in the making of the Breast Plate is to remember that it must be constructed of the best that we have; that only perfect stones may be used, and that the student can only construct these jewels by developing within himself the conditions suitable to them. This is done by education and spiritual development of only the highest and best kind. There are many ways by which this may be done, but the only sure one is through a life of altruism, service, and brotherhood. While there is one stone missing from this Breast Plate, man cannot enter the presence of his Lord.

Now let us consider how the priest of the tabernacle uses the Breast Plate which he has made. First of all, it reflects the light of the Shekinah and allows him to see in the Holy of Holies where all is dark until these stones, through polish, reflect the light. We see in figure No. 3 how the stones serve as reflectors and are objects against which and through which the Hierarchies focus their power, each upon its respective stone, and these stones reflect the power to those whom the priest is guiding. Man is a sun in the making. The physical sun, as the occultist knows, is nothing but a reflector for the two spiritual suns behind it. The rays of the sun are reflected to man through the planets and the signs of the zodiac. In the same way, the Adept or Initiate, who is a high priest, reflects through the channels which he has developed, the powers which he has gathered from the cosmos. In this way, men are slowly becoming suns of God, and the twelve stones are the reflectors through which they spread the light to those below them.

It is also by reverse action that the lord sees reflected in these stones the states of consciousness reached by the twelve tribes; in the same way the

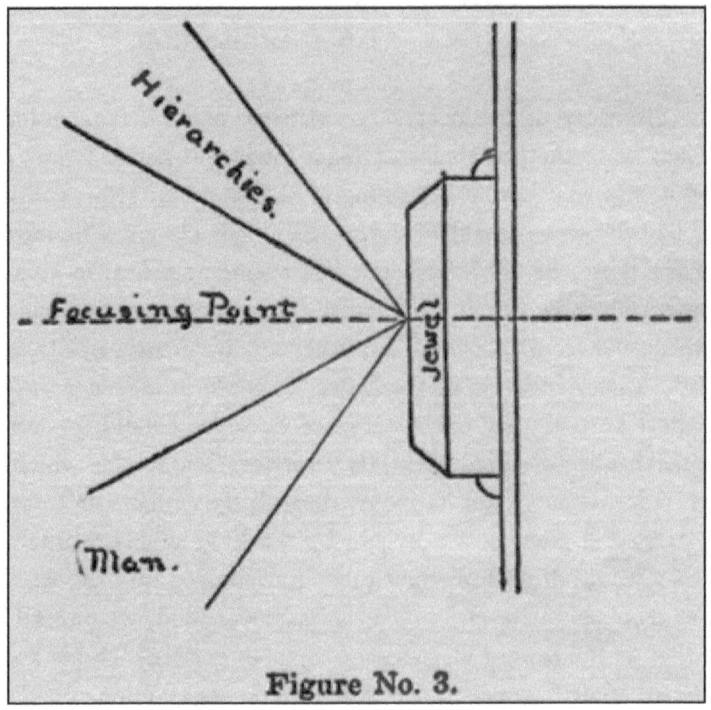

Figure No. 3.

spiritual centers in man show his position in evolution. The twelve stones symbolize the twelve convolutions of the brain, the development of which is individualizing man and differentiating him from the animal. Taking the heart of the priest as the Liberator, we find that the twelve stones are the twelve Elder Brothers that conceal him, and through whom his light radiates in twelve different colors, representing the twelve mystery schools, the seven lesser and the five greater. The Bible says, "Thou shalt put in the Breast Plate of Judgment the Urim and the Thummim." These two stand for the two poles of existence, which we understand as spirit and matter. The Urim and Thummim of the Hebrews are the same as the Yin and Yang of the Chinese. It is said that various combinations of these two principles make all things. As the student goes through life, let him realize that every temptation mastered and every purification of his body adds luster to the stones in his spiritual Breast Plate, and brings closer the day when he shall also become a high priest after the order of Melchisedec, who reflects to all who need them the powers of the spiritual Hierarchies through the living Breast Plate of his own soul.

KEY TO PHYSIC AND THE OCCULT SCIENCES
(Continued from last month.)

The discovery of the necessary existence of an eternal mind sufficiently leads us to the knowledge of God; for it will hence follow that all other knowing beings that have a beginning must depend on Him, and have no other ways of knowledge or extent of power than what He gives them; and therefore if he made those, he made also the less excellent pieces of this universe, all inanimate bodies, whereby his omniscience, power, and providence, will be established; and from thence all his other attributes necessarily follow.

Thus, a manifestation of the Deity is visible in all his work. There is not the smallest part of that immense space our eyes behold, or our imagination conceives, that is not filled with His presence. The worlds which revolve with so much order, beauty, and harmony, through the immensity of space, the sun, moon, stars, and planets, are upheld by the light of his countenance; but for which they would drop from their orbs, and plunged into the vast abyss, would return to their primitive chaos. To the mercy of God, we owe all the blessings of this life, as the reward of good and virtuous actions. To his anger, we justly attribute all violent concussions of the elements, famine, plague, pestilence, etc. brought on a wicked and abandoned people, like the storm of the fire and brimstone on Sodom and Gomorrah. The vengeance of the Deity cannot be more awfully described than by David in his Psalms, which should act as a timely warning to those atheists and unbelievers and to those wicked, idolatrous and polluted countries against whose detestable crimes these terrible scourges have been so often sent. The shaking of the earth; the trembling of the hills and mountains; the flames of devouring fire darting through the firmament; the heavens bending down with forked thunderbolts; they're riding on the clouds, and flying on the wings of a whirlwind; the bursting of the lightnings from the horrid darkness; the tremendous peals of thunder; the storms of fiery hail; the melting of the heavens; and dissolving into floods of tempestuous rains; the earth opening and swallowing up her inhabitants; the rocks and mountains cleaving asunder, and disclosing their subterraneous channels, their torrents of water, and bituminous fire, at the very breath of the nostrils of the Almighty, are all of them circumstances which fill the guilty mind with horror and dismay, and admirably express the power, the presence and omniscience of God!

To what has been stated above, I would earnestly recommend an attentive perusal of what I have written in the first volume of my complete Illustration of the Occult Sciences, from page 71 to 80; whence it will be manifest to the full conviction of the most obstinate atheist, (if such a thing can really exist) that there is a God, all powerful and intelligent; supremely perfect; eternal and infinite; omnipotent and omniscient; who endures from eternity to eternity and is present from infinity to infinity!

But though, from the nature and perfections of the Deity, he is invisibly present in all places, and nothing happens without his knowledge and permission; yet it is expressly revealed in Scripture, and admitted by all wise and intelligent authors, that he is visibly present with the angels and spirits and blessed souls of the departed in those mansions of bliss called Heaven. There he is pleased to afford a nearer and more immediate view of himself and a more sensible manifestation of his glory, and a more adequate perception of his attributes, than can be seen or felt in any other parts of the universe; which place, for the sake of pre-eminent distinction, and as being the seat and center from whence all things flow and have their beginning, life, light, power and motion, is called the interior or empyrean heaven.

The position and order of this interior heaven or center of the Divinity has been variously described and its locality somewhat disputed amongst the learned; but all agree as to the certainty of its existence. Hermes Trismegistus defines heaven to be an intellectual sphere, whose center is everywhere, and circumference nowhere; but by this he meant no more than to affirm, what we have done above, that God is present everywhere and at all times, from infinity to infinity, that to say, without limitation, bounds or circumference. Plato speaks of this internal heaven in terms which bear so strict a resemblance to the books of Revelation, and in so elevated and magnificent a style, that it is apparent the heathen philosophers, notwithstanding their worshipping demi- or false gods, possessed an unshaken confidence in one omnipotent, supreme, over-ruling Power, whose throne was the center of all things and the abode of angels and blessed spirits.

To describe this interior heaven in terms adequate to its magnificence and glory is utterly impossible. The utmost we can do is to collect from the inspired writers and from the words of Revelation, assisted by occult philosophy, and a due knowledge of the celestial spheres, that order and position of it which reason and the divine lights we have to bring nearest to the truth. That God must be strictly and literally the center from whence all ideas of the Divine Mind flow, as rays in every direction, through all spheres and through all bodies cannot admit of a doubt. That the inner circumference of this center is surrounded, filled, or formed by arrangements of the three hierarchies of angels is also consonant to reason and Scripture, and form, what may be termed, the entrance or inner gate of the empyrean heaven, through which no spirit can pass without their knowledge and permission; and within which we must suppose the vast expanse or mansions of the Godhead, and glory of the Trinity, to be. This is strictly conformable to the idea of all the prophets and evangelical writers. From this primary circle or gate of heaven, Lucifer, the grand Apostate, as Milton finely describes it, was hurled into the bottomless abyss; whose office, as one of the highest order of angels, having place him near the eternal throne, he became a competitor of dominion and power, with God himself! But Him the Almighty Powder Hurl'd headlong flaming from the ethereal sky.

With hideous ruin and combustion, down To bottomless perdition, there to dwell In adamantine chains and penal fire! — Milton, Paradise Lost.

OF NATURE

No one expression, used by authors, or spoken amongst men, is in general variously applied or so little understood as the word Nature. When speaking of the nature of a thing, we most commonly mean its essence; that is, the attributes or cause which makes it what it is, whether the thing be corporeal or not; as when we attempt to define the nature of a fluid, of a triangle, etc., oftentimes we confound that which a man has by nature, with what accrues to him by birth; as when we say that such a man is noble by nature. Sometimes we take nature for an internal principle of motion; as when we say that a stone by nature falls to the ground. Sometimes we understand by nature the established course and order of things. Sometimes we take nature for an aggregate of powers belonging to the same body, especially a living one, in which sense physicians say that nature is strong, weak, or spent; or that in such-and-such disease, nature left to herself will perform the cure. Sometimes we use the term nature for the universe or whole system of the corporeal works of God, as when it is said of a phoenix or any imaginary being that there is no such thing in nature. Sometimes, too, and that not unfrequently, we express by the word nature a kind of semi-deity or supernatural spirit presiding over all things.

This general abuse of the word nature is by no means peculiar to the English people or language; it prevails more or less in all countries and amongst all sects and seems to have been copied from the fabulous ideas of the ancients. Aristotle has written a whole chapter expressly to enumerate the various acceptations of the Greek word that is written in English nature; and among Latin writers there are not less than fifteen or sixteen different acceptations of the same word, with advocates out of number for their interpretation. The bulk of them insist that the word nature radically means the system of the world; the machine of the universe; or the assemblage of all created beings; in which sense they speak of the Author of nature and call the sun the eye of nature, because he illuminates the universe: and the father of nature because he warms the earth and makes it fruitful. Others, understanding the word in a more confined sense, apply it to each of the several kinds of beings, created and uncreated; spiritual and corporeal; thus, they say divine nature, angelical nature, and human nature, meaning all men together who possess the same spiritual, reasonable soul. In this sense the schoolmen and divines say, natura naturans, and nature naturata, speaking of God who is the natura naturans, as giving being and nature to all others; in opposition or distinction to the creatures, who are the natura naturata, as receiving their nature from the hands of another.

Nature, in a still more limited sense, is used for the essence of a thing; according to which the Cartesians say it is the nature of the soul to think; and that nature of matter consists in extension. Others more properly use the word Nature, for the established order and course of material things; the series of second causes; or the laws which God has imposed on every part of the creation; in which sense it is they say nature makes the night precede the day; nature has rendered respiration necessary to life, etc. According to which, St. Thomas speaks of nature as a kind of divine art, communicated to beings, which direct and carry them to the ends they were intended for; in which sense nature can be neither more nor less than a concatenation of causes and effects, or that order and economy which God has established in all parts of His creation. Others still more strictly consider nature as the action of Providence and the principle of all things; or that spiritual power or being which is diffused throughout the creation and moves and acts in all bodies and gives them peculiar properties and produces peculiar effects. In this sense, our modern philosopher Mr. Boyle considers nature as nothing else but God acting himself, according to certain laws he himself has fixed. This corresponds very much with the opinion of a sect of ancient philosophers, who made Nature the god of the universe, whom they conceived to preside over and govern all things; but this they acknowledged to be only an imaginary being, and that nature meant no more than the qualities or virtues which God implanted in his creatures, but which their poets and orators had figuratively personified as a god.

Aristotle, with a view of concentrating these ideas of nature into one point, as best adapted to the works of an infinitely perfect and all-powerful Being, defines nature, principium et causa motus et ejus in quo est primo per se, et non per accidens; which definition being mistaken by the Stoics, they form hence conceived the principle of nature to be a certain spirit or virtue diffused throughout the universe, which gave everything its motion by the invariable order of inevitable necessity, without liberty or knowledge. This induced the idea of a plastic nature, which several learned modern writers have described to be an incorporeal created substance, imbued with a vegetative life, but not with sensation or thought, penetrating the whole created universe, being co-extended with it, and under God, moving matter so as to produce the phenomena, which cannot be solved by mechanical laws; active for ends unknown to itself, not being conscious of its own actions, and yet having an obscure idea of the action to be entered upon. In support of this plastic nature, Dr. Cudworth argues thus: "Since neither all things are produced fortuitously or by the unguided mechanism of matter, nor God himself may reasonably be thought to do all things immediately and miraculously, it may well be concluded that there is a plastic or formative nature under Him, which as an inferior and subordinate instrument executes that part of His providence which consists in the regular motion of matter; yet so as that there is also, besides this, a higher providence to be acknowledged, which, presiding over it, doth often supply the defects of it, and sometimes over-rule it, for as much as this plastic nature cannot act electively, nor with discretion." This doctrine, he conceives, had the suffrage of the best philosophers of all ages, Aristotle, Plato, Empedocles, Heraclitus, Hippocrates, Zeno, and the Stoics, and the latter Platonists and Peripatetics, as well as the chemists and Paracelsians, and several modem writers.

Now, I am clearly of the opinion that notwithstanding these great authors have so obstinately contended for the definition of the word, and for the principles and construction of Nature, yet they all in reality meant one and the same thing, only giving different explanations of the same ideas; and if their arguments are closely pursued, and compared with each other, they will all tend to show that the anima mundi, or soul of the universe, was that they meant by Nature.

This anima mundi, as we have before seen, is a medium investing the whole interior heavens, and consists of a pure ethereal substance or spirit; which, as it more immediately resides in the celestial regions, is the second or next cause under God that moves and governs the heavens and heavenly bodies, stars, and planets; which bodies having received their first existence from the fecundity of the same spirit, in the act of creation, are by an influx of sympathetic rays, and by light, heat, gravity and motion, nourished and sustained, upheld and continued in the same regular course, and in the beautiful order we see them. From the celestial regions, the same influx of pure ethereal spirit descends into every part of the immeasurable space, and is diffused through the mass of this world, informing, actuating, and uniting the different parts thereof into various substances; and being the primary source of life, everywhere breathing a spirit like itself, it pervades all elementary bodies, and intimately mixing with all the minute atoms thereof, constitutes the power or instrument we call Nature, forming, fashioning, and propagating all things, conformable to the ideas or will of the Divine mind, in the first act of creation.

ASTROLOGICAL KEYWORDS

Aquarius is of special interest to the student of occult and religious philosophy because it is the herald of the coming age and under its beneficent rays many great changes will take place in world affairs. Old Saturn will crystalize that which is incapable of progression while the benevolent rays of Uranus will unfold and develop the highest and finest in the individual and in the world. The man with the pitcher of water on his shoulder is Aquarius and during his reign brotherhood, cooperation, humanitarianism, and fellowship will take the place of the world contentions of today. Under the rays of Aquarius, science will progress as it never has before, especially those finer sciences which are as yet so little understood. It is an air sign and the conquest of the elements by means of ever-increasing mentality will continue favorably under the rulership of this wonderful sign.

Its general keywords are as follows:

Hot, Whole, Moist, Fortunate, Aerial, Sweet, Sanguine, Strong, Masculine, Hyemal Diurnal, Southern, Western, Obeying sign, Fixed, The day house of Saturn, Human, Rational, Ruled by Uranus, Speaking, Detriment of the sun.

Aquarius, while scientific, produces in the undeveloped native a rather careless temperament. They act first and think afterwards, fired by Uranian impetuosity. They do things suddenly without thinking, take great chances and gamble with mind, body and soul. Are fond of travel and their most general characteristics are listed below:

Good disposition, Vivacious, Nervous, Excitable, Idealistic, Temperamental, Quick tempered but easily forgive, Enthusiastic, Humanitarian, Intuitional, Scientific, Inventive, Fond of all kinds of Hazards, Make many friends and are very well liked.

Physical Appearance:
Well set, Healthy, Robust, Not tall, Strong, Long face.
Delicate complexion—clear but rather pale, Sandy, dark flaxen or brown hair, Hazel eyes, usually large Graceful and elegant in carriage, Fairly heavy.
Health:
Aquarians are often thoughtless and do not take proper care of themselves or are too busy doing other things and overlooking the necessities of guarding their health. They are not usually long lived, and their most prevalent diseases and ailments are listed below:
Lameness, Fractures of limbs, Gout, Coagulations of the blood, Cramps in various parts of body, Diseases incident to the legs and ankles.

Domestic Problems:
Aquarius usually enters into matrimony very hastily and has more than one marriage during a lifetime. Aquarius is a fruitful sign and usually raises quite a family, fond of children but often neglectful of them. On the other hand, an undeveloped Aquarius will not have children around and lacks maternal or paternal instinct.

Countries Under Influence of Aquarius:
Arabia Denmark, Petrea, Lower Sweden, Tartary, West Philia, Russia, South part of Bavaria.

Cities Under Its Control:
Bremen, Pisa, Hamburg, Trent.

Colors:
First part, deep indigo, blue Second part, ethereal blue Grey, Sunlight color.
According to Ptolemy, the stars on the shoulders of Aquarius are like Saturn and Mercury; likewise, those in the left hand and face. The stars in the thighs have the influence of Mercury and a little of Saturn. Those in the stream of water have the power of Saturn and the moderate of Jupiter. Henry Cornelius Agrippa and Francis Barrett have the following to say concerning the sign of Aquarius: of the Twelve Orders of Blessed Spirits, the martyrs are ruled by Aquarius; of the Twelve Angels over the Twelve Signs, Gabriel; of the Twelve Tribes, Zabulon; of the Twelve Prophets, Habakkuk; of the Twelve Apostles, Matthew; of the twelve months, January 20th to February 20th; of the twelve plants dragonwort; of the twelve stones, crystal; of the twelve main parts of the

body, the lower legs and ankles; of the Twelve Degrees of the Damned and of Evil Spirits, the apostate; of the twelve metals, lead.

Keywords of Pisces:

Pisces the twelfth and last sign of the Zodiac is especially connected with the Christian faith. Its symbol is the two fishes so often found in ancient Christian sculpture or engraved upon the walls of the catacombs. The Master Jesus is called the Fisher of Men, for He brought to the world the Piscean religion of unity and spirituality. Those born under Pisces are especially mystic and psychic, for it is the greatest of those signs. It is not a fortunate sign, however, and the life of the Piscean is filled with ups and downs, mostly downs. But it is the great educative, humanitarian, spiritual and unifying sign of the Zodiac. Its keynote is harmony, but its great danger is negation, and a great deal of mediumship is found under Pisces, a very dangerous condition against which the student is warned perpetually. Pisces is a little different from any of the other signs and its types are the easiest told of all of the twelve.

Listed below are a few of its leading keywords:
Pisces the last sign of the Zodiac:
Cold, Moist, Watery, Phlegmatic, Northern, Nocturnal, Bicorporal, Common, Hymel, Effeminate, Idle, Sickly.

General Characteristics:
Pisces is very peculiar in many ways. Jupiter gives it power and dignity while Venus usually adds grace of thought but not of body. It is the most luxurious sign of the Zodiac, and its keynote is solid comfort. It usually dislikes exerting itself, but is most always forced to do so. It is not a combative sign but prefers comfort by compromise. It is mediumistic, psychic and, with training, an occult sign.

Its general description is:
Spiritual, Intellectual, Ruling, Cheerful, Literary, Artistic, Musical, Subject to irritability, Comfort-loving, Nervous, Sometimes melancholy, Slow moving, Usually misunderstood.

Physical Appearance:
The native is usually heavy, short, or tall according to the position of Jupiter. Usually thick, Head bent downward, Round shouldered, Peculiar waddling,

Stooping walk, Brown hair, Sanguine complexion.

Health:

Pisces always enjoys poor health and really learns to appreciate it. Its ailments are centered in the liver and stomach, sometimes the kidneys.

Spiritual, Intellectual, Ruling, Cheerful, Gout, Lameness, Liver complaint, Ulcerous sores Indigestion—sometimes chronic Heart burn. Poor circulation. Headaches. Eye trouble. Teeth trouble. And feet trouble.

Pisces ruling the feet, ankles, and toes, is usually noted for tender pedal extremities and, as it usually carries heavy avoirdupois suffers from falling arches, soft and burning feet and stunted toes.

Domestic Problems:

Pisces is rather varied in this line, usually fairly fortunate but often deceived by the marriage partner. If of a low type of Pisces can become very brutal and tyrannical in the home and until developed is subject to drink, dope, and all forms of excesses, including mediumistic obsession.

A well-developed Pisces is very wonderful and lovable in the home because of their easy-going disposition and their willingness to concede to the desires of others. Pisces is a very fruitful sign and is fond of children.

Color:

White, Light blue, Glistening shades, Watercolor.

According to Ptolemy, the stars in the head of the southern fish of Pisces have the influence of Mercury and, to some degree Saturn; those in the body, like Jupiter and Mercury; those in the tail and the southern line, like Saturn and Mercury. In the Northern fish, the stars in the body and backbone resemble Jupiter and Venus to some degree; those in the northern line, like Saturn and Jupiter. The bright star in the knot acts like Mars and some Mercury.

According to Henry Cornelius Agrippa the sign of Pisces has the following correlates: of the Twelve Orders of Blessed Spirits, confessors of sin; of the Twelve Angels over the Twelve Signs, Barchiel; of the Twelve Tribes, Ephraim; of the Twelve Prophets, Joel; of the Twelve Apostles, James the Younger; of the Twelve months, February 20th to March 20th; of the twelve plants, aristolochy; of the twelve stones, the sapphire and chrysolite; of the twelve principle members of the body, the feet; of the Twelve Degrees of the Damned and of Devils, the infidels; of the twelve metals, tin after its ruler Jupiter.

GREAT SAYINGS OF THE RABBIS
From the Talmud

"To be patient is sometimes better than to have much wealth."

"First learn, and then teach."

"Teach thy tongue to say, 'I do not know.'"

"Thy friend has a friend and thy friend's friend has a friend; be discreet."

"The weakness of thy walls invites the burglar."

"If a word spoken in its time is worth one piece of money, silence in its time is worth two."

"Two pieces of coin in one bag makes more noise than a hundred."

"The rivalry of scholars advances science."

"When a liar speaks the truth he finds his punishment in the general disbelief."

"The day is short, the labor great, and the workmen slothful."

"Silence is the fence around wisdom."

"Truth is heavy, therefore few care to carry it."

"Jerusalem was destroyed because the instruction of the young was neglected,"

"Commit a sin twice and it will not seem to be a crime."

"The thief who finds no opportunity to steal considers himself an honest man."

"There are three crowns; of the law, the priesthood, and the kingship, but the crown of a good name is greater than them all."

"Despise no man and deem nothing impossible; every man hath his hour and everything its place."

"Unhappy is he who mistakes the branch for the tree, the shadow for the substance."

AUTHOR AND MANAGING EDITOR

Darrell Jordan is an acolyte of the August Fraternity, former Noble Grand-IOOF and Freemason. He is also a member of the Theosophical and Philalethes Societies.

Darrell Jordan

BOOKS BY THE AUTHOR

- Illustrations of Masonry
- Surviving Document of the Widow's Son
- The Undiscovered Teachings of Jesus
- The Initiates
- Jefferson's Bible
- Master Masons Handbook
- Forgotten Essays - W.L. Wilmshurst
- Forgotten Essays - Waite
- Forgotten Essays - H. Stanley Redgrove
- The Writings of Sigismond Bacstrom M.D.
- Forgotten Essays — Reincarnation
- Masonic Writings of George Oliver
- Masonic Lectures by Wellins Calcott
- The Fellowcraft Handbook
- Secret Societies
- Vibration and Life
- Key to the Rosicrucian Characters
- The Revelation of John
- Life and the Ideal
- The Philosophical History of Freemasonry
- The Magic of the Middle Ages
- Musings of a Chinese Mystic
- The Life of the Soul
- Christian Mysticism
- Krishna and Orpheus
- The Eleusinian Mysteries & Rites
- The Crucifixion Letter
- The Mystic Key
- You Paid What?
- The Illustrated Pioneer History of the America
- Montana Freemasons 19th Century
- Washington Freemasons 19th Century
- Idaho Freemasons 19th Century
- Rock Metaphysics
- Emblems: Jean Jacque Boissard and Otto van Veen
- Emblems: Nicholas M. Meerfeldt
- Alchemy Art: Manly P. Hall
- Emblems: Manly P. Hall
- Alchemy Art & Symbols
- Splendor Solis

For the latest information, please visit author's book site: Parallel47North.com/collections/esoteric-books

If you have any question, suggestion, or feedback, please contact: info@Parallel47North.com

www.ingramcontent.com/pod-product-compliance
Lightning Source LLC
Chambersburg PA
CBHW020247010526
44107CB00002B/142